PRAISE FOR T̶H̶E̶ G̶R̶A̶N̶D̶ T̶O̶U̶R̶

T0116012

"This unflinching new biography ⟨...⟩
while vividly capturing his wild and ⟨...⟩

"Refreshingly written."
— *Pittsburgh Post-Gazette*

"Kienzle conducts a dazzling, somber, often sad, but always candid tour of
the legendary life and award-winning music of George Jones. . . . Kienzle
delivers a cracking good story. . . . Kienzle weaves stories about Jones's songs
with stories of Jones's life, creating a richly colorful tapestry. This moving
biography keeps Jones's voice alive and underscores his central role in American music history."
— *Publishers Weekly*

"*The Grand Tour* . . . doesn't shy away from shining light into the dark corners
or giving the highlights of the late George Jones' life a close, critical look."
— *Winnipeg Free Press*

"Veteran country music journalist/historian Rich Kienzle accomplishes a
tour de force in *The Grand Tour: The Life and Music of George Jones*. Crafting
a blemishes, blisters, and scars profile of 'Possum,' the author never glosses
over any[thing]."
— *Austin Chronicle*

"This brief but richly written bio by longtime music scribe Kienzle is the most
comprehensive look at the wild life, musical career and, most important, inner
workings of [George Jones]."
— *Houston Press*

"Rich Kienzle's comprehensive bio of George Jones is a great read and a dispas-
sionate chronicle of his drive-in movie of a life." — *Vintage Guitar* magazine

"Kienzle takes you seamlessly and carefully through Jones' life"
— *Pittsburgh City Paper*

"[*The Grand Tour*] is perhaps the most honest portrayal of one of music's most
controversial figures."
— *Library Journal*

"Writing with rich detail, music critic and journalist Rich Kienzle chroni-
cles the stumbles and falls but also the many musical triumphs in 'No-Show'
Jones's remarkable life."
— *Shelf Awareness*

DEY ST.
AN IMPRINT OF WILLIAM MORROW PUBLISHERS

The Grand Tour

The Life and Music of George Jones

Rich Kienzle

DEY ST.

THE GRAND TOUR. Copyright © 2016 by Rich Kienzle. All rights reserved. Printed in the United States of America. No part of this book may be used or reproduced in any manner whatsoever without written permission except in the case of brief quotations embodied in critical articles and reviews. For information address HarperCollins Publishers, 195 Broadway, New York, NY 10007.

HarperCollins books may be purchased for educational, business, or sales promotional use. For information please e-mail the Special Markets Department at SPsales@harpercollins.com.

A hardcover edition of this book was published in 2016 by Dey Street Books, an imprint of William Morrow Publishers.

FIRST DEY STREET BOOKS PAPERBACK EDITION PUBLISHED 2017.

Designed by Paula Russell Szafranski

Library of Congress Cataloging-in-Publication Data has been applied for.

ISBN 978-0-06-230992-1

17 18 19 20 21   OV/RRD   10 9 8 7 6 5 4 3 2 1

For Lloyd Green, Harold Bradley, Bob Moore, Pig

Robbins, and all the Nashville A-Teamers

who recorded with George

CONT

ENTS

PROLOGUE

● ● ● ● ● ● ● ● ● ●

Grand Ole Opry House, Nashville, Tennessee

October 12, 1981

ould he or wouldn't he show up?

That was the overriding question the night of the annual Country Music Association Awards, set to be a second triumphal year for George Jones. Though he was considered the greatest living country singer by both fans and the music industry, nearly three decades of self-destructive alcoholism, a trait inherited from his daddy, had taken a personal and professional toll, earning him a reputation for unreliability and the derisive nickname "No Show Jones." His more recently acquired taste for cocaine had left behind a growing trail of missed concerts, angry fans, incoherent performances, arrests, multiple lawsuits, and growing debt, much of it from endless purchases of vehicles and homes he couldn't afford. The media who began following him during his turbulent six-year marriage to fellow star Tammy Wynette continued to chronicle a seemingly endless stream of legal issues, incidents, arrests, and failure to appear at concerts. Those who knew the simple, decent, and painfully humble man beneath it all feared the worst.

Through it all, the one thing that endured—and kept the vast majority of fans and fellow performers in his corner—was the music. The previous year, George was honored for a hit single he didn't even want to record, one that took his producer, Billy Sherrill, nearly three years to cobble together, starting with multiple rewrites on the song itself. "He Stopped Loving Her Today" was the sorrowful tale of a man whose obsessive love for a woman ended only with his death.

The record was a bolt from the blue, a moving, jarring reminder of the raw power of traditional country in an era dominated by lushly orchestrated "countrypolitan" hits by Kenny Rogers, T.G. Sheppard, and Dolly Parton and the outlaw sound of Willie Nelson and Waylon Jennings. It summarized the raw, emotive, and searing vocal passion and interpretive genius on which Jones's reputation stood for nearly a quarter century. His performance packed such a visceral wallop that one knew, even on first hearing, that the song would endure as an example of what country music, freed of any showbiz facades, was always supposed to—expected to—embody. A year before, the CMA had honored "He Stopped Loving Her Today" as Song of the Year, and George as Male Vocalist of the Year. Unbelievably, it was his first CMA Award in that category. This year, he was up for his second Male Vocalist award. The public, even those beyond the country audience, were well aware of the travails of George Jones.

Tonight, Rick Blackburn, vice president and general manager of CBS Records in Nashville, parent to George's label, Epic Records, hoped for the best. After all, he'd been telling everyone who'd listen that George had turned things around. The Associated Press had recently run a story brimming with hope, George declaring that after the bad times, he'd turned a corner.

The truth was quite the opposite. George was to be at the Opry House, site of the broadcast, at 7:30 central time. He'd sing "He Stopped Loving Her Today" onstage and join Barbara Mandrell, the show's cohost, on her recent hit "I Was Country When Country Wasn't Cool." He'd added a brief vocal contribution on her recording. They were longtime friends. Mandrell first toured with him when she was a thirteen-year-old singer and pedal steel guitarist. This year, she was nominated for the CMA's top honor: its Entertainer of the Year Award.

George's handlers, Blackburn and his latest manager, Alabama-based Gerald Murray, had ample hurdles just getting him fit to appear. He'd drained most of a fifth of whiskey and, totally out of it, was ready to battle, a stance he often assumed when he was drunk. They ran the kicking, cursing star through cold showers, pumped him full of coffee, and got him dressed, to a car, and to the Opry House. Even in a fancy brocaded show outfit, he looked raw and dissolute, at least twenty years older than his fifty years. He was flanked in his seat by road manager Wayne Oliver on one side, Murray on the other. Hostile toward his girlfriend, Linda Welborn, he'd demanded she sit in the balcony. Blackburn had the unenviable task of warning the show's producers the star would be in no shape to sing "He Stopped Loving Her Today." The TV folks were not happy, and had to do some quick shuffling.

The show began running through awards and performers until Rosanne Cash, clad in a country-girl getup that didn't reflect her more cutting-edge musical style and joined by fellow singer Gail Davies, read the Male Vocalist nominees: George, Ronnie Milsap, Willie Nelson, Kenny Rogers, and Don Williams. When George's name was announced as the winner, he strode unsteadily up the aisle, shaking a few hands along the way. When he got there, he embraced Cash and Davies, accepted the award from a tall blonde, and then, blinded by the stage lights and totally looped, walked toward the mike. Looking out from the podium, he could recognize only fellow performers and friends: singer Johnnie Wright and his wife, Kitty Wells, who'd opened the door for female country artists with her 1952 hit "It Wasn't God Who Made Honky Tonk Angels."

"Well, I'm one of the Jones Boys, and I just wanna say one thing." He momentarily stared at the artillery-shell-shaped award. "Well, I'm very proud. I still love Johnnie Wright and Kitty Wells." He pointed toward the crowd, then continued, "Thank you very much. We love country music and it's 'bout time it got back to Nashville!"

There was nothing to do but continue. Mandrell, who'd been through two wardrobe changes, came out to sing "I Was Country" prior to the Entertainer Award announcement. A cameraman stood in the aisle next to George's seat in the audience. It was precisely what George, knowing he couldn't pull anything off, had feared. "Whatever you do," he'd grumbled to Murray, "don't you let her come down here and try to get me to sing that part." During a guitar break, she called, "Are you out there, George? You *are* there! Come on up here, George!"

Someone slipped George a hand mike. He looked toward the stage, smiled, made a noise, then, pointing to his throat, silently begged off.

Mandrell wasn't having it. "I'll come get ya!" she amiably hollered from the stage.

As she went into the next verse, she floated down the steps to the aisle.

George, still smiling, growled to Murray, "I *told* you!"

With a microphone cord that had only so much line, she implored, "Meet me halfway, George!" He fumbled down the aisle and behind his smile had totally forgotten the two lines he sang on the record.

Cueing off Mandrell, he barely sang the lines "country . . . from my hat down to my boots." Trying to save the moment, Mandrell remarked, "I love the way you do that."

"That's country!" he quipped unsteadily.

He tried but could barely squeak out the tag line "I was country when country wasn't cool" before pecking Mandrell on the cheek and the lips. As he walked back to his seat, she exclaimed, "The greatest . . . George Jones!" as applause swelled.

Her decades of stage experience allowed her to smooth, but not totally save, the moment. Millions of viewers saw the CMA Male Vocalist of the Year, for the second year in a row, too fucked up to do the thing he did better than nearly anyone in the world. Those who followed the tabloid coverage of his exploits saw the latest installment, live, on network TV. Given the steady stream of scandal, even as he made the greatest music of his career, it was little wonder much of Nashville and many fans concluded that any day, George would follow his longtime idol, Hank Williams Sr., whom he'd met when he was eighteen and who died drunk and drugged up in the backseat of his Cadillac, into the darkness.

Grand Ole Opry House, Nashville, Tennessee

September 30, 1992

The thick, graying cape of hair was heading toward white, the sideburns shorter. Quite a bit heavier and clearly healthier, clad in a black western tux, white shirt, and string tie, he stood on the Opry House stage holding a hand mike and tore into his current single, "I Don't Need Your Rockin' Chair." Written specifically for him, the churning novelty tune celebrated the legend who, in the end, had staunchly refused to go gently into anyone's good night. His voice was huskier, yet packed the same emotional power as when he recorded "The Window Up Above" in 1960.

The record included symbolic cameos by ten of Nashville's young Turks: Garth Brooks, whose phenomenal rise marked a clear if controversial generational shift to a more pop-rock style of country, joined Clint Black and Joe Diffie, both of whom walked a line between modern and traditional. Neotraditionalists included Alan Jackson, just beginning his own rise to stardom with a style far closer to George's; Vince Gill, who first emerged as a force in the mid-1980s; and Mark Chesnutt, a honky-tonker from George's home area around Beaumont, Texas. Also representing the traditionalists, Kentuckian Patty Loveless, who got her start in bluegrass, sang with Pam Tillis, daughter of veteran singer-writer Mel Tillis, who had shared many wild times on tour with George. Rounding things out were the R&B-flavored T. Graham Brown and edgy outlaw Travis Tritt.

Steady on his feet, George sang with ease about "not being ready for the junkyard yet" and feeling "like a new Corvette." Behind him, the curtain opened wider, and flanking him were Jackson, Brown, Loveless, Black, Gill, Diffie, and Pam Tillis. With them: Marty Stuart, the rooster-haired antiquarian who blended a more rocking style with the traditional vintage country George had staunchly revered since childhood. As the performance ended, Randy Travis, another neotraditionalist star of the 1980s whom George deeply admired, strode out in a black fringed jacket, carrying a plaque.

"I have the best job in the house tonight," Travis said as George bowed his head slightly, deferring to the occasion.

"You know there's nobody sittin' at home watchin' tonight or nobody in this audience that wants to see you retire to your rockin' chair by any means, but we *do* want you to enjoy bein' the next member of the Country Music Hall of Fame."

The standing ovation came. George, clearly moved but not tearful, as many other living inductees had been, reacted with his characteristic blend of awe and modesty.

"I don't believe it! Greatest thing! Thank you so much," he said. "I don't know what to say. Only thing I can say is that country music has been awful good to me throughout a whole bunch of years, and I'll tell you what—I'd just like to thank a few people. I'd like to thank the good Lord above, first of all, because he made it all possible, surely. And I naturally gotta thank all the fans in the *whole wide world,* especially the country music fans. It's been a great career and I ain't over it yet and I ain't through and I ain't givin' it up and I don't need no rockin' chair.

"But I'll tell you what. I want to thank one more person, for makin' it *real* possible for me bein' able to be on this stage tonight to receive this award. Between her and God, she's been one of the greatest ladies in the whole wide world. She saved my life, and I'd just like to acknowledge my wife, Nancy, if you'll do it."

At that point Nancy Sepulvado Jones, beaming and tearful, stood to acknowledge the applause—and collective gratitude. Everyone in the audience and at home knew she was the catalyst, the long-needed anchor who finally allowed George to learn to love himself enough to control his urges, to set aside seven years of nearly fatal cocaine abuse. Sticking by him in some of his worst moments put her at risk as well. Now the coke was gone and the drinking, at long last, reduced and controlled.

"I won a lot of awards, not braggin', a lot of awards over a period of years. And each and every one of 'em was fantastic. They made you feel great, they kept you goin' and made you try harder and work harder, but this has got to be the greatest one in the world. It's made my day. It's made my whole life. Thank you so much! I love you!"

And with a wave, he and Travis strode offstage. George Glenn Jones, who climbed to stardom from East Texas poverty, who fell to the depths and then some, had risen in utter triumph, having overcome demons that destroyed many friends and musical heroes.

HE WAS A COMMON MAN GRACED WITH AN UNCOMMON TALENT. DURING HIS life, he was considered by peers and fans to be the greatest living country singer. In death he remains, to many, the greatest country singer of all time.

His expressive vocal style earned him laudatory nicknames like the "Rolls-Royce of Country Singers." His admirers included two masters of American song, Frank Sinatra and Tony Bennett. It's easy to see why. Jones's deeply emotional singing makes him a transcendent figure in American music, one who influenced and continues to inspire generations of singers. While he wrote some of his own material, Jones was above all a master interpreter on a par with Sinatra, Bing Crosby, Bessie Smith, Johnny Cash, Barbra Streisand, Patsy Cline, Elvis Presley, Ray Charles, Nat King Cole, and Billie Holiday.

Certainly his fan base differed from that of longtime friends Johnny Cash or Willie Nelson, whose blend of the visceral and cerebral appealed to broader audiences. Jones was what he was and never made a conscious effort to broaden his impact and fame beyond his sizable core of fans. Unlike Cash and Haggard, George didn't offer social commentary as one of his goals. Waylon and Willie challenged Music Row to attain creative freedom; Jones, even at his worst, always embraced the Nashville establishment.

Except for a few early day jobs and two years in the marines, singing is all he ever did. Beginning as a young man mimicking Hank, Acuff, Monroe, and Frizzell, Jones used his heroes as a footing, a foundation to create a unique, elemental, and chilling vocal presence of his own. He slowly evolved into a stylist capable of conveying levels of meaning that explored and defined a lyric at a level even the composer may not have thought possible.

The voice was a raw nerve put to music. Jones reached deeply into a lyric to capture a song's essence, infusing the correct amount of emotion (or emotions) into each word. He sang of love and joy, of spirituality and zany nonsense. Yet above all that was his consummate ability to explore pain, sorrow, heartbreak, and emotional desolation. Over time, his singing grew more expressive and compelling, particularly when he channeled his real-life pain into songs, most of them written by others, that uncannily seemed to echo his state of mind at that moment.

He was born into poverty in a harsh, inhospitable region of East Texas, the youngest of eight children initially raised in an environment that in many ways hearkened back to nineteenth-century America. His mother, raised in a devout Christian home, was loving and deeply religious. She taught him moral values and exposed him to music, specifically the traditional hymns she sang in backwoods churches. George's father wrestled with his own demons, stemming from the death of his eldest daughter when she was eight. Loving and hardworking when sober, sloppy and at times brutal when drunk, he demanded his talented son sing on command and beat him when he wouldn't comply. It remained burned into George's psyche.

That led to a conundrum that plagued George Jones through much of his life, the two sides of his personality long in conflict: simple virtue, charity, and empathy on one side; nihilism, self-destruction, and violence on the other. His talents became both a blessing and a curse. At times, in his harshest moments of despair, he felt unworthy of his gifts, undeserving of the financial successes and mass acclaim that came his way. Material comforts and luxuries meant everything and nothing. He would change cars like many change socks or shoes. He'd purchase high-end items such as boats, and then, often while drunk, sell them for a fraction of what they'd cost him.

His failures were as spectacular as his triumphs. Jones was married four times and had one common-law relationship. He had four children and was, for the most part, a colossal bust as a father. He could be a loving parent when he was present but for the most part functioned as an absentee father, either because of domestic problems or, barring that, his endless touring schedule. Sometimes on tour he simply vanished, failing to appear for contracted performances. That could have undermined his career. Instead it became part of the mythology surrounding him, along with the famous tale of him traveling to and from a Texas liquor store on a riding lawn mower.

While his exploits weren't initially covered in the mainstream media, that changed after his 1969 marriage to Tammy Wynette, the hot female country star of the moment. She arrived in an era when women were just beginning to carve significant niches in the country field. "George 'n' Tammy" became one word to many fans. Their joint tours, hit duets, regular battles, separations, and reunions became fodder not only for the tabloids but for their record company, who produced and released songs, both duets and solo performances, that seemed to reflect the current status of their marriage. Their 1975 divorce didn't allow Jones to escape media scrutiny. His personal life and his finances spun out of control, pushing him further into the spotlight. Cocaine joined the bottle as a primary intoxicant. His tours often came unglued when he went on a bender or appeared at a show too dissolute to sing a word. Gentle and good-humored when sober, his irresponsibility and occasional violence when out of control only added to his mystique. As his stature grew, his substance abuse constantly jeopardized his vocal abilities, which miraculously survived the worst of his excesses for many years.

Those feelings of inferiority and occasional self-loathing remained. When he overcame his fears playing for an audience of hippies and his core blue-collar fans at a 1976 gathering, he was triumphant. Offered a prestigious showcase booking in New York a year later, he agreed, only to flee before he could be flown there, convinced he was unworthy and uncomfortable with the notion of performing for the celebrities and media stars invited to hear him. At his lowest, mentally and physically, in an era before rehab became respectable, even commitments to hospitals didn't help. Consequently, few expected him to live long. Yet amid that dark time, he emerged with the song destined to stand among his many triumphs as his definitive statement: "He Stopped Loving Her Today."

Jones's death spiral seemed fixed when he met Nancy Sepulvado in 1981. Their relationship heralded a new beginning, though his turnaround wasn't immediate. With no background in music, this simple, blue-collar woman fell in love with the man, not the star. She'd endure his worst, be an innocent bystander at incidents including a cocaine arrest that would likely end the career of any other country singer. Slowly, particularly after the couple moved back to his home territory of East Texas, where he had family, Jones realized he had a true partner, the support he hadn't had or taken advantage of in the past. The couple married, and by the early 1980s he began to gain an equilibrium he hadn't had before. The cocaine vanished; the drinking continued, but he had greater control over his intake, enabling him to largely avoid the binges. There were backslides, including a near-fatal 1999 vehicle accident near his Franklin, Tennessee, home. Nonetheless, a man many expected would die in his late forties or early fifties endured and flourished for three more decades. He lived to enjoy—and gracefully accept—a stream of honors including his 1992 induction into the Country Music Hall of Fame, his 2003 National Medal of the Arts, and the 2008 Kennedy Center Honors.

Even these more sanguine years had bittersweet moments. George's fans and peers continued to revere him, but the passage of time diminished his once-routine successes on records as younger generations of singers, some inspired by him, began to dominate the music. Decades of heavy smoking eroded the respiratory system that regulates every vocalist's skills and power. Singing that was once effortless, even in his darker periods, gradually became more difficult. Yet he persevered until his Final Grand Tour, conceived to conclude with his retirement. He died in 2013, clear of mind, fully aware the end was approaching.

All of this history fuels a cumulative perception that George Jones is defined by wildness, drinking binges, fistfights on the road, and endless tales of bad behavior that took place around Nashville, northern Alabama, and every other place where he traveled or performed. Documented stories and legends are told, retold, and explored. And that is a vital part of the story. His domestic issues, cavalier irresponsibility with money, and inability to meet commitments or his responsibilities are all essential to the narrative, vital to understanding his simple yet complex makeup. Much of his life was an open book, free of many of the show-biz facades constructed to help performers control their narrative. George himself admitted that at times when he missed shows, an agent or manager would suggest claiming illness. More than once, Jones responded, "Tell 'em I was drunk!" Nonetheless, he was in many ways impossible to fully know or understand, a condition rooted in the Big Thicket area of East Texas where he grew up. Thicket men literally beat their own trails, to hell with what anyone thought.

There was, however, another equally important part of that narrative. Jones's life and music are inseparable. The music often triumphed even during his worst personal moments. His evolution from twangy imitator to distinctive new voice, from influential vocalist to master of his craft, is as important as his personal failings. Exploring that musical side—how he found songs and recorded them; the perspectives of the public, those involved in creating his records, and Jones himself—is pivotal to understanding the story.

I've attempted to take the long view, examining not only his life and the events that shaped him from start to present, but simultaneously exploring his immense musical legacy, all in a clear chronological context. I've examined how he was perceived by the media of the times and spoken to people who knew him well and saw him at his best and worst on the road, at home, and in the studio. Like any other prolific artist, he recorded gems and throwaways, and noting a lapse is not denigrating an entire career.

I hope that if I've achieved anything, I've chronicled and explored his life and art and taken a step or two toward defining his pivotal place in country music history—and, more important, his stature in American popular music and culture.

There was and will be only one George Jones. His life is part of the American fabric. Even so, it's the voice—*always* the voice—that has defined that life for posterity.

CHAPTER 1

. . . .

1931-1953

It's a story that persists today: the Ghost Light of Bragg Road, built on an old railroad line in the Big Thicket near Saratoga, Texas. No one seems sure if it's swamp gas, car headlights, a dead railroad worker's ghost carrying a light, or what, but Bragg Road to this day has the nickname "Ghost Road."

The legend is understandable. The Thicket, in southeast Texas, was a huge and forbidding region of piney woods, bayous, swamps, and backwoods, more like Louisiana than the Texas prairie. It stood out against the largely flat and arid background of the Lone Star State. Remote and untamed, it dominated five rural counties at its largest and covered between two and three million acres. The Brazos River bordered it on the west, the Sabine River on the east. The town of Nacogdoches marked the northern border. It once ran south until not far from the Gulf Coast.

Nature, not man, held the cards. Dense woods and wild creatures within the Thicket made it a sort of terrestrial black hole, a place that explorers and even Native Americans largely avoided due to the potential for entering and never exiting. The area has seven types of hickory trees, according to a Department of the Interior survey, not to mention multiple types of oak and cypress. A similar diversity applies to the vines and shrubs there. At one time, the Thicket had junglelike wildlife in its midst: coyotes, wolves, bears, ocelots along with bobcats and foxes. Alligators, turtles, snakes— some of them lethal—and lizards were abundant.

Inevitably, civilization intruded. Nineteenth-century outlaws on the lam from some other part of the country began settling there in part because of the isolation. Confederate deserters arrived during the Civil War. They faced a difficult life in the Thicket, which wasn't the optimal place to plant crops and was highly vulnerable to flooding. Settlers had to be resourceful just to stay alive. When lumber companies saw vast, seemingly endless acres to be harvested in the 1880s, the region began attracting workers willing to cut down the trees.

The Thicket developed its own unwritten code, where laws mattered less than a rugged libertarianism. People left others alone unless their space or rights were being violated. For those who got in someone else's way, the resolution was often swift and violent. Husbands were expected to provide for their families, wives were to handle domestic chores and accept whatever the husband dished out. Breadwinners who did not provide adequately were considered unsavory. Racism and violence against minorities were part of everyday life, one reason many African Americans and Latinos avoided the area. Just as violence, domestic and otherwise, was common, drinking was part of the austere lifestyle, the booze largely homemade. Gunplay, not surprisingly, was also part of everyday life, whether aimed at a bear or at somebody who provoked a fight or stole something from someone else. The region became a hotbed of Christian fundamentalism delivered in primitive, ramshackle churches matching equally primitive, ramshackle houses built of logs and wood.

J.F. Cotton, who settled in one area of the Thicket, discovered a mineral spring there before the Civil War and later found oil beneath the ground. He did little with it at the time, but in the 1880s, businessmen began promoting the springs to attract people seeking their therapeutic value. A hotel was constructed there and the growing community dubbed Saratoga, named for upstate New York's Saratoga Springs. The government opened a Saratoga post office in 1884. After Spindletop, the first major oil field in Texas, was discovered south of the Thicket, in Beaumont, in 1901, the region became open to exploration, including the Thicket itself and the area around Saratoga. Other settlements grew, including Kountze, Thicket, and Sour Lake. The oil fields did in the springs, and the Gulf, Colorado and Santa Fe Railroad ran a branch into Saratoga to service the lumber and oil activities.

The town was laid out with three sections reflecting the community's phases of growth. Old Town was adjacent to the site of the springs; New Saratoga adjoined the oil fields that came next. Depot Town sat near the railroad station. By the time of the Depression, however, the oil fields were largely tapped out and the lumber industry had drastically diminished the Thicket. A 1936 survey found it covered no more than a million acres. Conservationists viewed it as a laboratory for biodiversity worth preserving before it disappeared, an effort that increased after World War II. To protect what remained, President Gerald Ford signed legislation creating the Big Thicket National Preserve, administered by the National Park Service, in 1974.

George Washington Jones had Alabama roots. His ancestors had left there for Texas in the first half of the nineteenth century. Frank Jones, his grandfather, had been a Confederate officer whose son, David Raleigh Jones, born in Nacogdoches in 1872, married Mississippi native Mary Elizabeth Farris, a tough, volatile woman who enjoyed a drink or two and whose family had a reputation for hard living. The couple had separated by the time of George Washington Jones's birth in Lufkin, Texas, on January 10, 1895. Living with his mother and her family, he grew into a tall, strong man who enjoyed the bottle, played the harmonica, and danced, but also possessed a powerful work ethic that never left him.

Clara Patterson's ancestors also hailed from out of state. Her mother, Martha, was born in Mississippi before her family moved west and settled in the Thicket. Her Florida-born father, Jepton Littleton Patterson, known as Uncle Litt, was a deeply religious farmer. He not only imparted his fundamentalist spirituality to his fourteen children—twelve daughters and two sons—he also constructed a church on his property. Clara, the couple's seventh child, was born in Nona, Texas, on March 10, 1896. Her love of family and religion were seamless. As she matured, she became a fine singer and formidable organist, the last young woman one would think would fall for someone like George Washington Jones.

When they met in the tiny settlement of Thicket, Texas, northwest of Saratoga, each found much to like about the other, leading to a move totally out of character for Clara. The couple secretly married on August 14, 1915. Clara's father, well aware that his new son-in-law was part of the rowdy Farris clan, was not happy. The couple settled in the Thicket, moving from rented house to rented house through the region over the next twenty-five years. They both realized mere survival required backbreaking labor in the thick, hot, piney woods and taking whatever work could be found.

The census of 1920 revealed George Washington Jones, twenty-four, and Clara Patterson Jones, twenty-three, renting a home in Hardin County, in the middle of the Thicket. They had one child, Ethel, born in 1918. George's listed occupation was "teamster," connected to the local logging industry. The couple and their expanding family scraped out a living through sheer determination. George did whatever he could to provide for the family, delivering and selling ice and whatever else brought in money. When the oil fields tapped out, his specialty became carving and shaping the wooden slats, or staves, that make up barrels. He didn't come about the lumber honestly, raiding the nearby forests for the right wood. They grew their own food, and Clara's frontier-era approach made use of everything she had available. When a hog was butchered, she combined the fat with lye to make soap for a family that was growing fast.

Herman, their first son, was born in 1921, followed by Helen in 1922 and two consecutive sets of twin daughters, Joyce and Loyce in 1925 and, in 1928, Doris and Ruth. Dr. Alfred William Roark, who had an office in back of a local drugstore in the area, was one of the few physicians around. He often used a bicycle to maneuver through the backwoods. Delivering babies was common for Roark, who'd delivered Ethel and knew the Jones family well. When he required help in emergencies, he often summoned George Washington Jones, who developed a skill for tending to wounds and setting broken bones that made him a sort of primitive EMT or physician's assistant.

Ethel, the firstborn, was special to her father, who doted on her within the couple's limited means. When she became ill in 1926, George and Clara tried to take care of her. A hospital might have helped, but the money wasn't there, and George's Thicketeer nature led him to refuse any charity. Dr. Roark did what he could, but it wasn't enough. Ethel died February 28, 1926. Her shattered parents buried her at Felps Cemetery, northwest of Saratoga. Clara's deep religious faith helped her cope with the overwhelming grief, but for George Washington Jones, the loss of his first and favorite child forever changed him. He could dull the pain by plunging into the hard work required to support his family. When work ended, after the next week's groceries were purchased, he began to anesthetize the pain with regular drinking binges that led to alarming personality changes. He became boisterous, belligerent, and even verbally or physically abusive.

The 1930 census showed thirty-five-year-old George and thirty-three-year-old Clara residing in a house near Saratoga with an estimated value of $150. While the census taker mistakenly listed his trade as "stove maker," the form correctly categorized the job as part of the "timber" industry, whose trees he was poaching for the wood. The children were Herman, Helen, "Jocee" (Joyce), "Lous" (Loyce), "Doriss" (Doris), and Ruth. Clara's occupation was "housewife." In early 1931, she was again pregnant. Dr. Roark was present to deliver the eighth and final Jones child on September 12, 1931. George W took the kids to a nearby home while Dr. Roark saw to Clara and delivered her twelve-pound son, heavy enough that the physician accidentally dropped him, breaking his arm. Telling the kids they had a new baby brother, George Washington Jones brought his brood home to find the infant's fracture had already been set. The couple named him George Glenn Jones, but to the family, and everyone else in the vicinity, he was Glenn, a name that stuck to him into adulthood. Clara rarely called him anything else.

She doted on her youngest son, as did his sisters. On Sundays she took them to nearby church meetings. Clara noticed he seemed responsive to music, sometimes hymns, or the old folk tune "Billy

Boy," which she often sang to him at home. He eventually began trying to sing himself, and his uncanny ability to remember a melody and even sing it back impressed many. Clara kept him constantly by her side, as if something catastrophic might happen. But she couldn't always keep her eyes on him. Sometimes the baby, who had little use for clothes, would run buck naked to neighbors, grinning all the way. As he entered his toddler phase, more folks noticed Glenn's clear, strong voice in church, a source of pride to Clara, Herman, and the girls. Music became a respite from hard work, and when George Washington Jones was in a good humor, he sometimes pulled out his harmonica and played as Clara happily led their children in singing hymns. Later, when the family acquired a wind-up record player, Glenn found joy in the primitive mountain songs of the Carter Family.

Within a year of Glenn's birth, the family relocated to a house in the Depot Town area. Like others in the Thicket, they existed much like nineteenth-century pioneers. The family often lived on gravy and bread and whatever vegetables were available. They took baths in washtubs. When Dr. Roark wasn't needed, Clara treated common ailments with home remedies. Toys had a different connotation around the Thicket than they did in more affluent areas. On Christmas, any playthings the Jones children received were tiny and few. When Glenn was old enough to handle a chore, he was assigned the job of loading the iron stove with wood chopped for that purpose. The first time he tried, anxious to do well, he overloaded it, the intense heat nearly ruining the stove before it had to be doused with water. As he grew, the boy, unaccustomed to any other life, had little idea of his poverty, like many other Thicketeers. Shy but friendly, he loved solitude and often walked deep into the woods to daydream or sing songs at the top of his lungs.

Still haunted by Ethel's death, George Washington Jones remained sober and evenhanded when he worked. It's difficult to dismiss the enormous pressures on him to provide for his family. Making staves became impossible when timber companies who owned the forests posted private guards to stop anyone—by whatever means necessary—from filching lumber for any purpose. With Prohibition repealed, the always resourceful Jones, fully aware he lived in a dry area, found a new vocation: brewing and selling moonshine and beer.

CLARA PASSED HER STRONG MORAL CODE, ROOTED IN THE TEN COMMAND- ments, to her children and expected them to follow it to the letter. Glenn once ran afoul of that rule when he stole a pocketknife from a neighbor's home. When the neighbor told Clara, Glenn admitted the theft, produced the knife, and got a whipping for his trouble, one he knew he deserved. Clara's simple Christian values and belief in charity became a lifelong touchstone for her son, who would help others without hesitation, often without being asked.

The problem came with the undeserved violence the family suffered at the hands of their patriarch.

George W's taste for alcohol wrought immense psychological havoc and physical abuse on the family he worked so diligently to support. It became a ritual. He'd frequently stumble home drunk in the middle of the night, tearing up the house and waking the kids to demand they sing for him, using his belt on any who balked. Glenn and Doris were often singled out. Well aware of his youngest son's singing talents, George W increasingly focused on Glenn. When they could, Helen and her sisters helped their little brother sneak out an open window. Clara was not silent. Her husband's drinking offended her sensibilities, and she railed at him about it. For her trouble, she found herself in his line of fire, beaten and battered around.

For George Glenn, it was a paradox: being coerced to do the one thing he loved doing more than anything else—singing—or face a belt whipping. It became one of a number of deep scars that led to depression, conflicts, and feelings of worthlessness that didn't fade as he grew into adulthood. As he became one of the great singers of his time, beloved by fans and admired by peers, his shyness remained, aggravated by a gnawing sense he was some-how undeserving—particularly when he drank. Given what he endured in his youth, he would identify with the underdog his entire life.

George W was not always so irresponsible. He acquired a Zenith battery radio in the late 1930s that allowed the family to sample the wider world beyond Saratoga. Glenn, not surpris-ingly, gravitated to music on various stations in Beaumont and to the east in Louisiana. But it was the Grand Ole Opry, heard from Nashville on WSM's fifty-thousand-watt clear-channel sig-nal, that truly captivated him. The Opry began in 1925 as the WSM Barn Dance, conceived by ex-Memphis newspaperman-turned-announcer George Dewey Hay, formerly an announcer on the country's first such rural-oriented radio show: Chicago's National Barn Dance on WLS. In Nashville, he created a specific, rural-South concept for the program that contrasted with the Barn Dance's broader musical content. The early Opry presented performers from middle Tennessee. Many were string bands like the Gully Jumpers; among the solo performers were fiddler Uncle Jimmy Thompson, black harmonica virtuoso DeFord Bailey, and rollicking elderly singer and banjo strummer Uncle Dave Macon. With the powerful WSM signal, the Opry's popularity expanded nationwide throughout the 1930s.

Glenn found two new musical heroes on the Opry. One was Roy Acuff. An east Tennessee singer and fiddler, the onetime baseball player turned medicine-show performer had developed a powerful singing voice performing at venues that often lacked microphones. He'd worked around Knoxville since 1934. A 1938 guest performance on the Opry led WSM to invite the thirty-five-year-old singer and his band to join the show that year. Acuff quickly became the Opry's preeminent personality. Propelled to national stardom, he and his Smoky Mountain Boys had an unforgettable dynamic: his fiddling and rough-edged, deeply emotional vocals were accompanied by a raw, traditional string ensemble. Mixing secular numbers like his signature song "Wabash Cannonball" with gospel favorites like "The Great Speckled Bird" earned him a huge following across the country.

The Opry welcomed Bill Monroe and the Blue Grass Boys in 1939. Monroe, a singer-mandolinist from Rosine, Kentucky, had already achieved considerable success with his guitarist brother Charlie as the Monroe Brothers, a close-harmony vocal duet. When the brothers parted ways, Bill devised a new, dynamic approach to string-band music with his group, centered around a strong backbeat, intense high-harmony vocals, aggressive fiddle solos, and his own fiery mandolin playing. Glenn was captivated by the fervor in Acuff's voice and by both Monroe's eerie high tenor vocals and the Blue Grass Boys' sound, tighter than that of Acuff's musicians. If things were calm on Saturday nights, Glenn would crawl into bed next to his parents to listen, asking them, if he dozed off, to wake him if Acuff or Monroe came on. Soon he had fantasies about his own Opry stardom, telling anyone who would listen about this seemingly impossible goal.

Sixteen-year-old Helen departed the Jones household in the fall of 1938. She'd met twenty-year-old Wayvard Thomas "Dub"

Scroggins, a farmer from Kerens, Texas, northwest of the Thicket and not far from Dallas. He knew about old man Jones and his abuse and when he beat Helen yet again, an infuriated Dub solved the problem by marrying her in Saratoga on October 21, 1938. The couple, who would have five kids of their own, would remain a positive touchstone in George Glenn's turbulent life. Known for ingenuity and earthy common sense, Dub became a lifelong hero to George.

GLENN'S LIFE WAS NOT ALL HYMNS, THE OPRY, AND BEATINGS. HE BECAME A rambunctious kid who developed a sly, ornery sense of humor he carried into adulthood. His older brother Herman and his wife, Evalina, lived nearby; when her husband was away, Evalina, fearing the hobos who roamed the area, rapping on doors begging for money and food, kept their screen door latched. Knowing this, Glenn would tease her by rattling the door and uttering hobolike requests. Sober or drunk, he played similar tricks on family and friends for decades, and some of his fellow country stars weren't exempt from them.

The Joneses departed Saratoga in 1940 for the larger Thicket town of Kountze (pronounced *Koontz*), northeast of Saratoga. It had a railroad stop that gave the family greater freedom to travel. They could take a train to visit Beaumont, the port city built around oil development, shipping, and shipbuilding connected to the Gulf of Mexico by a large ship channel. Clara found the First Gospel Tabernacle in Kountze, pastored by the Pentecostal evangelical team of Wilbertine Burl Stephen, known as Brother Burl, and his singing, guitar-playing wife, Annie Pharris Stephen, known as Sister Annie, who also taught Sunday school.

LITTLE GLENN'S ABILITY TO REAR BACK AND INFUSE OLD HYMNS WITH FEEL-
ing led the Stephens to take him, with his parents' approval, along
to revival meetings they held throughout the area, at Kountze's
H&H Store, and in other nearby hamlets and larger towns. After
Burl did the preaching, Annie would sing hymns Glenn already
knew, such as "Canaan's Land" and "Farther Along." Since he
knew how to drive his daddy's used vehicles, Glenn wound up
educating Burl on the niceties of driving and gear shifting. Singing with Burl and Annie in various settings became basic training
for Glenn. It instilled in him the fundamentals of how to project
and reach an audience in ways his casual singing or the old man's
command performances never could.

Glenn had a respite from his family for a couple summers when
he visited Helen and Dub's farm, joined by Ruth and Doris the
second year. The Jones family's days in the area of the Thicket, however, came to an end for an entirely different reason: the Japanese
attack on the United States Navy base at Pearl Harbor on December 7, 1941.

For impoverished laborers throughout the South still struggling
to recover from the Depression, the war offered an escape from
poverty. In Texas, Gulf Coast shipyards, gearing up to produce
new vessels for the war effort, needed laborers, skilled and otherwise. Though many Texans headed west to California, opportunities nearer home were abundant. The Joneses moved to Beaumont,
where, at the venerable Pennsylvania Shipyard, George W found
employment that was more secure and lucrative than any jobs he'd
done in the Thicket. Formerly the Beaumont Shipping and Dry-
dock Company, it had turned out ships for World War I. The influx
of defense workers and their families led to a housing shortage
and culture shock for the city as Beaumont's population quickly

rose from 59,000 to 80,000. Around the country, the federal government began building public housing for the newcomers and their families. Beaumont's huge six-hundred-unit Multimax Village was one such project, created by the Federal Works Agency. While stark and utilitarian, the government-subsidized Multimax apartments had running water and electricity, new amenities to some who settled there.

At some point in 1942, George W and Clara took Glenn to Jefferson Music, where his daddy bought him a sunburst Gene Autry cowboy guitar. Glenn later put his name on the back of the instrument as "George Jones," noting his age as eleven. Glenn needed some guidance on playing it, and a better guitar instructor was just a train ride away: Sister Annie. She taught him some basic chords on one of his return trips to Kountze. When he returned for his next visit, she discovered he'd mastered everything she'd taught him and even expanded on it. Glenn had a small library of tunes in his head along with all those ancient hymns. He could sing Acuff or Bill Monroe songs and a myriad of other country songs he heard on the radio. One day, he wandered into downtown Beaumont with his guitar and began singing in front of a penny arcade on Pearl Street. Soon coins were flying into a cup someone put on the ground. When he quit singing two hours later he had twenty-four dollars, a princely sum for an eleven-year-old. He promptly blew it on a meal and in the arcade, but he realized the potential. He continued singing downtown and later set up a shoeshine stand, singing when he wasn't polishing footwear.

A kid singing country songs and hymns on the streets was a tranquility Beaumont needed by 1943. The massive and rapid population boom had led to problems. Multimax could not handle all the newcomers, and soon poor whites who'd arrived from rural areas found themselves in a situation they considered unpalatable:

coexisting closer to blacks than they ever had in the past. That tension culminated in June when a white woman declared she'd been raped by a black man. The incident sparked rioting, with whites rampaging through black neighborhoods until all available lawmen, the Texas Rangers and the Texas State Guard among them, were brought in to restore order. For one day, June 19, A.M. Aikin, the acting governor of Texas, imposed martial law in Beaumont.

FORMAL EDUCATION WAS NEVER HIGH ON THE JONES FAMILY'S LIST OF PRIORITIES. Glenn's report cards were far from acceptable. He had to repeat seventh grade, but the income from singing on the street gave him the incentive to quit school for good. Things at home, however, weren't much better. Herman had married, and his other sisters were moving on with their lives. Glenn, still at home, had to deal with his daddy's onslaughts, like the times the old man brought friends home and forced performances from the kids. Clara sometimes left for a while to visit her married children. Glenn did the same, visiting his sisters for a respite. As Glenn grew into his teens, the old man's meltdowns grew less tolerable, and after one confrontation, he simply headed out of town.

It's not clear how he knew Clyde Stephens, a kid who resided in Jasper, Texas, fifty-eight miles northeast of Beaumont, but Glenn took off heading north and looked up Stephens when he arrived in Jasper. Knowing George's love of music, Stephens introduced him to young Dalton Henderson. The two became fast friends and Glenn wound up living with Henderson and his parents. By his own account, with Clara not around to warn him against such things, Glenn did his first serious drinking there. One bit of partying with some new friends got him four days in the Jasper County jail. Glenn and Dalton bummed rides to sing in bars all around the area. For a while they sang live on Jasper's KTXJ radio. Glenn's personality made him a favorite of the Henderson family, although at times he could become as explosive as his daddy. The Jasper interlude lasted only a few months before he decided to move on. Eventually he wound up back in Beaumont, living with family members or friends.

Eddie and Pearl Stevens were regulars on the club and dance-hall circuit around Beaumont. The middle-aged husband-wife duo were a self-contained act. Eddie sang, strummed guitar, and occasionally blew a harmonica on a wire rack around his neck; Pearl sang and played upright bass. Their repertoire centered around crowd-pleasing, meat-and-potatoes country favorites and hits of the moment. Mondays through Fridays, from 4:05 to 5:00 every afternoon, they hosted a live show over Beaumont's KRIC radio that also allowed them to promote their upcoming gigs. One night they were performing at Playground Park, a combination of carnival rides and an outdoor honky-tonk, when Glenn, toting a new acoustic guitar with an electric pickup, came in with a buddy. When his friend asked the Stevenses if Glenn could sit in, they were fine with it. In his autobiography, Jones recalled, Eddie "told me what he was going to play, and I must have impressed him because I knew everything he did, which was mostly Hank Williams and Ernest Tubb songs." George became the couple's new lead guitar man. They had plenty to do: the radio shows, plus four nights playing the local circuit, including Playground Park. For that, George received $17.50 a week. He continued living where he could, bunking with various musicians wherever he could find someone willing to let him stay. At other times he stayed with Eddie and Pearl.

FOURTEEN-YEAR-OLD LUTHER NALLIE WAS AN ASPIRING GUITARIST WHEN HE first saw George with the Stevenses in 1948, picking guitar and singing occasional harmonies with the couple. As he was with his family, George was still known to many as Glenn. On radio, Nallie remembered, "*Every* once in a while they'd let George sing. Eddie kind of had his own style. He sang [in] just a normal country voice. Didn't sound like anybody. Eddie was a good MC. Pearl— she looked older than Eddie—played that bass, very simple. She'd sing 'Make Room in Your Heart for a Friend.' When George was playin' with them, he added a little relief on the instrumental part. Eddie used to call him 'Glennie Boy.' He'd say, 'Now here's Glennie Boy gonna sing a song for ya!'"

He generally got on well with the couple, even when Eddie's drinking at the end of the night sometimes forced Pearl to drive everyone home. Over time, his solo spots started gaining attention among Eddie and Pearl's fans, Nallie remembered. "They all called him Glenn. They'd say, 'You know Glenn Jones?' They loved him. They loved the way he sang." If there was a conflict, it involved the "kitty" Eddie set up at shows for tips from the crowd, especially for requests. George's singing earned him his own tips, causing occasional dustups when Eddie pushed him to throw his tips in with the rest. He often flatly, angrily refused.

As he gained greater stage experience, George found a new idol who, to him, surpassed Acuff and Monroe: Hank Williams. Eight years George's senior, Williams got started singing around Alabama as a teenager. In those days he busted his ass to emulate Acuff's emotional vocals and using them as the basis for his own style. Unlike Acuff, Hank also possessed a rare, innate genius for writing simple tunes that conveyed humor, anger, sarcasm, or deep emotional pain. He'd learned the ropes of performing on the radio in Montgomery and in rural Alabama honky-tonks, some so violent he bought the original members of his Drifting Cowboys band blackjacks for self-defense. Occasionally, he sacrificed a guitar on an assailant's head. While his youthful taste for booze evolved into full-blown alcoholism, in 1946 he had the good fortune to connect with Fred Rose, a veteran pop and country songwriter who'd formed the Acuff-Rose song publishing company with the business-savvy Roy Acuff. Rose, who published Hank's songs, became a benevolent father figure to the young singer. He got Hank a short-term recording contract with a small New York label, then maneuvered him into a new contract with the larger MGM label and became his producer. The year 1947 brought four hit singles in a row, beginning with "Move It On Over," followed by "Honky Tonkin'," "I'm a Long Gone Daddy," and "Mansion on the Hill," all Williams originals. That notable start didn't impress officials at the Opry. Aware of his reputation as an unreliable boozer, the show was reluctant to even offer him a guest shot. Less concerned was Shreveport's KWKH Louisiana Hayride, a Saturday-night Opry-like stage and radio show launched in April 1948. The Hayride welcomed him as a cast member that August. Randall Hank Williams, Hank and his wife Audrey's only child, was born in Shreveport in May 1949.

Hank's rising fame took a drastic turn after he recorded a song he'd picked up from fellow Alabama singer Rex Griffin. "Lovesick Blues" was a 1920s pop number that Rose saw little value in recording. When an obstinate Hank stood firm, the producer relented. In May 1949, it knocked George Morgan's ballad "Candy Kisses" out of the No. 1 spot. The single was still riding high when MGM issued a new single May 13: "Wedding Bells," a ballad that Hank didn't write. Neville Powell, KRIC's program director, knew Hank personally, and when Powell heard he was playing Beaumont's Blue Jean Club, he invited Hank to swing by Eddie and Pearl's broadcast to promote the new record. For George, it became a life-changing experience: a chance to meet his hero, man to man.

Hank, advised that George was an Acuff fan, gave the kid a tip or two that George recalled years later. "When he found out that I loved him and was singin' his songs—you know, someone put it to him I sounded just like him—he said, 'I'll tell you. I was a pretty good imitator of Roy Acuff, because he was my favorite, but I soon found out they already had a Roy Acuff, so I started singin' like myself.'" George, who intended to be at the Blue Jean Club, asked Hank to sing "I Can't Get You Off of My Mind," a tune he'd recorded about two years earlier. Hank agreed. The point of the KRIC visit, however, was to promote "Wedding Bells." He sang it accompanied by Eddie, Pearl, and George. Anxious to play the song's guitar intro, George was disappointed when Hank barreled right into the vocal. Any disappointment was mitigated that night when about midway through the show, George remembered, "He said, 'I want to do this song for a young man, George Jones, who wanted to hear it' . . . and I just couldn't believe it." Hank achieved his own goal on June 11. Invited to the Opry as a guest, his showstopping performance of "Lovesick Blues" landed him a place in the Opry family.

George, after the better part of two years with the Stevenses, was ready to perform on his own in 1949, working the same clubs he'd played with Eddie and Pearl. He picked up his own lead guitar man: Luther Nallie, now fifteen. "He was really a very nice person," Nallie said. "He always wanted to be a singer. He was what he was; he never did change what he was. I'll say to this day he was the best country singer I ever heard. Of course he . . . loved to sing Hank Williams songs. He liked Acuff and he liked Lefty

Frizzell . . . George could imitate some of those guys."

The two had one minor point of contention. George had never studied guitar beyond the simplest licks and chords. When Nallie, who'd learned to play the complex, jazzy western-swing guitar favored by bandleaders like Bob Wills and Cliff Bruner, played rhythm behind George, it sometimes led to oil-and-water moments onstage. "I'd make one of them jazz chords, and George'd go, 'What was that funny sound?' Our playin' was a little out of phase, but at that time, we needed each other. I needed a job and he needed me. And we made it through. I was young but every now and then I'd sip on a beer and we'd be ridin' along somewhere, and we'd go to singin' and we'd do it sometimes out playin'. George used to like 'Maple on the Hill.' We did it high [in harmony] and he had me singin' that high part to it."

While admiring his friend's singing, Nallie felt sympathy for George's offstage life, saying, "He'd stay with one family and then another, but he didn't actually have a home." George Washington Jones also became an occasional irritant. "I never met his mother," Nallie added. "But his dad used to come out and he was an alcoholic. He'd come around tryin' to bum money from George to buy some booze. And George'd get upset.

"George never really had a home. That's what was bad."

Nallie remembered the pair had a regular circuit, starting with Lola's and Shorty's on Pine Street.

"Lola's and Shorty's was right there by the shipyard, right by the Neches River. And it was a knock-down, drag-out place. We played another place out there on Highway 90, just a little ways out of Beaumont, called Miller's Café. It was kind of a drive-in beer joint. We played inside but we had the speakers goin' outside because people would sit in their cars and drink beer and listen to the music. They had carhops that would go back and forth and they had people inside, too, and they'd serve hamburgers, stuff like that. They had another place a half mile further down called Glenn Vista. We'd play on Sunday from one to five at Miller's Café, and then we'd go over at Glenn Vista from six till closin' time. I was flat worn-out. But we made a little money. George was pretty good. They'd put money in the kitty and we'd split it up. They paid a little something, like five dollars, which wasn't bad back then. I was livin' at home."

George's guitars, Nallie remembered, were catch-as-catch-can. "He kind of borrowed guitars. I don't know if he had one of his own or not. He had friends that he stayed with that were musicians and he'd use one of theirs. We were still playin' beer joints and then later on we added a fiddle player, Robert Shivers, and another one by the name of Lloyd Gilbert, and later on as time went on George got up a band with the drums and the whole shot." He enjoyed creating onstage comedy, sometimes at Luther's expense. He'd cede the microphone to his partner, whose specialty vocal was the dramatic 1950 hit ballad "Cry of the Wild Goose," a pop hit for Frankie Laine and a country success for Tennessee Ernie Ford. As he sang, "Tonight I heard the wild goose cry," George started honking, goose-style, behind him, cracking up the crowd and deflating Nallie's presentation.

George drank during this time, but Nallie insisted it wasn't yet a major problem when they were performing. Offstage was another matter. George and Nallie joined the owners of Lola's and Shorty's for a day of fishing on their small boat, equipped with an outboard motor and an ample supply of beer. Fortified with more than a few beers, George took the wheel only to hit something that damaged the propeller. When Luther raised the motor from the water to effect a temporary fix, a laughing, drunken George began rocking the boat.

It was at Playground Park that George first encountered the Bonvillian family: the patriarch, known as Willie; his wife, Claudia; and their daughter, Dorothy Ann, who'd come to Beaumont from Houston. Dorothy had been born in Houston in 1929. For Willie, going to bars and enjoying live country music on weekends was a respite from his job as a superintendent of the painting division of G. Sargl, Inc., a large Beaumont general contractor Nallie knew well, noting, "They would do like big buildings and they must have had thirty, forty painters, people workin' in that department."

The entire family seemed fascinated with the young singer. Willie liked his voice enough to buy him a portable PA system and a decent guitar. Overwhelmed by the attention, George took a liking to Dorothy. When he proposed, she accepted, but their wedding on June 1, 1950, proved awkward. The upwardly mobile Bonvillians seemed discomfited by Clara Jones and her backcountry ways, and by George's insistence that Brother Burl, a true backwoods preacher, officiate. Since he and Annie were doing revival meetings in Port Arthur, the wedding was held there. Even in the wedding photo, with both mothers separated by the happy couple, the more urbane Claudia Bonvillian looks uncomfortable.

The disconnect became all too clear when the couple moved in with the Bonvillians. Willie might have loved his son-in-law's singing, but he also knew music wasn't going to support a wife, much less a family, on hit-and-miss payments from Playground Park, Yvonne's, Miller's, or anywhere else. He laid down the law. Playing music in bars was fine on weekends, but his new son-in-law needed a day job with steady pay, and he happened to have one in mind: work as an apprentice housepainter for Sargl. George tried it, hated it, and quit, leaving Willie highly displeased. He landed a job driving a delivery truck and moved Dorothy and himself into an apartment. George's job history became even more checkered when he bailed on the delivery position and, later, a job at a funeral home. Soon the couple returned to the Bonvillians. With Dorothy pregnant by early 1951 and the marriage in free fall, George was back playing clubs, which disgusted his in-laws and ramped up the tension. As the conflicts escalated, George moved out.

George and Dorothy's parting ways benefited Nallie on two levels. "Willie had bought George one of those Bogen PA systems, the kind where the two speakers fit together and the amplifier fits in the middle and you take it apart, spread the speakers out. When George quit and left and all that, Willie took [the PA] back. Well, I was still playing out there with somebody else, and the first thing, I got George's job paintin'. Willie put me to work. I said, 'That PA system, I'd like to have that. How much do you want for it? I don't have any cash.' And he said, 'Well, I'll take $120 for it, and you can pay me ten dollars a month.' That's what I did, and I had that set for a long time. Willie was a real nice guy. But he didn't take any baloney from anybody."

George occasionally headed elsewhere. In Houston, he showed up at Cook's Hoedown, a dance hall known for presenting local western swing acts like Dickie McBride's Ranch Hands. He didn't leave a great impression. George Ogg, who played sax and clarinet with the band, told researcher Andrew Brown about seeing George with his guitar, singing on the bandstand steps during intermissions. Calling him "the sorriest presentation I ever saw in my life," Ogg noted, "you could insult him and he'd smile at you."

His pantheon of musical heroes increased by one in 1950–51, this one born not far away: Lefty Frizzell, from Corsicana, Texas. In the fall of 1950, his raw Texas honky-tonk swept America with the hit single "If You've Got the Money, I've Got the Time," a lively drinking song, and the single's B-side, the ballad "I Love

You a Thousand Ways," Frizzell originals recorded at Jim Beck's studio in Dallas. George became enamored of Frizzell's phrasing, the way he'd stretch out certain one-syllable words for effect—"way" became "way-a-hey," and so on—and worked to master Lefty's vocal style as well. For a time, George played guitar and sang with the Rowley Trio, who later worked with Lefty. Jerry Rowley; his wife, Evelyn; and his sister, Vera "Dido" Rowley, had an early-morning show on Beaumont's KFDM that often took requests on the air for songs, listeners choosing who would sing them. George stuck around for a while, but the early-morning hours were more than he wanted to handle.

Lefty had Beaumont ties. His new manager was a local businessman, Burl Houston Starns, known as Jack, who knew little about country music. His wife, Neva Starns, however, had considerable experience managing and booking local country acts. They owned Neva's, a dance hall/café on Voth Road in the northern end of Beaumont. Starns guided Frizzell's career, which included an entire stage show with supporting acts and his own band. He kept Lefty touring constantly, traveling to distant shows in his own plane.

Meanwhile, George's domestic situation worsened. On July 23, 1951, Dorothy Bonvillian Jones filed for divorce in the District Court of Jefferson County, citing George's drinking and propensity for violence. Four days later, the court ordered him to refrain from bothering his wife and set support payments for the unborn infant at thirty-five dollars a week, with an added $466 for medical bills relating to her pregnancy. When he failed to fork over the required amount, the judge jailed him on August 24. Five days later, his sister Loyce bailed him out. A month later, the scenario repeated itself when he was jailed again on September 28. Dorothy gave birth to Susan Marie Jones in Beaumont on October 29.

With two jail visits under his belt, George finally had to face the reality Willie Bonvillian knew from the start: singing in East Texas beer joints wouldn't cover child support, and sure as hell wouldn't keep him out of jail. The judge hearing his case offered one sure solution: enlisting in the military, where family-support payments were automatically deducted and forwarded. It was, however, not the optimal time to sign up. Since June 1950, America, along with the United Nations, was in an undeclared war—or "police action"—in Korea battling the Communist North Koreans. The military draft was in full swing. It wasn't what he wanted, but given the realities, namely the fact that the Bonvillians and Jefferson County courts and sheriff were set to pounce at the first late check, he had little choice. George was amazed to find waiting periods for the army and navy, but not for the marines. On November 16, 1951, George Glenn Jones enlisted for two years in the United States Marine Corps with nary a bit of enthusiasm. He'd left in anguish, Dido Rowley remembering him in tears before his departure. Little wonder. The odds he'd wind up in Korea were high.

Assigned the serial number 1223231, he underwent his basic training at the Marine Corps Recruit Depot in San Diego and dodged a huge and literal bullet. The Corps sent him not to Korea but to Moffett Field, a naval air station near San Jose, south of San Francisco. His MOS (military occupation specialty) was that of basic infantryman. Despite the war, he'd spend his entire enlistment there, holding no rank higher than Private First Class, with the classification of Rifleman. He lived for leaves and weekends, when he could take his guitar to the area's clubs and dance halls. One of his early favorites: Tracy Gardens in San Jose, where nineteen-year-old steel guitarist Bobby Black and his guitarist brother Larry spent their Saturday nights playing as members of the house act, Shorty Joe Quartuccio's western swing band the

Red Rock Canyon Cowboys. Local musicians and even strangers who felt they could sing routinely asked to sit in with the band, who were happy to oblige.

One night George, in uniform, approached the bandstand wanting to sing. Black never forgot the crowd's reaction. "Right away, he was a hit because he sang the songs they were playin' on the radio, mostly Frizzell and Hank Williams. I remember him singing 'Always Late,' 'Mom and Dad's Waltz,' 'Cold Cold Heart,' and all that kind of stuff. He sounded like Hank and Lefty, another reason why people liked him. There wasn't anybody around these parts that could do that. You had to have a certain quality to your voice, and George had it." His lack of ego also impressed Black, who called him "kind of quiet and unassuming—just a good ol' country boy, and although we didn't suspect at all that he would someday be a star, it was obvious that he had what it took to become one. I recall [him performing] maybe three or four times," Black continued. "It wasn't every Saturday. We'd get him up to sing a few numbers and everybody always wanted to hear him . . . He would just sort of vanish. We just called him 'George the Singin' Marine,' and later 'Burr-head.' At that time, he was lookin' for a place to go, to hear a country band, and maybe just get up to sing with somebody."

That desire caused him some grief at Moffett Field. He later admitted to going AWOL. It's not clear if that was the specific offense that on April 21, 1952, after a summary court-martial, earned him ten days in the brig. It didn't stop his extracurricular performing. He met Cottonseed Clark, a popular Bay Area disc jockey and promoter based in nearby Oakland, who'd started promoting country and western swing dances there in the forties. Clark began doing shows at the Foresters of America Hall, better known as Forester's Hall, a popular gathering spot in nearby Redwood City, where George earned the nickname "Little Georgie Jones, the Forester Hall Flash." At least once he traveled to Los Angeles, where some accounts have him appearing as an occasional guest on Cliffie Stone's Saturday-night *Hometown Jamboree* TV show from El Monte Legion Stadium. On October 27, he wound up in the infirmary at Moffett Field with some unspecified malady.

His marine buddies, who'd heard him sing around camp, knew how much he admired Hank Williams. Much had changed for Hank in the years since George had met him. He'd become one of the nation's top country stars, charismatic onstage when able to sing, but too often he either took the stage drunk or not at all. Pain from back surgery had got him addicted to chloral hydrate prescribed by a quack "physician." After he missed various broadcasts and stage appearances around the nation, the Opry suspended him in 1952, but the Louisiana Hayride quickly took him back. Many hoped a New Year's Day 1953 gig in Canton, Ohio, would begin his redemption and eventual restoration to the Opry ranks.

When George came into his barracks New Year's morning, one of his friends told him, "Your buddy's dead," and handed him the morning paper, revealing Hank had died in the backseat of his baby-blue Cadillac en route to Canton. The coroner's later findings of a simple heart attack were, of course, bullshit. Hank had been whacked out of his gourd on booze and chloral as eighteen-year-old Charles Carr chauffeured him north. During a stop in Oak Hill, West Virginia, Carr found his passenger cold to the touch. Reading the story, a devastated George sat on his bunk crying over the loss of a hero he'd actually met. The image of Hank stoned in a Caddy would haunt George for decades.

As her son had never been a letter writer and perhaps felt no great desire to stay in touch with his family, a worried Clara had to write his superiors to get him to communicate at all. On April 18, 1953, he got another leave. He came back to Beaumont dragging along a woman he claimed was his wife, and hung out with friends before returning for his last few months of service. At some point another letter arrived from Beaumont. This one wasn't from Clara, but from Jack Starns. Aware of George's singing and impending discharge, Starns told him about a new record company he'd cofounded and urged him to get in touch when he returned home that fall. His separation from the Marine Corps began October 28, when he was reassigned to a facility in Oakland, California. He was back in Beaumont in November. He had to keep eyes in the back of his head and maintain his support payments, lest the Bonvillians and the courts wind up nipping at his heels. Nonetheless, buoyed by the note from Starns, George Jones was ready to resume his music career.

CHAPTER 2

1953–1961

East Texas was the last place Bobby Black expected to be at this point in his life.

The twenty-year-old steel guitarist had left the San Francisco Bay Area to join Blackie Crawford and the Western Cherokees, Lefty Frizzell's former backup group. Fronted by singer-guitarist Crawford, they were a large, versatile unit capable of backing honky-tonkers of Lefty's stripe or playing hot, danceable western swing of the type Black played in the California dance halls. One day, Black and Cherokees pianist Burney Annett arrived at Beaumont's Railway Express to take delivery of a custom-built pedal steel Black had ordered from builder Paul Bigsby before he left California. Anxious to see the new instrument, the two men enthusiastically tore open the wooden crate, removed the hard-shell case, and opened it. As a crowd gathered around the rich, curly maple guitar with its stainless-steel hardware, Black heard a familiar voice.

"Hey, what are *you* doin' here?"

He turned and saw a smiling, newly civilian George.

"Man, what are *you* doin' here?"

"This is where I live, man! I'm not in the marines anymore!"

Black asked if he was still singing. When George replied he was, Black said, "You should go to Nashville."

"Yeah," George answered. "I'm thinkin' about it."

The Cherokees had more to do than play dance halls. They were the house band for Starday, Beaumont's new record company, a partnership of Jack Starns and Houston jukebox kingpin and record retailer Harold Westcott Daily, known to all as Pappy. The label's name was a mash-up of the names *Starns* and *Daily*.

Even when managing Frizzell, Starns was far from a longtime country music fan, but he succeeded in part due to his wife Neva's experience in the business, booking acts and running her Beaumont club and dance hall. The family lived next door. In May 1951, with Lefty riding high, the Starnses added a second dance hall by purchasing the legendary Reo Palm Isle in Longview, Texas. Jack had guided Frizzell for about a year before the two fell out over a two-year option to renew the management contract that Lefty claimed had been added without his approval. After legal parrying, it cost Lefty $25,000—all the cash he had—to get Starns out of his life. The Western Cherokees, however, decided to stick with Jack, not Lefty. Jack had an idea how to use that windfall. With Neva handling her end, he'd launch a record company focused on Texas talent. To make it work, he'd need someone with hands-on record company experience.

Born in Yoakum, Texas, in 1902, Pappy Daily, was a former marine and baseball player who'd worked for the Southern Pacific

Railroad in Houston. In the early 1930s, with the nation laid low by the Great Depression, he began distributing jukeboxes through his Southcoast Amusement Company, an increasingly lucrative field despite the dire economic times. He expanded into retailing after World War II with Daily's Record Ranch, a Houston retail store that also featured live performers, as Nashville's Ernest Tubb Record Shop later did. His connections led him to become the Texas distributor for California-based Four Star Records, who recorded West Coast country acts like T. Texas Tyler and the Maddox Brothers and Rose. Four Star owner Bill McCall, notorious for his slippery business dealings, wanted to tap the Texas market and needed a talent scout and producer who could find regional acts, record them, then ship him the finished recordings.

Daily came up with an impressive list of local honky-tonk talent: Smilin' Jerry Jericho, Eddie Noack, Hank Locklin, and, from Shreveport, Louisiana, Webb Pierce. His amiable, supportive nature led Locklin to nickname him Pappy, but relations between Daily and McCall turned less cordial. McCall's reputation for not paying people applied to Pappy's efforts as well. He never got a dime for his Four Star production work or expenses. When they parted ways, Pappy could add record production to his extensive music portfolio. The only Four Star employee in California he got along with was Don Pierce, also no McCall admirer.

Exactly how Starns and Daily connected isn't completely clear, but they were planning Starday by 1952. Having jumped ship at Four Star, Pierce, still in LA, helped the partners create the Starday Recording and Publishing Company with a music publishing company known as Starrite. *Billboard*'s June 27, 1953, edition announced the new label, identifying the founders as "well known c & w manager Jack Starns, Jr., and his wife, Neva." After Starday's first three singles, one of them by Crawford and the Cherokees, were ignored, fortunes suddenly changed when Jack and Neva discovered Arlie Duff. The twenty-nine-year-old Warren, Texas, schoolteacher, songwriter, and singer had a raw, nasal voice and a number of original tunes including the exuberant "Y'All Come," inspired by a phrase his grandmother used. Starns recorded Duff, accompanied by the Cherokees, at a Houston studio. Soon after the late 1953 release of "Y'All Come," it became Starday's first national Top 10 country single. The song's stature grew when Bing Crosby's cover version reached the pop Top 20.

Starns had set up a makeshift studio in his home. Some recall it located in the living room; others in an enclosed back porch. He purchased a Magnecord portable tape recorder and microphones and fastened egg cartons to the walls to deaden the sound. His fourteen-year-old son Bill would work the recorder, flipping a light switch on and off to signal the singers and musicians when to begin and end a take, a quick and dirty way of getting records done and ensuring a steady flow of releases. By year's end, George Jones, back on the local honky-tonk circuit, was ready to record.

HE AND HIS GUITAR ARRIVED AT THE STARNS HOME ONE DAY IN JANUARY 1954. The Western Cherokees were there to back him, although Jimmy Biggar had replaced Bobby Black, who'd returned to California. Also at the session was Big Thicket native Gordon Baxter, a local broadcaster and author who chronicled the Thicket and had his own musical aspirations. George brought five original songs: "No Money in This Deal," "For Sale or Lease," "Play It Cool," "You're in My Heart," and "If You Were Mine." After working out loose arrangements and making sure everyone was ready, Bill Starns hit the light switch. George kicked off "No Money," the Cherokees falling in behind him, Burney Annett energetically pounding the piano as fiddler Little Red Hayes played rhythmic double-stops. George's animated vocal wasn't quite enough to mask his nervousness. It was a start, but not a terribly good novelty song. Even a shout-out to twin sisters Joyce and Loyce couldn't save it.

It was glaringly apparent on the remaining numbers that the advice Hank Williams gave George about finding his own style had gone out the window. The wry "Play It Cool" and the ballad "You're in My Heart" were blatant Hank imitations, with Biggar reproducing the high-register licks of Hank's longtime steel player Don Helms. On "For Sale or Lease" and "If You Were Mine," George unabashedly channeled Lefty, and Biggar imitated the steel-guitar flourishes Jim Kelly had made a trademark on Lefty's early hits. The egg crates may have helped dampen the echo, but they didn't filter all outside sounds. George recalled hearing eighteen-wheelers flying north and south on Voth Road during the session.

Starday wasted no time trying to generate interest. *Billboard*'s January 23 "Folk Talent and Tunes" section announced George and Baxter had been signed (no Baxter recording was ever released). When "No Money" was released, the March 6 issue, ignoring the technical flaws, declared, "Lively country novelty has a good catch-phrase." "You're in My Heart" elicited a more accurate evaluation: "Country weeper derives directly from the Hank Williams school . . . Jones belts it out with fair effectiveness," essentially (and justifiably) damning the performance with faint praise.

When George met Pappy in person, the old man asked him to sing some other material. He obliged, invoking all his musical heroes, which led to Daily posing a now immortal question, worded slightly differently depending on the source:

"George, you've sung like Roy Acuff, Lefty Frizzell, Hank Williams, and Bill Monroe. Can you sing like George Jones?"

"I don't understand," George cluelessly responded. "Those guys are who I like."

Finding his own singing style may not have been his priority at the moment, yet George, elated to have a record out, visited local radio stations with copies of "No Money." Dropping by KLTW in nearby Pasadena, Texas, he asked disc jockey "Tater" Pete Hunter to play it. Hunter obliged without comment. Off the air, George asked Hunter what he thought. Hunter wasn't impressed. George, not offended, kept the comment in mind.

Starday wasn't enough for Jack and Pappy. With weekly barn-dance stage and radio shows like the Opry and Hayride going strong around the country, on March 13, 1954, they launched the Grand Prize Houston Jamboree. Broadcast from City Auditorium over KNUZ radio and TV, the sponsor was Grand Prize Beer, a product of Houston's Gulf Brewery, founded by industrialist Howard Hughes. Among the cast: Hank Locklin and the rest of the Starday roster—Blackie Crawford and the Cherokees, George, Arlie Duff, Sonny Burns, and Patsy Elshire. George's exuberant performances made him one of the show's more popular acts. When he wasn't working honky-tonks and dance halls, he earned extra money accompanying other Starday singers, contributing a flat-picked acoustic solo on Duff's recording of the traditional "Salty Dog."

In May 1954, nineteen-year-old Houston-born John Bush Shinn III, later known as Johnny Bush, was living in San Antonio. He was visiting Houston to see his uncle, Smilin' Jerry Jericho, the popular local singer Pappy recorded for Four Star in the late forties. More recently Jericho had recorded for Starday, and was en route to perform at the Jimmie Rodgers Memorial Festival in Meridian, Mississippi. Before they headed east, Jericho and his nephew stopped by City Auditorium, where Jericho was to play the Jamboree.

"I saw this young man who was literally tearin' the crowd up. He would bounce out there and do about five lines of a song and just walk off. And people would just scream and holler and do everything but tear the seats up. I thought, 'Who in the world is this?' I've never seen anything like it. At that time, he was apin' Lefty Frizzell and Jimmy Newman. He hadn't quite gotten into his own yet, but it was phenomenal how he was goin' over, and I said, 'Man, this guy has got to go!' He was knockin' people out. He was getting standing ovations. He'd sing a few lines of a song, leave the microphone, run back into the wings, and they'd have to bring him back. He never would finish a song. He had 'em in the palm of his hand and he knew it."

Backstage, Bush asked Tommy Hill, the Western Cherokees' guitarist, about the young singer.

"That's George Jones," Hill replied. After the show, Bush accompanied Jericho to a gig at Cook's Hoedown. "George come down after the show, and that's when my uncle introduced me to him. He came down there and sat at a table with a friend, didn't get up to sing."

GEORGE FOUND A NEW BEST FRIEND AT THE JAMBOREE: GALVESTON NATIVE and Starday artist Clyde Burns Jr., known to all as Sonny. A year older than George, he first gained attention around Houston. He signed to Starday, and his energetic rendition of "Too Hot to Handle" did well enough for Starns and Daily to take a greater interest. With "Y'All Come" now yesterday's hit, Sonny's records began catching on regionally while George's languished. Thinking Sonny's stronger sales might boost George's visibility, Pappy teamed them for harmony duets on "Heartbroken Me" and "Wrong About You."

While their duet singles sputtered and died, the Burns-Jones camaraderie did not. The bottle became common ground. "George didn't need any encouragement on the drinking," Starday and Jamboree artist Patsy Elshire told Andrew Brown. But the George-Sonny bond seemed to kick George's boozing into overdrive. When he and Sonny began working together, George got a better perspective on the Houston club scene. As he drank harder, the results began reflecting George W. Jones at his worst: paranoid, aggressive, and belligerent. George's diminutive stature and height of five foot seven didn't prevent him from squaring off with anyone of any size he thought was getting on his case.

One night at Lola's and Shorty's, it nearly got him killed.

George was onstage with a fiddler when he spied a solitary man in the crowd. Being two car payments behind, he sensed the stranger's reason for being there. On a break, George confronted the man, who admitted what George suspected: he was there to repossess the car. George proceeded to pound the shit out of him. Landing punch after punch, he didn't see his adversary pull the razor that sliced through George's leather jacket into his torso. He didn't realize he was bleeding until two of his friends yanked the man off and pummeled him. George left in an ambulance; it took ninety stitches to close the lengthy wound.

With monthly support payments a priority and income from singing in joints anything but steady, George began spinning records fifty-five minutes a day over at KTRM in Beaumont. The radio station was as much frat house as radio station, where on-air pranks between staff were common. George, anything but a polished personality, habitually broke reel-to-reel tapes and mispronounced words when he read commercial scripts on the air. The job allowed him to advertise his upcoming local appearances. Johnny Bush, who heard him on KTRM, remembered him imitating Simon Crum, singer Ferlin Husky's comedic hillbilly alter ego. "Between records, he would ape Simon Crum. He would do that laugh and you'd swear he was Simon." George found another new buddy in the station's top personality: beefy twenty-four-year-old Jiles Perry Richardson, from Sabine Pass, south of Beaumont. Like George, Richardson had lived in Multimax as a kid and knew his way around a guitar. During high school he parlayed a part-time KTRM announcing job into full-time employment.

Moving around East Texas and the Gulf Coast, with and without Sonny, George found honky-tonks had a different status depending on the area. In rural East Texas, there were never a ton of them. Texas music researcher Andrew Brown points out that in Baptist areas, cities and counties (including the Thicket) were dry. In other places, honky-tonks were relegated to the outskirts of town. One exception: Port Arthur, where the heavily Catholic (and Cajun) population meant bars and clubs weren't pushed to the city limits. That also wasn't a problem in Houston. George was playing at a honky-tonk known as Amma Dee's on Canal Street in late August or early September 1954 when he stopped by a nearby Prince's drive-in. In business since 1934, Prince's was, and remains, a beloved local chain known for burgers—and carhops. He set eyes on one: eighteen-year-old Shirley Ann Corley of Tenaha, Texas, north of the Thicket.

Shirley came to Houston that summer to escape rural poverty. After her father, Bryan Corley, died in a railroad accident, her mother remarried to a man who farmed and did little else. After high school graduation, she headed for the city for the summer, expecting to return home and marry her steady boyfriend from high school. When that relationship fell apart, she signed on at Prince's. George urged her to come see him at the club. They married on September 14. The flames of youthful romance initially blinded both as they entered what for George was his second square-peg-round-hole relationship. Throughout their fourteen-year marriage, Shirley could never fully accept her husband's unyielding commitment to his career. She wasn't pleased when he insisted they relocate from Houston to Beaumont, where cheaper housing was easily found. They moved into a one-story home at 2650½ Magnolia Street. Beaumont's city directory listed him not as an entertainer or singer, but as an announcer at KTRM. Between that salary, income from the honky-tonks, and what he was paid for playing the Jamboree, he cobbled together a living.

Starday had a publicity shot of George that showed him with slicked-back hair, most of it covered by a white cowboy hat, wearing a light-colored embroidered western shirt. Every Starday act had such photos, even those whose records, like his, made few if any waves. The real turbulence involved Starday's cofounders and their diverging perspectives about the company. Starns, ever the manager-promoter, felt as he did at the start: the label was a marketing tool for whatever act or acts he managed. Daily, supported by Pierce, who assumed the title of president and handled the business affairs from LA, sensed the label was set for growth. Starns and Neva were about to divorce. Starns, who'd had his ups and downs in the business, finally opted to abandon his music interests, selling his half of Starday to Pappy. His daughter told Starday authority Nate Gibson her father declared, "I've had enough of these hillbillies!" After the divorce, Starns remarried and began retailing mobile homes in the Deep South. Neva moved to Springfield, Missouri, home of the Ozark Jubilee, and continued to manage acts.

With Pappy and Pierce running Starday, Pappy still produced records around Houston. He had access to better recording facilities thanks to a backdoor investment in Bill Quinn's Gold Star

Studio in Houston, originally a homegrown operation similar to the Starns living room setup. George and other Starday acts recorded there. He remained popular on the Jamboree, yet record sales continued to lag, his vocals enthusiastic but still too imitative. He may have wanted his own voice, but he kept on invoking his heroes when he sang.

George became fast friends with Frankie Miller, a singer and Columbia recording artist from Victoria, Texas, who joined the Jamboree cast sometime in early 1955. George's stage presence also impressed him. "The people really liked him from the first time I saw him. They used to encore him on that show. He'd sing some of the things he had out, but he would sing other songs, and man, they would just love him." George kept the crowds laughing with self-deprecating wisecracks. Miller remembered the time George had a barber buzz his slicked down hair, returning to the haircut he sported in the marines. "He would come out with that flattop and say, 'I got this flattop. You all can see my big ears now!'" Miller took special note of George's physical approach to singing. "He would kind of bow his legs [and crane his neck] and kind of grit—sing through his teeth a lot, with his mouth almost shut." Alcohol, Miller recalled, didn't interfere with George's performances at that point. "We worked at a lot of clubs together. He was always good. I never saw him when he couldn't do a show. I've seen him so damn drunk almost that he couldn't hardly walk. And he would get out onstage and sing like a damn mockingbird. No matter how much drink he had, he'd get that guitar and sing. Of course, after the show, down in the dressing room, he'd be drunker than hell, but he never missed a show when I was with him."

For club work, George had a band: steel guitarist R.C. Martin, guitarist Donnie Broussard, drummer Lennie Benoit, and pianist Pee Wee Altenberry. They generally carried no bass unless Raymond

Nallie, Luther's brother, sat in. "If it had a Falstaff [beer] sign, we played there," Martin recalled. "There was the Super 73 Club in Winnie. We never did play [in Beaumont] at Yvonne's with him or the Blue Jean Club. Smaller clubs. There used to be a lot of them. Played in Louisiana. Just around that area there. Sundays, we played out in a drive-in theater on a flatbed truck. That was a job we had for quite a while with him. He often played four hours at a clip."

Like most regional singers playing local clubs, George couldn't pay his sidemen much. Martin remembered how the musicians wrangled a two-dollar raise when they played the Super 73 Club, thanks to Raymond Nallie. "George was payin' us ten dollars, which was [union] scale," Martin said. "He was makin' pretty good money . . . about one hundred or a little better a night. When we drove up, Raymond was outside. He says, 'Stop right here. Don't go in. Don't take a step in.' We said, 'What's the matter?' He said, 'He's gonna pay us twelve dollars a night, or we're not gonna play.' George come out and him and Raymond argued around for a while and he said, 'Okay, I'll pay you twelve dollars a night.' And we went and played the job."

George bought a used 1951 Packard to get to gigs, complete with his name and label painted below the chrome trim, along with BMT. TEX and a phone number. Luther Nallie rode with him on one job. "George came by to pick me up after he got that contract with Starday. He bought him a Packard from some used-car dealer and it was kind of a bright purple and he had all the way across in yellow letters, GEORGE JONES . . . STARDAY RECORDING ARTIST. He came by and picked me up in that thing. He thought that was really something."

George in those days was still a man of the Thicket, holding on to the mind-sets and prejudices he grew up with.

"I was in San Antone on a show he did," Frankie Miller

remembered, "and a young black guy come back to the drinkin' fountain! George said, 'You can't drink there! Get the hell away from there!' Run his ass away from that drinkin' fountain." Over time, his views would evolve, not unlike those of Johnny Cash and other singers raised in the Deep South. "We were raised like that," Johnny Bush commented, "and we had to get over it."

His redemption on records came through an old Thicket pal and amateur poet: Darrell Edwards. Twelve years older than George, they knew each other in Saratoga. Edwards served in the Coast Guard, heard about George's singing, and reconnected with him. The two would begin kicking ideas around. He gave George a wry, catchy number titled "Why, Baby, Why" with enough potential that it also impressed Pappy. George, who added some ideas of his own, got a cowriter credit. He took it to his next date at Gold Star in the summer of 1955. Some accounts indicate Sonny Burns was expected at the session—since Pappy saw "Why, Baby, Why" as a George-Sonny duet—and that George overdubbed vocal harmonies after Sonny, likely on a drunk, didn't show.

The Hank Williams–style vocal aside, the catchy chorus of "Why" ("Tell me why baby, why baby, why baby, why, you made me cry baby, cry baby, cry baby, cry") gave it a commerciality his previous records lacked. Three more Edwards numbers went to tape that day, including a wrenching ballad titled "Seasons of My Heart" that again featured George relying on Lefty's characteristic habit of stretching words. As always, despite the improved studio, production values remained nonexistent. As George later admitted to Nick Tosches, "There was no such thing as production at Starday," noting the arrangements were hurriedly done, and even bad notes didn't much concern Pappy. "If we went a little flat or sharp in a place or two, they'd say 'The public ain't gonna notice that, so put it out.'"

Pappy and Don Pierce paired "Why" and "Seasons" on a single, promoting "Seasons" as the stronger tune. In an August 7, 1955, form letter sent to "country music DJ's" with a copy of the disc, Pierce thanks them for past support, then turns on the hard sell, declaring, "Right now, we have a record that in our opinion is about the best we have ever released. We hope we can ask you occasionally to 'really lay on one' for us and we think George Jones 'SEASONS OF MY HEART' is worthy of special consideration." He adds, "The reverse side 'WHY BABY WHY' is also very strong." Clearly, Pierce sensed the ballad was the stronger performance and the one more likely to make radio take notice.

George doubled down on self-promotion. On August 24, he heard about a Louisiana Hayride traveling show at the high school football field in Conroe, Texas, north of Houston. Headlining was the Hayride's hottest singer: Sun recording artist Elvis Presley, supported by Hayride favorite and future star Johnny Horton and singer Betty Amos. George arrived before showtime and cajoled MC Horace Logan into letting him perform, explaining he had a new Starday single about to drop. Logan agreed. Pierce had clearly miscalculated which tune would prove stronger. In their October review of the single, *Billboard* reported that "Why Baby Why" was scoring big in Memphis, Texas, and Louisiana, momentum that had begun in September and continued through most of October. The Hayride booked him for an October 1 guest appearance. The timing was fortunate, since George and Shirley welcomed their first son, Jeffrey Glenn Jones, that fall. But if the public liked "Why Baby Why," so did former Hayride star Webb Pierce (no relation to Don Pierce). Pappy recorded Pierce for Four Star in 1949. After becoming one of the Hayride's top stars, Pierce landed a Decca recording contract, joined the Opry, and became one of America's top country singers. His honky-tonk hits for Decca—"Wondering," "Back Street Affair, "There Stands the Glass," "Slowly," and others—showcased his distinctive, expressive tenor. Pierce wanted to record "Why" as a duet with Hayride pal and fellow Decca artist Red Sovine.

In Nashville, Webb was considered a great singer, but a hard-nosed businessman and a mercenary when it came to the bottom line. Pierce claimed he learned business fundamentals working as a department manager at Shreveport's Sears Roebuck before becoming a full-time performer. He and Opry manager Jim Denny co-owned Cedarwood, a Nashville song publishing company. Pierce often aided new songwriters, including newcomer Mel Tillis, by recording their tunes—provided they gave him half ownership. The line usually worked when he'd tell them half of something was better than all of nothing. Many times, he was correct. This time, Webb didn't ask for a piece of the song. Supposedly, remembering Pappy's early support, he offered to delay his version of the song to give George a head start and more exposure.

Whether he did or didn't make such an offer, Pierce and Sovine didn't record "Why Baby Why" in Nashville until October 27, 1955. Decca rush-released their single. It took off, yet didn't dent the momentum of George's. The two versions ran neck and neck in regional markets that fall, as Tennessee Ernie Ford's "Sixteen Tons" grabbed and held the No. 1 position nationwide.

George's single continued to rise. He became a Hayride cast member on February 4. A week later, Pierce and Sovine's "Why" knocked "Sixteen Tons" out of No. 1. George's version reached No. 4 in store sales. In all, he was triumphant. He had his first national hit, and Starday had a single whose success outdid "Y'all Come."

Bob Sullivan was KWKH's engineer even before the Hayride began in 1948. He'd seen future icons appear on the stage at Shreveport's Municipal Auditorium: Hank, Webb, Elvis, Jim Reeves, Horton, Johnnie and Jack, Kitty Wells, and others. He, too, marveled at George's onstage physicality. "I called it hard singin'. When he would sing one of his songs, if the note was high, he would bow his neck up. And you could tell that he was workin' at it. And we used to laugh at him. Once in a while he'd come offstage and some old boy'd say, 'I didn't see you bow your neck tonight!'" His flair for cutting up onstage continued as he worked Elvis imitations into his act.

While Hayride acts commonly drank backstage, Jones took things to another level. "He was the nicest guy in the world," Sullivan admitted. "But when he got drunk, he got mean drunk. He would cuss and raise Cain and they would have to keep him away from a microphone, 'cause he didn't watch what he was doin'. I saw him one night, he was so drunk they wouldn't put him on for his last song." Every artist did two or three appearances during a Hayride broadcast. When the show ended, KWKH followed with a disc-jockey program from the studio, cohosted by a different Hayride artist each week, driven to the studio from the auditorium. One week it was George's turn. He began the evening in good shape, but, Sullivan added, "By the time he did his third appearance on the Hayride, he started drinkin'."

When the time came to take him to the studio, things were in free fall. "He was so drunk he couldn't stand up," Sullivan continued. "And they had two girls, one was on each side of him, draggin' him to the studio. He was ready to go on, but he was so drunk he was out of it. He showed up at the station and the DJ got up, opened the door, and invited him in. He saw the shape he was in. He said, 'Girls, don't bring him in. I'm not puttin' him on the air!' They never did ask him anymore because he was unreliable."

Pappy released another single from the Houston session,

this one the jaunty "What Am I Worth." Topping out at No. 7 nationally, it gave him back-to-back Top 10 singles, bringing more national attention his way. Around that time he also recorded a vintage tune that over time became a Jones standard. "Ragged but Right" was his adaptation of Georgia singer-guitarist Riley Puckett's 1934 recording of "I'm Ragged but I'm Right." But where Puckett jauntily sang of being "a thief and a gambler" who's "drunk every night," George, probably at Pappy's insistence, jauntily sang of being "a tramp and a rounder, and I stay out late at night." The single, never a hit, remained part of his onstage repertoire throughout his active career. It also marked a new chapter. The vocal sounded less derivative, and it seemed that at last, all those misguided attempts to find his own voice were beginning to pay off. That was even more apparent on his optimistic original "You Gotta Be My Baby," his third Top 10. The Hank, Acuff, and Lefty overtones began to recede. He tested his vocal range on this tune, his twangy tenor easily dropping to a deep bass as he infused the playful lyrics with a natural lightheartedness.

THE HIT SINGLES GOT HIM TOURING NATIONALLY. HE GOT A GOOD TASTE OF THE road on one early trip. Booked in New Orleans during Mardi Gras, he hauled ass to the show, doing ninety through Bay St. Louis, Mississippi. The local cops took exception, arrested him for speeding, and threw him in jail. He had to call home, and money had to be wired to get him out. While he got to New Orleans in time for the show, his hotel room was robbed and he lost a watch and rings. One tour took him to the San Francisco area, where he looked up Bobby Black, who was playing with a band at the 1902 Club in downtown Oakland.

Black was surprised to see him walk in out of the blue. "I could tell he'd been drinking," he said. "I introduced him to the band. Nobody there had probably ever seen him before, but they were all familiar with 'Why Baby Why.'" George agreed to sing it during the band's next set, leaving time for a few more drinks. When he was introduced and the band kicked off the song, Black recalled, "George sounded as if he'd never done it before and just barely got through it, forgetting words along the way. I don't think anybody there that night really believed that he was George Jones. On our next break, I took him across the street to the Doggie Diner and got him a hot dog and some coffee. He then just disappeared into the night."

George still got off imitating Elvis onstage, but by the spring of 1956, the twenty-one-year-old from Memphis was becoming a worldwide phenomenon with the rockabilly sound he accidentally developed at Sun Records and continued at RCA, about to revolutionize popular music. Nerves became frayed in Nashville's growing country music industry. For a time country record sales fell, and some country stations jumped ship and embraced the rock 'n' roll format. Pappy's business sense told him this rock business wasn't fading anytime soon. He and Don Pierce decided they'd better jump on the bandwagon fast. Young rockers would soon be pounding on Starday's door, and many would join the label. But for now, Pappy opted to kick-start things using the existing roster, George included. Knowing George always needed money, he gave his star vocalist a direct order: write a couple of these rocking-type songs he could record. Elvis impersonations aside, George didn't mind others doing rockabilly. But while the idea of singing it himself was a notion he despised, finances trumped personal taste and he dashed off two simple rockers: "Rock It" and "(Dadgummit) How Come It." If he spent more than fifteen minutes writing either one, it would be surprising. Their lyrics, little more than random, free-associative clichés, reflected his contempt for the idiom. Beyond the money, the notion that Pappy would use him—Starday's top act—to capitalize on a sound alien to him left him furious.

From the first flurry of hard-strummed A chords on his acoustic guitar, clearly inspired by the opening of Presley's "That's All Right," George, driven by a powerful confluence of booze and anger, screams the "Rock It" lyrics as Hal Harris's pulsing Chet Atkins–Merle Travis finger-style electric guitar percolates beneath him, the same way Scotty Moore played it behind Elvis. At times it sounded as if he was creating some sort of barbed satire of rockabilly. But there was also a clear, liquor-driven undercurrent aimed directly at Pappy: *You want this kind of shit? Okay, here!* If "Rock It" is grotesque, "How Come It," kicked off by Doc Lewis's boogie-woogie piano, is simply sloppy as George rushes through the vocal, the band barely able to follow him. The final number, a cover of "Heartbreak Hotel," was so messy it resembled Stan Freberg's savage 1956 parody of the Presley hit. Pappy wasn't that discriminating. He had something rocking to throw out there. But few bothered to buy it. That some rockabilly scholars and fans view "Rock It" as powerful and fiery is a hard premise to accept when the songs are placed alongside the best by Presley, Charlie Feathers, or Carl Perkins. The best rockabilly is intense, free, and loose. "Rock It" and "How Come It" were chaotic and uptight.

Thoroughly disgusted, George demanded Pappy not issue the single under his name. Drawing on his love of cartoons, he offered the pseudonym "Thumper Jones," a play on the character Thumper Rabbit. Pappy agreed. Discussing the single forty-five years later, George said, "That oughta show you how bad I hated doin' it because I didn't want anyone to know it was me. I'd have done anything in those days to make a dollar, because I was hungry." *Billboard* might have called "Rock It" "country blues with an engaging beat" when reviewing the single, but radio and the public disagreed. Few stations played it, and sales were minimal. The passing of half a century didn't temper George's contempt for that bit of his history. In a 2006 interview, he called the record "a bunch of shit" and the "worst sounding crap that could ever be put on a record." His aversion to singing rock himself didn't preclude his admiration for the music of two black rock singers: Little Richard and Chuck Berry. Berry was especially admired by other rock-averse country singers because of his skill as a songwriter. Ernest Tubb had a hit 1955 adaptation of Berry's "Thirty Days."

George didn't have to worry about the "Heartbreak" cover, released by Pappy under the name "Hank Smith and his Nashville Playboys." It was part of another Daily moneymaking idea. He'd produce cover versions of country hits, sung by George and unknown vocalists trying to impersonate the original singer, accompanied by a band roughly copying the original arrangement. He'd market them on radio as cut-rate singles and LPs. Finding hungry young singers willing to record these covers wasn't hard. Among those who jumped on board for the money: Roger Miller and Donny Young, the future Johnny Paycheck.

There was no small irony in Pappy, who'd pushed George to quit imitating other singers, paying him to mimic (with varying degrees of success) Johnny Horton on Horton's hit "One Woman Man," Ray Price on "Run Boy," Carl Smith on "Before I Met You," Marty Robbins on "Singing the Blues," and Faron Young on "I Got Five Dollars and It's Saturday Night." Pappy marketed the discs via two popular late-night country disc jockeys with a national reach. One was Chicago's Randy Blake, the other Paul Kallinger, who worked at Del Rio, Texas, station XERF, his program broadcast over megawatt transmitters across the border in Mexico. The common thread with these and the Thumper single was predictable. George declared that Starday "would pay me two hundred or three hundred dollars, which I needed real bad at the time, to go in there and do those type of things."

Beaumont acknowledged George's growing fame when the *Beaumont Enterprise* ran a July 6, 1956, profile of him. Reporter Milton Turner declared, "He plays the guitar like he sings— enthusiastically. The result is he breaks about three or four guitar strings at each performance. This native Beaumonter is breaking other things too!" The story went on to claim "Why Baby Why" had sold half a million copies, a likely exaggeration. Turner also noted George's recent awards, such as his Best New Artist of 1956 Award by *Country and Western Jamboree* magazine. Turner's propensity for exaggeration peaked when he claimed the Thumper "Rock and Roll" singles were "rolling to the top—fast."

Pappy and former Starday employee Gabe Tucker, now in Nashville managing Ernest Tubb, focused on moving George to the next level: Opry membership, or a permanent place in the show's cast of performers. Tucker, who'd worked for Colonel Tom Parker when the Colonel managed Eddy Arnold, was familiar with the highly political Opry environment. He secured George a guest spot for August 4. The 780-mile drive from Beaumont to Nashville was clear sailing compared to the bullshit he faced before he could set foot in front of a WSM microphone.

Opry guest spots did not always end well. Elvis's sole appearance in 1954 ended on a sour note when arrogant, conniving Opry manager Jim Denny, who disliked his performance, suggested he go back to truck driving. At the Ryman Auditorium, unspecified backstage bureaucrats claimed "union rules" barred George from playing his own guitar onstage since he wasn't a member of Nashville's Local 257, a red herring conceived to let guests know their place. Sober and nervous, George was terrified. As Ernest Tubb introduced him, Opry stalwarts Little Jimmy Dickens and George Morgan intervened. Dickens handed George his own guitar; Morgan sent the timorous newcomer onstage, where he breezed through "You Gotta Be My Baby" before walking off. He decided not to push an encore. The Machiavellian nonsense aside, the appearance led Opry management to offer George that coveted membership a week later, making him a part of the show's artist roster. He performed on August 25 as a member. Over a decade and a half before, George Glenn lay in bed Saturday nights with Clara and George W listening on the battery radio and amusing family members by boldly declaring someday he'd appear on the Opry. Now, like Hank Williams, he was part of the Opry family after just one guest appearance.

On records, his momentum wasn't slowing down. "Just One More," a morose barroom weeper George wrote himself, became his most successful single yet, reaching No. 3 on *Billboard*'s country charts. It also showed his voice continuing to develop beyond his roots. The B-side, "Gonna Come Get You," jaunty and upbeat, had an amiability similar to "You Gotta Be My Baby." George's first hit duet with a female singer came well before Melba Montgomery or Tammy Wynette: "Yearning" teamed him with Hayride vocalist Jeanette Hicks, who'd been recording since 1953. Issued in early 1957, the single made it to No. 10, though George simply harmonized behind her lead. Even as his stature grew, his ties to Brother Burl and Sister Annie remained strong. He added melodies to three of Burl's religious poems and recorded them, adding fervent vocals to "Boat of Life" and turning "Taggin' Along" into a stunning, tent-meeting-revival tune complete with hand clapping, enhanced by Hal Harris's electric guitar. George adapted another of Burl's poems, "Cup of Loneliness," into a plaintive ballad, one he would record with the same intensity as the other two.

"Why Baby Why" scored in *Billboard*'s Top Country and Western Records of 1956 chart, in the "Best Sellers in Stores" and "Most Played on Juke Boxes and on Radio" categories. George's original compositions were getting around, attracting attention beyond Starday artists. Ray Price had a Top 10 single with the Cajun-flavored ballad "You Done Me Wrong," which bore both George's and his name as composers. Jimmie Skinner recorded George's "No Fault of Mine."

Pappy became the sole owner of Starday after buying out Starns. Don Pierce still remained president, but the company's fortunes were about to take a turn. Mercury Records president Irving Green and Art Talmadge, the label's vice president, realized they needed to boost the company's weak country music presence. Their solution: teaming up with Starday to create a joint Mercury-Starday operation based in Nashville with George as the flagship artist. Pappy, working mainly from Houston, would continue to oversee his business interests and produce other singers. Pierce would handle the business end and do some production. None of this would tempt George to move his family to Nashville. Shirley wouldn't want it, and he seemed to have little interest in putting down roots there, not when he could hang out and party in local hotels when he was there for the Opry or any other purpose. The Opry connections, however, demanded a greater Nashville presence. His new booking agent, former fiddler J. Hal Smith, who also managed Ray Price, worked out of Nashville.

George started recording in Nashville in 1957, using the Bradley Film and Recording Studio on Sixteenth Avenue South, an old house purchased by Owen Bradley, soon to become one of Nashville's preeminent producers, and his guitarist brother Harold. They built a studio in the basement. Hoping to attract industrial filmmakers, they attached a Quonset hut, a prefab, half-cylindrical corrugated metal building widely used by the military during World War II. When a producer filmed a series of color movies there featuring Opry artists, the Bradleys built wooden sets inside the hut resembling the interior of a barn. Those sets, left behind after filming ended, inadvertently rendered the studio an acoustic marvel perfect for recording. It became known to all as Studio B, or just the Quonset Hut, one of Nashville's most iconic studios. George would do the bulk of his Nashville recordings there, but did his second Nashville session at RCA Victor's newly opened studio on March 18, 1957, resulting in the hit "Too Much Water," credited to George and Sonny James. Among the Nashville musicians on the date: T. Tommy Cutrer, Hank Garland, fiddler Shorty Lavender, and pedal steel guitarist Lloyd Green. "Water" became the first of many Nashville hit singles Green would play on over the next three decades.

GEORGE'S TV VISIBILITY STEPPED UP WITH OCCASIONAL APPEARANCES ON *Town Hall Party*, the weekly Compton, California, stage show hosted by Tex Ritter that was filmed and syndicated nationally as *Ranch Party*. He made a February 1957 appearance on *Ozark Jubilee*, the ABC variety show broadcast from Springfield, Missouri, hosted by former Opry star Red Foley. The road was a constant as he performed on so-called package shows with a specific group of stars at stops around the country. He generally got along well with his costars, yet the amounts of booze ingested by all could change that. Sober, he had Clara's noblest attributes. A binge summoned forth the obnoxious, abusive spirit of George Washington Jones. If he realized what he'd done after sobering up, remorse set in and apologies flowed—until the next whiskey was poured. He and fellow Opry star Faron Young proved to be natural combatants. Both were short and slight; the liquor could turn them aggressive, hostile, and foulmouthed. Each could easily provoke the other. They took a crack at the same groupie during one tour. At another stop, they got into a verbal battle as a local radio personality interviewed Faron live on the air, with the local mayor and his wife standing by. Backstage at another show, Faron got into it with the equally feisty Little Jimmy Dickens. George jumped to Dickens's defense, and in seconds, George and Faron were battling as the audience heard pounding and screaming. Afterward, both appeared onstage in what was left of their fancy, expensive Nudie suits. Most of the time, Faron came out on top in these confrontations.

Still writing songs, George created a few with up-and-comer Roger Miller, one of Pappy's Starday hit cloners, now recording for Mercury. Miller, who was about to establish his compositional genius with hits for Ray Price, Ernest Tubb, and Jim Reeves, co-wrote two of George's more cheerful, effervescent recordings from this period: "Nothing Can Stop My Loving You" and "Tall, Tall Trees." Neither were hits, but they reflected his continued evolution into a vocalist able to evoke emotions across the spectrum. He rolled around the country in the fall of 1957 with Johnny Cash and Jerry Lee Lewis, still appearing at country concerts despite his success as a rocker. Later that year, George joined Rusty and Doug Kershaw, Lone Star honky-tonk fountainhead Floyd Tillman, and Canadian singer Wilf Carter for a swing through New Jersey.

Among his close friends within the Opry community was Stonewall Jackson, the onetime Georgia sharecropper who carried that moniker as his legal name, not a stage identity. Stonewall, too, had had a horrific childhood and abusive father, and he also sensed he had what it took to appear on the Opry. In early November 1956, just a few months after George joined the cast, Jackson drove his truck into Nashville hoping to land a spot on the Opry. In pure storybook fashion, the dream came true in days. He connected with Fred Rose's son Wesley Rose, who'd taken over the Acuff-Rose music publishing firm after his father's death. Jackson went from being an Opry guest to a member and, soon after, a Columbia recording artist. Both from the backwoods, Stonewall and George had much common ground, and that included heavy drinking.

Neither felt any pain after playing a club in either Albuquerque (George's memory) or Texas (Stonewall's recollection). They stopped at a bar to pick up some six-packs for the road when a huge cowboy, walking into the place as they left, hurled a bottle toward them that barely missed Stonewall. George, already well lubricated, turned around in a fury. "Did you throw that bottle?" he snarled at the cowboy. "Yes, I did," the man admitted. That did it. As usual, ignoring his weight disadvantage, George took a swing at the guy and missed. The cowboy threw a punch that landed George facedown in a mud puddle. Other men began kicking him. Stonewall came to his aid and yanked George out of the mud before he drowned. For his trouble, the cowboy and friends beat Stonewall so badly that his eyes swelled shut. Both recovered, but yet another stage outfit was trashed; they had to buy civvies to finish the tour. On another tour, George heaved the coffee table in his room through a plate-glass window. Stonewall had fun of his own, sweeping up the glass and scattering it inside George's room with a large rock that made the destruction look like an outside job.

Stonewall had a bigger problem. So far, his records for Columbia weren't moving. George changed that in 1958 when they appeared together with Ernest Tubb at a fiddlers' gathering in Crockett, Texas. A few inmates from a nearby prison had permission to attend, one a convicted murderer George and Stonewall chatted with. They asked how long his sentence ran. His reply, that he had been inside eighteen years and "I still got life to go," registered with both. George claimed he wrote it and earmarked it for Johnny Cash; Stonewall later claimed they cowrote it but agreed that Stonewall would record the song and George would take sole writer credit and not record it. "Life" became Stonewall's first hit single, saving his recording contract.

George's responsibilities at home increased in July 1958 when Shirley gave birth to a second son, Bryan Daily Jones, named for Shirley's father, Bryan Corley, the middle name inspired by an obvious source. George's chart successes continued. "Color of the Blues," written by Lawton Williams, composer of the country standard "Fraulein," became a landmark of sorts. The plaintive number, reflective yet unabashedly pained, reflected the stops-out vocal expressiveness that earned George the admiration of his peers.

His early hero Acuff had a similar skill. In the early 1940s, Fred Rose, his future partner in Nashville's Acuff-Rose song publishing company, was known as a successful pop songwriter. After watching Acuff sing "Don't Make Me Go to Bed and I'll Be Good," a maudlin tune about a dying child, Rose later recalled, "Suddenly I said to myself, 'Are those tears splashing down the guy's shirt?' They were, and that's when I got it—the reason people like hillbilly tunes. 'Hell,' I said to myself, 'this guy *means* it.'" In the same way Hank Williams had cultivated a deeply emotional, Acuff-inspired skill, so did Little Jimmy Dickens. Known primarily for sassy novelty hits like "A-Sleepin' at the Foot of the Bed," Dickens was admired by fans and artists alike for his ability to deliver raw, emotional ballads in a style clearly inspired by Acuff.

George kicked the bar up several notches. He discussed this in an extended 2006 *Billboard* interview with Ray Waddell, explaining, "When I sing a song, whether it's in the studio or onstage, I try to live the story of that song in my mind, my heart and my feelings. That's why [the songs] come out like that. I feel the hurt that people have, especially everyday working people. I'll be in the studio and just get so involved in it I almost have a tear come out." There's no reason to dispute this simple explanation, which has precedent in the field of drama: a technique known as Method acting, or just "the Method." It's been used by some of America's greatest actors, among them Marlon Brando, James Dean, Robert De Niro, Johnny Depp, Jack Nicholson, Al Pacino, Meryl Streep, Shelley Winters, and Marilyn Monroe.

The concept, often credited to Russian actor Constantin Sergeyevich Stanislavski and later refined by American actor and acting teachers Lee Strasberg and Stella Adler, involves actors focusing on and drawing from their own past real-life experiences relevant to a scene, reliving them in a way that brings greater passion and authenticity to their performance. While it's unlikely George, despite his love for movies and TV, had any awareness of the Method concept, he had resources to create his own variation of the idea. The pain and occasional joys he had with George W, the virtues Clara ingrained into his personality, his goofy, ornery sense of humor developed in childhood, and other life experiences gave him a deep wellspring he could draw from. That sensitive, empathetic side and lifelong identification with the underdog permitted him to do precisely what he conveyed to Waddell. He would immerse himself in a song's lyric and context, drilling so deeply into its emotional essence that he would become the person in the song, living the scenario in his mind. The result: decades of emotionally moving and memorable performances. It's present on the darker ballads but also on more upbeat fare like "Gonna Come Get You" and

"Tall, Tall Trees." Both were love songs with proud, unabashedly rural lyrics, reflecting a cheeriness that felt neither forced nor contrived. He could infuse a novelty with a loopy vocal edge that put the madcap comedic intent right in the listener's face. Certainly he didn't bat a thousand or achieve emotional nirvana on every number he recorded. But when the song and his psyche were at one, whether straight or enhanced by intoxicants, he offered performances that inspire and amaze decades later.

As his recorded triumphs continued, the Mercury-Starday merger proved less successful than everyone had hoped. Many of their other releases didn't sell. Some acts moved on to other labels. Mercury decided they would pursue country acts on their own. Starday would revert to independent status, but without Pappy, who would retain George and keep him on Mercury. He'd sell his shares to Pierce, and they'd divvy up the master recordings and songs. As sole owner, Pierce would keep Starday independent and move the entire operation and himself to Nashville. Pappy already had a new company in Houston with the single-letter name of D Records. Like Starday in the early days, it would focus on regional talent. One early signing: J.P. Richardson, who'd recorded the boogie-driven "Chantilly Lace," released under the name the Big Bopper. Pappy sold the master of "Lace" to Mercury, whose rerelease took it to the pop Top 10 and made it a standard of early rock 'n' roll. Another Richardson original, "Running Bear," an upbeat tale about a love affair between two Indians, went to singer Johnny Preston, who recorded it in Houston. Behind Preston, Richardson and former Jones manager Bill Hall sang backup as George added rhythmic "Ooh-uhh ooh-uhh" chants.

George and Richardson remained friends, cowriting country songs like "Treasure of Love" and "If I Don't Love You (Grits Ain't

Groceries)." George took both, plus "White Lightning," to his September 9 session at Bradley's basement studio, arriving well juiced up and ready to go. Buddy Killen, who played bass on the Opry and was vice president of the nascent Tree Music publishing company, had been cutting demo recordings with local session players, most of them very capable second-tier musicians. One was guitarist Floyd Robinson, able to play deep, twanging boogie licks; the other, Hargus Robbins Jr., was a gifted Tennessee pianist affectionately known as Pig, blinded by a knife mishap when he was three.

For Robbins, recording with George became a step up in a career that would take him to the select group of Nashville studio musicians known as the A-Team. "I'd been doing some demos for Buddy and he called me one day and said, 'Hey, can you cut with George Jones?' I said, 'Why, hell, yeah!' So I showed up and we got lucky," he said.

They needed the luck. George arrived able to sing yet thoroughly hammered. After finishing two numbers, the band dug into "White Lightning," J.P. Richardson's frantic, madcap chronicle of a backwoods moonshiner being tracked by lawmen that included "G-men, T-men, revenuers, too." George's condition slowed down the progress. The drunker he was, the more takes he would foul up, requiring everyone to start over. Killen, who developed a punchy, aggressive bass intro, wore the skin from his fingers as the false starts continued. The hastily created arrangement, reminiscent of a Chuck Berry song, was effective, enough to make the song a smart country-rock hybrid. With Robinson's throbbing guitar moving along, Robbins played swirling piano chords not unlike Lafayette Leake's accompaniment on Berry hits like "Nadine." George doubled down on the lyrics, his boozy performance enhancing the song. As much as he had pissed and moaned about Thumper Jones two years earlier, any reservations he had about recording a more polished rocker like "White Lightning" were muted.

Given the condition his hands were in after the session, Killen wasn't pleased with what it took to nail down the song. Robbins, by contrast, was more than satisfied at the outcome. "I was so thrilled just to be on [a session with] a name artist. I didn't stop to analyze it or anything. I just did my job best I could do and was thankful." For over two decades, Pig would play piano on nearly every Jones session for Mercury, United Artists, Musicor, and Epic.

As Mercury prepared to release "White Lightning" in February 1959, the dead of winter, Richardson toured the Midwest in a bus with Bobby Vee, Buddy Holly, and Ritchie Valens. He, Holly, and Valens, wanting off the bus, boarded a chartered plane out of Clear Lake, Iowa, on February 3. All three and the pilot died when the plane crashed in a field shortly after takeoff. Six days later, "White Lightning" was released and exploded across the country, Richardson's death making it a bittersweet triumph. As George's first No. 1 single, it stayed atop the *Billboard* country chart five weeks and made a showing in the lower reaches of the pop charts.

His success kept him on the road constantly, away from Shirley and his sons at home, feeding Shirley's misgivings about the marriage and her largely justified suspicions about what was going on with the women he (and nearly every other star) encountered on the road, where every male singer pretty much had his pick of groupies (referred to by some as "snuff queens") wherever he played.

The money was now good enough to buy his first home in Vidor, across the Neches River from Beaumont in Orange County, notorious as a hotbed of Ku Klux Klan activity and known as a "sundown town"—at one time there, signs graphically warned blacks, NIGGER, DON'T LET THE SUN SET ON YOU IN VIDOR. In other words, be out by sundown or face unspecified and possibly lethal dangers. Segregation was a way of life throughout the South, and East Texas at that time was a hotbed for it. Vidor became a destination for many Beaumont residents anxious to escape the changing racial population, a phenomenon known as "white flight." George's parents had lived there for years, but for George, it was more than that. After growing up in a virtual time warp in the Thicket and pinching pennies in their days living in Beaumont, he finally had the money to give his family the suburban living so many aspired to in the 1950s.

Song ideas could materialize anywhere, even when George was idle at home. That's where in 1959, sitting in his den with bacon frying in the kitchen, he conceived one of his greatest adultery ballads: "The Window Up Above." He wrote and sang it from the perspective of a husband who assumed he had a happy marriage, only to discover that his wife was involved with another man when he saw them together from his upstairs window. He later told writer Nicholas Dawidoff, "It was around 7:00 A.M. and my wife was cooking breakfast." He told Alanna Nash, "I wrote that in about fifteen or twenty minutes. I just came off a tour. And I don't know what made me write it. I had no problems at home, or nothin'. I just got home, hadn't been there long and I got the guitar out in the den and sat down and the idea just came to me from somewhere." The song, like most of his other originals, reflected George's greatest strengths as a composer: simplicity, economy of language, and a complete lack of pretense. It's regrettable he didn't write more.

There were more tours, with alcohol-fueled bad behavior and, naturally, more fights. In the late spring of 1957, George was working with Jimmy Newman, Patsy Cline, and Mel Tillis. After a show in Colorado Springs, everyone went to a nearby dance hall to unwind. In a 2013 reminiscence, after George's death, Tillis remembered sitting in the front seat next to Newman, who was driving. George was in the back seat, and his arm had only recently healed after a fracture. Now, drunk and aggressive, he started in on Mel.

"I don't know the reason why," Tillis told *Billboard* reporter Ken Tucker. "But he got onto me about something and I turned around and here come a fist at me. I just grabbed his arm and held it. I didn't know he had just broken his arm and I broke it again. I didn't mean to do that. We took him to the hospital and they patched it up." A sober George apologized to Tillis the next day.

When George passed out drunk in a North Dakota motel shower stall, his ass covering the drain, Faron Young had to yank him out of there before he drowned. Sidemen had similar perspectives of George's childish behavior. Veteran steel guitarist Howard White toured with Jones several times. In his memoir, he remembered being at the wheel when George, a passenger, pitched a beer can at the windshield, prompting a sharp rebuke from White. On a South Dakota jaunt with George and singer Ernie Ashworth of "Talk Back Trembling Lips" fame, White remembered George throwing Ashworth's thermos out the window. Ashworth sat quietly for a time before quietly saying, "You shouldn't ought to have done that, George." Despite it all, White concluded, "We all knew George had a good heart."

After setting up Starday's distribution, warehouse, and studio complex on Dickerson Road in Madison, just outside Nashville, Don Pierce got a taste of George's whiskey-fueled paranoia when the singer dropped by his offices and began asking questions about his record sales. George was dissatisfied with the answers he got. Pierce tried to defuse things by giving George $900, to no avail.

As George began slamming things around in the office, Pierce called the police, and George slept it off in a cell overnight. The next day, sober and contrite, realizing what he'd done, he returned and apologized profusely to Pierce. He had a similar issue with Pappy. The story would be repeated time and again for nearly three decades, the product of his bifurcated Jekyll-Hyde personality from the Thicket.

Needing a follow-up to "White Lightning," George turned to Darrell Edwards and two other writers for "Who Shot Sam." Despite being an unimaginative musical clone of "Lightning," it managed to reach the country Top 10 and even made a modest showing on the pop charts. Unfortunately, Pappy, sensing more life in the "Lightning" formula, didn't know when to quit. He went to the still once too often with "Revenooer Man," a weak if rocking moonshiner knockoff penned by Donny Young.

Other songs reflected more conventional Nashville standards, among them George's spot-on performances of Roger Miller's magnificently loopy story-song "Big Harlan Taylor" and Eddie Noack's clever drinking ditty "Relief Is Just a Swallow Away," playing on an Alka-Seltzer commercial from that era. He continued honing his growing ballad skills with "Accidentally on Purpose," another Edwards lament and one of his most accomplished early laments. It centered around the theme of a man dealing with a situation where the woman he loved had married someone else. George's ideas about making records required some adjustment, Pig Robbins remembered. "Back in the beginning, he wanted to play guitar [with the studio band]. Which was pretty much a no-no when you're tryin' to sing and they're trying to get the mix down and all that kind of stuff, and sometimes he'd miss chords and that sort of thing. Or if he got over the line, he might change the melody and everything at a certain point."

Around the time "Running Bear" became a hit for Johnny Preston, Mercury released the LP *George Jones Sings White Lightning and Other Favorites*. The cover featured a right-profile shot of George, staring straight ahead, his flattop cut standing tall. It was almost certainly the album that inspired Nashville drummer, announcer, and disc jockey T. Tommy Cutrer to bestow the nickname "Possum" on George. Others credited Slim Watts—his friend from KTRM—with the nickname, but in later years, George cited Cutrer as the originator. He was known as Possum for life, though he had occasional love-hate issues with that nickname.

The year 1960 kicked off with a January tour of the Midwest with Johnny Cash, Bill Monroe, Norma Jean, Carl Perkins, and Carl's fellow ex-Sun rockabilly labelmate Warren Smith through Iowa, Nebraska, and Kansas. Spring included extensive sessions in Nashville, yielding a less successful yet riveting take on Luke McDaniel's masterful ballad "You're Still On My Mind" and, most notably, a searing performance of "The Window Up Above," George's first-ever recording with a Jordanaires-style vocal chorus behind him.

George's musical obsessions could drive friends to distraction, as Frankie Miller remembered. That summer, he guested on ABC's *Jubilee USA,* a rebrand of the network's longtime country variety show *Ozark Jubilee,* produced in Springfield, Missouri. During one Springfield visit, he roomed with Charlie Dick, Patsy Cline's husband. At the time, George was smitten with Miller's recording of "Young Widow Brown," written by two Lubbock, Texas, disc jockeys: Sky Corbin and the other credited on the label as "Wayland Jennings." Jones loved the record so much he played it thirty times, singing along and driving Dick to distraction. Frankie Miller and George occasionally sang it together: "We used to sing it onstage when I was with him," Miller said. "He'd say, 'You want harmony or melody?' I said, 'Whatever you want.' He'd say, 'I'll sing harmony!'"

THE OPRY MIGHT HAVE BEEN HIS BOYHOOD DREAM, BUT HE LEFT THE SHOW AT some point in the early 1960s. He would return in 1969, depart yet again, and, according to Opry historian Byron Fay, return once more—this time to stay—in 1973. Later in 1960, he moved Shirley, Bryan, and Jeffrey to a larger, newly constructed home on Hulett Street in Vidor.

In spite of being a national act, George wasn't carrying his own musicians. On tours, another singer's band might back him; in clubs he'd work with the house band. In the late fifties and early sixties, many stars carried harmony singers. Up-and-comer Buck Owens had hired sideman Don Rich to handle fiddle and vocal harmonies. Ray Price's Cherokee Cowboys had a steady stream of vocalists filling that role, among them Van Howard, Roger Miller, and Donny Young, later followed by a Texas boy named Willie Nelson. One night in 1960, newly discharged army vet and aspiring vocalist George Riddle stopped by George's room at the Hermitage Hotel, where the star was doing some partying. As he heard George talk about hiring a harmony singer, Riddle was truly in the right place at the right time. Eager for the chance, he took the job and remained with George, witnessing and participating in some of his craziest escapades, for the next five years.

Released in the fall of 1960, "The Window Up Above" was a straightforward performance, as raw and simple as his previous work. Along with the pedal steel and solo fiddle, however, was a vocal chorus, the sort of embellishment used by Chet Atkins or Owen Bradley. It would not reach No. 1, but it nevertheless established itself as one of his great ballad performances and finest compositions.

George loved the fancy, rhinestone-spangled western suits in style at the time. He was a regular customer of the famous Hollywood western tailor Nudie Cohn, who made virtually all of George's show outfits and had to have been kept busy given the number of them ruined by his carrying on. He had Nudie create a suit honoring "Window," the back of the jacket depicting a man looking out a window. With his characteristic disregard for material things, he wore it for a while. When he tired of it, he'd sell the suits, usually for less than he paid, something he'd later do with more expensive items including fancy vehicles and boats.

Frankie Miller, recording for Starday, was George's top clothing customer. Mentioning a famous Starday color publicity shot of himself in a red Nudie suit, Miller said, "I bought that red suit from George for one hundred dollars. Genuine Nudie-made suit when Nudie was makin' the suits himself. [George would] get tired of 'em. I bought three or four suits from him. He would throw 'em in the back of the bus and I'd meet him somewhere and go back there, dig through 'em, and find one I wanted." Miller acquired the "Window Up Above" suit, but added, "I gave that back to him because Shirley and him had a little museum [in Beaumont]—out on the end of Fifteenth Avenue—so he could put it in the museum."

So far, George had been making raw, unabashedly twangy honky-tonk with some rockers thrown in. Yet things had changed since the days of "Why Baby Why." Rock 'n' roll's popularity led two of the town's major producers, Chet Atkins at RCA and Owen Bradley at Decca, to try a new approach with some artists: cutting back on the fiddles and steel guitar and using a muted, neutral rhythm section and vocal chorus behind singers. It would become known as the Nashville Sound. The rudiments had shown up occasionally on Nashville recordings in the early fifties, but Capitol's Ken Nelson really got the ball rolling in 1956 with Sonny James on the song "Young Love" and Ferlin Husky on "Gone." Atkins and Bradley began doing the same, recording country songs with smoother accompaniments. Atkins used it with Jim Reeves and Don Gibson; Bradley made it work with Bobby Helms and Patsy Cline. The idea of recording George this way seemed to make little sense given his popularity recording twang-laden honky-tonkers. It's not likely Pappy cared one way or another, as long as it sold. But Mercury had a new head of Nashville A&R named Shelby Singleton, whose wife, Margie, recorded for the label.

Darrell Edwards came through again with "Tender Years," an eloquent, stately romantic ballad. George's performance would differ from anything he'd done in the past. As with "Window Up Above," it would include a muted pedal steel but also a vocal chorus, very likely the Jordanaires, and an addition: the soprano voice of Nashville singer Millie Kirkham, heard on Husky's "Gone." While pedal steel guitar remained prominent, on this recording it fit into a less prominent musical context. The rhythm section, with Pig Robbins adding a brief, graceful solo, was smoother, solidly in the Nashville Sound mode. Given his conservative musical tastes, it's difficult to think George was totally comfortable with this softer background. Nonetheless, he delivered a stunning, mature performance reflecting his capacity to evolve while retaining the straight-ahead delivery so many admired. A harbinger of what he'd do at Epic Records a decade later, "Tender Years" became his second No. 1 and remained at that position for nearly two months. A subsequent single, "Did I

Ever Tell You," a duet with Margie Singleton, gave him his second successful duet with a female vocalist when it reached No. 15 later that same year.

Much had changed in only a few years. George was beginning to leave his influence on the music of other performers, a step toward his eventual status as the Greatest Living Country Singer. His fluid vocal range and ability to move between high lonesome and low baritone, combined with his distinctive phrasing, set him apart from any of his peers, earning their admiration as well as his fans'. Buck Owens, who'd had his first national successes on records over the previous couple years recording honky-tonk shuffles in the Ray Price style, had a phrasing with obvious elements of George embedded within. "I thought that George was the greatest thing since sliced bread. I could not help it. If you listen [to the records of my] early years, you're sure gonna hear George, because he was a big influence on me as far as the singers go."

Soon enough, George, his status continuing to rise along with his reputation as a hell-raiser, would be heard on a different record label.

CHAPTER 3

1962-1968

Bill Hall, George's former Beaumont manager, owned Gulf Coast Recording Studio. George did most of his business, such as management and bookings, in Nashville, but when off the road, he'd often drop by the studio to hang out with Hall and his partner, singer, songwriter, and producer Jack Clement. If they weren't at the studio, they'd hang out at Rich's Snack Bar across the street, where the Cajun food was authentic and the homemade chili was great.

The eccentric, iconoclastic Clement, a Tennessee native, ex-marine, and former bluegrass mandolinist, had formerly worked for Sam Phillips at Sun Records. At Sun, he discovered and produced Jerry Lee Lewis and later supervised Johnny Cash's Sun recordings before Cash left for Columbia Records. A hassle with Phillips led Jack to depart Sun in 1958. After running his own label, Summer Records, and working on and off in Nashville, he arrived in Beau-

mont in 1961 and joined Hall to organize a song publishing operation known as Hall-Clement Music.

One of Hall-Clement's writers was Dickey Lee Lipscomb,
who recorded as Dickey Lee. Clement knew him well, since Lee
had recorded several sessions at Sun. Lipscomb and Steve Duf-
fey wrote the pop ballad "She Thinks I Still Care." Few paid it
any mind, but Clement felt the song had potential. He had a
demo tape but hesitated to play it for George because the original melody sounded more pop than country. Throughout his
career, George never automatically embraced every tune thrown
his way and had a sixth sense when he felt a song was too "pop"
for him. Jack grabbed a guitar and began singing him the song,
subtly altering the melody to make it feel more country. Clement
recalled George finding another issue: the number of lines starting with the phrase "Just because." Raymond Nallie, Luther's
brother, told Nick Tosches that George had eyes on a portable
recorder they had at the studio, and that Hall told George he
could have "the fuckin' recorder" if he did the song. Clement
supposedly played him "She Thinks I Still Care" on several different occasions. George later disagreed with those accounts,
claiming he knew the song was right for him from the first time
he heard it, but the details in the accounts of both Nallie and
Clement tend to favor their memories.

The year 1961 saw Pappy working with Art Talmadge, his old
friend from Mercury, now at United Artists Records, a spinoff of
the film production company. The label, formed in 1957 to dis-
tribute soundtracks from UA-produced feature films, also released
jazz albums and pop collections. Pappy would bring George and
some of his masters from the D Records label to UA, including
material by Texas singers like Tony Douglas, Glenn Barber, and

"Country" Johnny Mathis (so named to differentiate him from the black pop vocal star who recorded for Columbia).

The father-son relationship between Fred Rose and Hank Williams lasted until Hank's death, but any similar dynamic between Pappy and George, if it existed at all, was showing signs of wear. It was probably inevitable. George, amid his drinking and hell-raising, was getting harder for Pappy to handle. As Pappy grew fed up with his star's misbehaving, he sought out an old face from Starday: George's old Houston buddy Sonny Burns. Now on the wagon, Sonny had quit music to drive a truck. Pappy signed him to United Artists, thinking his return would bring George into line by making him feel Sonny would be competition. It's not clear that gambit could ever have succeeded in taming George. He and Pappy would work together for another decade, but he had far fewer illusions about his old benefactor.

Why was George becoming so obstinate with Pappy? It's not clear. He didn't always pay close attention to contracts and money, but his growing antagonism may have stemmed from doubts about some of his old benefactor's business dealings. Pappy tied George to a contract that not only made him George's producer, it allowed him to move to any label willing to meet Pappy's terms. After selling his stake in Starday, he'd moved George to Mercury, then to United Artists, where Pappy produced George and other singers.

The best Nashville producers, Chet Atkins and Owen Bradley in particular, held the reins in the studio. They selected songs, sometimes in conjunction with the singer, and booked the session musicians. They might work with the musicians and singer to create an arrangement, or leave it to the musician in charge, the "session leader." In 1961, Pappy wasn't even that hands-on, and in later years George wasn't shy about making that clear. In a 2001 interview he explained what other Nashville musicians confirm: during his seventeen years in the studio with George, Daily at best played a peripheral role in production, regardless of the label. "A lot of people think he was the producer, but he really wasn't," Jones said. "He timed the songs in the studio and he wrote out the paperwork. That was about all he did. I worked with the musicians myself and we worked out the arrangements. I basically left it up to the musicians after we ran through the songs. I wanted them to be more a part of the production." Pig Robbins agreed. "Pappy was just the paper guy, you know. I'm sure Pappy was payin' for it in the end, but yeah, Pappy, he'd sit in there and hit the intercom every now and then and say, 'All right, boys, come on! I gotta get back to Texas here!'"

The bottle remained George's other collaborator. His reputation as one of Nashville's great drinkers was a given. The amount he consumed before and during a recording session could affect his performances in positive or negative ways. Too few drinks didn't loosen him up enough to delve into a lyric; too many left him sloppy or uncontrollable, to the point the session would have to be scrubbed. The right amount of alcohol, combined with his ability to interpret, unleashed every bit of his vocal power.

When he entered Bradley Studios on January 4, 1962, with many of his regular accompanists—Pig Robbins, Buddy Harman, and the Jordanaires among them—"She Thinks I Still Care" was the first song on the agenda. As the Jordanaires harmonized, George created another intensely focused, deeply emotional performance. With amazing precision, he gave the correct amount of emotional weight to every word, his performance adding up to a cathartic tale of a man's loss, masked by bravado. It may have been outside the composers' original vision, but with Clement's reworked melody, the performance became one of his finest. A second standout: D.T. Gentry's "Open Pit Mine," a dark tale of a western copper miner's adultery, murder, and suicide. A departure from George's usual honky-tonkers and laments, it had the feel of a nineteenth-century folk ballad, enhanced by George's solid confessional performance. In 2001 he said, "That was a true song. The boy that wrote it, he worked in the copper mines. Every time I'd go out to Arizona or New Mexico, the Indians, that's the first thing they want to hear." By day's end he'd recorded his first UA single and one entire album: *The New Favorites of George Jones.*

WITH THE ALBUM DONE, GEORGE, ALONG WITH PATSY CLINE, JOHNNY CASH, Carl Perkins, Gordon Terry, and Johnny Western, headed into the Midwest for an extended tour that would take up most of the month. George Riddle was along to sing harmony. After having no major hits since her 1957 groundbreaker "Walkin' after Midnight," Patsy was starting a roll, revitalized by her 1961 hit "I Fall to Pieces." Aggressive and profane enough to face down any alpha male, she held her own in such company. Also along on the tour was thirteen-year-old West Coast singer and pedal steel guitar prodigy Barbara Mandrell.

George and Riddle hit the road in a camper. Cash's Tennessee Three made up the core band, augmented by a couple West Coast pickers, one of them the respected Bakersfield guitar man Roy Nichols. Mandrell played steel guitar behind the others. George and Patsy (who affectionately called him "Jones") got on well, and his motorized digs allowed him to party with musicians and women as long, loud, and hard as he wanted without risking any shit from hotel desk clerks. He invited everyone, including Patsy and the teenage Mandrell, to join him at the camper to party.

George's intentions were likely innocent, but the invitation sent Patsy into protector mode. She made sure Mandrell traveled and roomed with her from then on. Years later, Mandrell, a lifelong friend of George's, considered touring with Patsy and playing steel for George a double honor.

On May 10, 1962, he performed at Carnegie Hall with a pilled-up Cash, the Carter Family, and Tompall and the Glaser Brothers. Nine days later, "She Thinks I Still Care" became George's third No. 1 and remained there six weeks. It became a two-sided hit when the B-side, "Sometimes You Just Can't Win," a raw, melancholy ballad, reached the country Top 20. One tour took George and Riddle to Bakersfield to perform at the Blackboard, the area's most popular dance hall, where every star of that time played. As usual, George didn't forget radio. While visiting KUZZ to promote his new single, he met a young ex-con just getting started in music. Merle Haggard had emerged from San Quentin in 1960 bent on making something of himself. Set to open for George that night, Haggard was in awe. George was puzzled, later recalling, "He wouldn't look me in the face. I couldn't figure if he was stuck on himself or just shy." Haggard recalled George being drunk backstage (something George denied) and kicking open the door of the club's office to see who was singing.

Nearly two years of touring with Riddle, still relying on house bands of varying quality and other singers' groups, wasn't cutting it anymore. In 1962, he tasked Riddle with hiring a four-piece band: guitar, pedal steel, bass, and drums. George dubbed them the Jones Boys. Like most such groups, the lineup changed, expanded, and contracted, but it continued until George's death in 2013. Initially, he bought a used bus for himself and the band. Not in the greatest shape and lacking air conditioning, the "Brown Bomber" made summer excursions grueling for everyone. With the band bitching about it, George settled the matter one night at a club in Chicago Heights, Illinois, when he drunkenly shot holes in the floor of the bus, assuming that would serve to ventilate the interior. He never considered that the holes let in dangerous exhaust fumes.

The on-tour antics didn't abate. Out with Cash and Merle Kilgore on a circuit supervised by Cash's manager Saul Holiff, George embarked on a demolition derby in a Gary, Indiana, hotel as Cash observed. Given his own reputation for trashing hotels, he had keen insights into the costs of breakables in any room. When George busted two lamps in Cash's presence, Cash calmly noted, "Two lamps. Ninety dollars." Ripping down a curtain brought a declaration that it would cost $100. George doubted Cash's figures, but when the tour ended, as Holiff ticked off deductions for the items trashed in Gary, he was stunned to find every amount except one matched Cash's estimates to the penny.

That August, United Artists claimed the *New Favorites* LP had sold fifty thousand copies, strong sales for a country album at that time. "She Thinks I Still Care" was the top single in *Billboard*'s Country Music Disc Jockey Poll, with *New Favorites* coming in third behind albums by Ray Price and Claude King. "Open Pit Mine" reached the Top 20. "A Girl I Used to Know," a Jack Clement ballad that resembled "She Still Thinks I Still Care," hit the Top 5 that fall. His growing successes led to an idea that resurfaced throughout his career: side businesses bearing the Jones name. In Beaumont, he opened a restaurant known as the George Jones Chuckwagon Cafe. Bill Sachs's "Folk Talent & Tunes" column in the December 29, 1962, *Billboard* reported that Jones, Riddle, and the Jones Boys, along with Johnny Cash, June Carter, and the Tennessee Three, played the *Big D Jamboree* on December 8. The next night, they performed at the Chuckwagon's opening.

With George on the road, Shirley, already seeing to Bryan and Jeff, would manage things.

George's Mercury recordings with Margie Singleton revealed the two had little real vocal chemistry. Things would be different with the next vocalist. Melba Montgomery was a product of south Tennessee. Born in 1938 in the hamlet of Iron City, her path to a musical career came through her family. Her father, Fletcher, was a music instructor. Willie Mae, her mother, strummed a mandolin. Her brothers Earl (nicknamed Peanutt), Cranston, and Carl Montgomery were singers and songwriters: Carl cowrote Dave Dudley's trucker anthem "Six Days on the Road." Melba toured with Roy Acuff and the Smoky Mountain Boys in 1958 and 1959, joining his show full-time in 1960. When he was off the road, she worked with Opry comedians Lonzo and Oscar and made her first records for their tiny Nugget label. George, who'd heard those early records, was impressed enough that he wanted to meet the young vocalist whose powerful, emotional delivery led some to call her "the female George Jones." It took two meetings. Melba recalled that at the first meeting in Nashville, George was drunk and remembered nothing of it.

They met a second time in January 1963 at the restaurant in Nashville's Quality Inn motel, with Pappy present. Melba brought along an original ballad, "We Must Have Been Out of Our Minds," written when she was on tour with Lonzo and Oscar. She remembered starting to sing it for Pappy, only to have George immediately jump in and harmonize. It was a far cry from those earlier duets he'd done. His cathartic, unfettered emotional phrasing blended perfectly with her raw, edgy mountain voice. The pair created a sharp, penetrating vocal blend not unlike the chilling harmonies of the Louvin Brothers or the high harmonies favored by bluegrass singers.

George and Pappy were stunned. Melba was pleased but not particularly startled by their vocal magic. "Actually, I wasn't surprised at all," she remembered in a 1994 interview. "I remember we just kinda fell right into singin.' It was a natural thing. We just both had the same feel and that helped us to do our phrasin' together."

As they toured and recorded together, the two developed a deep friendship. George got to know her brothers and her parents, who lived in northern Alabama. Her presence on the road didn't diminish George's on-tour misdeeds a bit. He once walked onstage drunk. Deciding his acoustic guitar was out of tune in the middle of "White Lightning" and thoroughly pissed off, he swung it by the neck, smashing its body on the stage, then walked off. He asked to borrow Melba's treasured acoustic guitar. Warily, she handed it to him, pointedly warning him not to repeat the beatdown on her instrument. He did not.

Montgomery vividly remembered her first recording session with George in January 1963, which produced four songs, including "We Must Have Been Out of Our Minds." "George and I used the same microphone and we never overdubbed anything," she said. "What you hear went down on the track as it went down. Not even the musicians overdubbed anything. George and I harmonized, blended well together, we just kind of knew where the other one was going with the lyric and . . . we wouldn't make any mistakes. So, we'd get a lot of songs on the first take." As Pig Robbins's Floyd Cramer–ish "slip note" piano burbled around them, they created a hypnotic, high lonesome synergy. Melba remembered it took only three takes to complete. "Until Then," a tune she and her brother Carl wrote, became the B-side. "Minds" reached No. 3 in the summer of 1963.

George's solo material blended filler tunes for albums with more remarkable singles like the powerful "You Comb Her Hair," a Top 5 single in mid-1963. Not all his strongest work was commercially successful, such as his magnificent performance of the soulful "The Old, Old House," an anguished Hal Bynum ballad. "In the Shadow of a Lie," an album cut, was a compelling murder tale in the style of Lefty Frizzell's hit "Long Black Veil." Cowritten by Jones and steel guitarist Dicky Overbey, it related a timeless old story with a new twist. A single man was secretly involved with a friend's wife. While the men fished from a rowboat, the married man fell into the water, and his adulterous friend stood by until the other man drowned before finally retrieving the body. Hailed for trying to rescue his friend, the survivor married his friend's widow, but was dogged by torment and guilt.

The stars knew that aside from pleasing their fans, they had to maintain close ties with local disc jockeys in every part of the nation—at the large, medium, and small stations alike. These were the interlocutors who brought their records to the public and at the time had considerable discretion over what they did and didn't play. For singers, sending personal notes, gifts, and Christmas cards and visiting the studios when in town were part of doing business and not considered payola. When Cactus Jack Call of KCMK in Kansas City died in a January 25, 1963, car crash, stars rushed to plan a benefit concert for Call's family, shooting for a date that could attract the biggest names.

George came to Kansas City to perform at the March 3 show with Patsy, Billy Walker, Dottie West, Cowboy Copas, Wilma Lee and Stoney Cooper, and Hawkshaw Hawkins. The benefit was successful, but tragedy quickly overshadowed it. Two days later, Cline, Hawkins, Copas, and Cline's manager, Randy Hughes, died when the plane Hughes piloted crashed near Camden, Tennessee. The collective grief of the close-knit Opry community and fans grew deeper when singer Jack Anglin, who with Johnnie Wright made up the duo of Johnnie and Jack, died in a Nashville car crash en route to a memorial service for Patsy, bringing the total to five accidental deaths in a month. George and the Jones Boys nearly added to those somber statistics. Traveling from a California date to a show in Salem, Oregon, on March 30, they were near Grants Pass when the bus swerved to avoid another car, slid off the road, went over a mountainside, and flipped over. George suffered broken ribs; Hal Rugg, his steel guitarist, was also injured. The others played without George, who was shaken enough to fly back to Vidor.

The partnership with Melba continued to thrive as they worked intensely to complete their debut album, *George Jones and Melba Montgomery Sing What's in Our Heart*, arriving at the sessions with songs to record. "A lot of times maybe George would bring in a song, or I'd bring in a song or a writer would bring one in and we'd just learn it right there," she said. Country Johnny Mathis wrote "What's in Our Heart," the second George-Melba hit. They picked up singer Onie Wheeler's composition "Let's Invite Them Over," their third successful duet, late in 1963. The blend of new songs and old, including two from the Louvin Brothers, helped them build a fan base for their duets. The album reached No. 3 on *Billboard*'s newly instituted Top Country Albums chart in early 1964.

What was happening with George and Melba on the road was another matter. Both publicly insisted nothing went on besides a musical and personal friendship born of a mutual love of music. Others saw it differently, believing the potential for a relationship existed, with George's drinking a major obstacle. There's no question the two were close friends, and that she seemed to understand George's impulsive nature. They also had ample common ground. Both were proudly rural, with similar tastes in music and living. They often relaxed on the road by fishing (George bought the fishing equipment), then cooking their catch. Over time, the friendship would put even more strain on George's marriage to Shirley as she began to hear the rumors about her husband and his duet partner.

George's tours teamed him with various combinations of stars in the sixties, among them Buck Owens, Loretta Lynn, Onie Wheeler, and Sonny James. Buck's career was taking off during this time. He'd set aside the Ray Price shuffle rhythms of his earlier hits on the tune that became his first No. 1 single: the driving, upbeat novelty "Act Naturally." It became the first of a series of No. 1s that gave Buck a greater profile and, despite George's humility, it led to a clash of egos. Buck and George might have had common Texas roots and childhood poverty, but Buck's family moved to Arizona and, finally, Bakersfield. George's desires were to sing, drink, and run a sideline like the Chuckwagon. Buck, determined to never be poor or hungry again, developed a level of business savvy and wealth few singers shared at the time. He owned his own song publishing company and would move into radio station ownership. George's humility and tendency to shrug off his talents didn't alter the fact that he had both an ego and an uncanny skill for finding some sly way to prank someone, be it friend or enemy.

When Buck, fully aware of his growing stature and raised profile, insisted on closing shows, he put himself on a collision course with George. On one show that also featured Loretta Lynn, Buck insisted on closing. This time, George didn't complain. Instead he and the Jones Boys dutifully went on before Buck—and played Buck's entire stage show, start to finish. At the end, George cockily strode offstage, faced his seething competitor, and (depending on who one believes) slyly remarked, "You're on!"

WITH HIS GROWING WEALTH, GEORGE TRIED TO TAKE CARE OF HIS PARENTS, buying them a home not far from his. Whatever he thought of his daddy, Clara remained a beacon for her son, one who could talk to him and calm him down. As for George Washington Jones, the old reprobate's ceaseless boozing had the entire family fed up with his derelict behavior and its effect on Clara. On November 22, 1963, the day all hell broke loose at Dealey Plaza in Dallas, the family committed George W to a state mental hospital in Rusk, Texas. Northwest of Vidor and the Thicket, it had an inpatient facility for alcoholics. They hoped for some degree of success. Soon after his release, though, he was back at the bottle.

JOINING FORCES WITH GEORGE BOOSTED MELBA'S STATURE. IN 1963 SHE EARNED *Billboard* and *Cash Box* magazine awards for Most Promising Female Singer. In January 1964 she teamed up with George for a second UA album, *Bluegrass Hootenanny,* that included Dobro player Shot Jackson and five-string banjoist Curtis McPeake. The odd title was meant to tie bluegrass to the term *hootenanny,* popularized by the folk music revival that had swept America. The material mixed bluegrass standards like "Blue Moon of Kentucky" with originals by Melba and her brother Carl, a cover of the Hank Williams gospel number "House of Gold," and similar fare. That a bluegrass-flavored record reached No. 12 on *Billboard*'s Country Album Chart said much about George and Melba's popularity as a duo.

George was booked for a major New York appearance on May 16–17, 1964. Promoter Vic Lewis's "Country Comes to Madison Square Garden" show was one more indicator of the music's growing audience. Lewis did not skimp on booking top-drawer talent for this presentation. George, Buck, Ray Price, Jimmy Dean, and western swing bandleader–steel guitarist Leon McAuliffe were all part of the lineup. The Opry contingent included Ernest Tubb, Bill Monroe, Dottie West, Webb Pierce, Bill Anderson, Stonewall Jackson, Skeeter Davis, and Porter Wagoner. Even the MC was part of the Nashville elite: Ralph Emery, who hosted WSM's all-night Opry Star Spotlight. Given the station's fifty-thousand-watt clear-channel signal, Emery's show had a nationwide reach. He played the newest singles and sometimes previewed upcoming releases. He also welcomed stars into his studio for off-the-cuff chat and occasional jam sessions.

To accommodate the huge bill, every act was instructed to perform only two songs, no more. That was especially important for the final concert, since the Garden had many unions. If the proceedings ran *one second* past 11:30 P.M., overtime kicked in for the venue's union employees and that would cost Lewis a ton of money. Drunk and still chewing on his rivalry with Buck, the designated closing act, George didn't give a damn about anybody's overtime. This time, going on prior to Buck, he didn't perform Buck's act but upped the ante. He simply ignored the two-song limit and continued to sing. Consternation spread backstage, with no one sure how to get him off—until Monroe, George's boyhood hero, devised a simple solution. Monroe enjoyed laboring at his Tennessee farm when he wasn't touring, giving him plenty of physical strength. He simply strode onstage, picked up the five-foot-seven Jones, and carried him off. Buck and the Buckaroos managed to take the stage, and ended their performance just forty seconds before the clock hit 11:30.

George lucked onto another strong number when he found the Don Rollins novelty "The Race Is On," which used horse racing as a metaphor for lost love. George's hard-charging performance sparkled, with quintessential A-team virtuosity as session guitarist

Kelso Herston added a twanging, throbbing guitar solo that gave George's already zesty performance a powerful kick. Released that fall, it would hold on to the No. 3 position for six weeks.

The 1964 British Invasion brought the Beatles and a new form of rock to the nation that spawned rock 'n' roll. In the country field, reactions were mixed. Many artists shrugged off rock. Buck admired the Beatles so much he and the Buckaroos began doing a Beatles routine as part of their show. Others mocked the younger musicians' long hair and flashy "mod" outfits. George got some exposure to the new sounds at San Antonio's Teenage World's Fair of Texas that June. Organizers booked clean teen acts like Diane Renay and Bobby Vee, along with the Marquis Chimps, George and the Jones Boys, and, from England, a virtually unknown quintet who called themselves the Rolling Stones. In 1964 San Antonio, where George's flattop haircut was considered normal, the Stones were booed and heckled by the audience. Stones bassist Bill Wyman, who kept a detailed diary of the band's early tours, mentioned the crowd's hostility in his book *Stone Alone* and recalled the Stones chatting backstage with both Jones and Bobby Vee. Richards, who cut his teeth on the music of Chuck Berry, Bo Diddley, Muddy Waters, and other blues and R&B greats, had never seen Jones perform before. In his autobiography, *Life,* he remembered watching George and the Jones Boys take the stage, thinking them "a bunch of cowboys." Familiar with soulful singing, Richards added, "When George got up, we went whoa, there's a master up there."

After five wild and harrowing years at George's side, through fights, binges, brawls, and onstage lunacy—including one harrowing escapade across the border in Mexico—George Riddle moved on by 1965. Most singers who carried bands had one musician designated as the front man, who opened the show and sang a few numbers before introducing the star. The Jones Boys' new front man was twenty-seven-year-old bass player, steel guitarist, and harmony singer Johnny Paycheck, who as Donny Young was part of Pappy's group of obscure singers covering hits and the composer of "Revenooer Man." He was actually Donald Lytle of Greenfield, Ohio, who did two years in a military stockade for hitting an officer before plunging into music. He fronted and sang harmony for Ray Price as a member of the Cherokee Cowboys. His Decca and Mercury recordings as Donny Young fizzled, but George's influence on his singing was undeniable. He found the right producer in 1964 with New York businessman Aubrey Mayhew, owner of Hilltop Records, and took the name Johnny Paycheck from a boxer. Around the time he joined the Jones Boys, he had his first hit single with "A-11," a honky-tonk lament that George himself could have recorded. Paycheck's vocal clearly reflected the Jones influence.

Both bona fide hell-raisers, Jones and Paycheck were sure to generate fireworks on tour. George did as he pleased, in full Jekyll-and-Hyde mode. He could show up relatively straight, seriously drunk, or not at all. Booking agents, management, and certainly the band and fans themselves had no idea what they were going to get at a George Jones concert. When the bus pulled into a Virginia venue in the Washington, DC, suburbs, Paycheck fulfilled the front-man role and prepared to introduce the boss. Backstage, a totally annihilated George balked, refusing to appear until Paycheck introduced him as Hank Williams. When he did so, George still didn't move, insisting he was staying put unless introduced as Johnny Horton. As the audience grew restless, a disgusted Paycheck made the introduction. As the Jones Boys played the intro to "White Lightning," George strode to the mike, sang a bit of the song, and walked off. The cops arrived to calm things down. George hid out in a bar down the street, concerned with the bottle, not the havoc he left behind. No one was going to make him sing, the way his daddy had, if he didn't want to.

Hanging out in Nashville, he partied with anyone and everyone. With onetime idol Lefty Frizzell now a close pal and drinking buddy, the two went on binges that lasted for days, at times hanging out in Frizzell's basement. Back in Vidor, George Washington Jones continued his endless consumption of booze until, for the first time ever, the bill unexpectedly came due. After undergoing surgery, the old man suffered a stroke, the mark of a circulatory system faltering under the weight of both advancing age and decades of alcohol. For George Glenn, who was at home when it happened, the event was cathartic, unleashing a maelstrom of love, guilt, and rage all rooted in his longtime love-hate relationship with his daddy. Sitting with Helen's husband, Dub Scroggins, clearly hurting, he raged about the old man's failings, a trail of anger that extended back to Saratoga.

His impulsive instincts front and center, George jumped into his Cadillac that night and mowed down a good bit of fencing around his house. The hired hands who tended to his horses called Dub, who found the Caddy totaled. Dub walked in to find George lying on a couch and angrily assumed the rampage was a by-product of another binge. He was amazed to find his brother-in-law totally sober. What that escapade cost George financially didn't assuage the pain. As Dub drove his brother-in-law to the hospital to see his daddy, George cried, declaring he felt inferior to both of his parents. To everyone's surprise, old George not only recovered: he set aside the bottle for good. Clara was obviously relieved, delighted to see a happy, sober husband at work, enthusiastically selling sewing machines door-to-door.

ALONG WITH RAISING JEFFREY AND BRYAN, SHIRLEY WAS INVOLVED WITH George's business interests besides the Chuckwagon. Occasionally, she saw to the Jones Boys' musical needs. Luther Nallie, working at a Beaumont music store, often dealt with her. "Shirley took care of everything, and she would call me and say George needs this or that, and I'd bring it out to him, out in Vidor. I think Johnny Paycheck was playin' bass with him at the time. [George'd] say, 'I need a bass amp,' and I'd put one together and bring it out to him and Shirley would pay me. Shirley took care of the payin'. She was a lot more responsible about payin' stuff than George was. She did a good job of it. He'd just call when he needed something or have Shirley call."

Contractually bound to United Artists for a given number of songs, George had fulfilled his agreement. Pappy already had a new place for him to land: Musicor Records, founded by Brooklyn-born songwriter Aaron Schroeder in 1960. Schroeder hit the mother lode writing the Elvis Presley hits "A Big Hunk o' Love," "I Got Stung," and "It's Now or Never." Musicor was affiliated with United Artists, and Schroeder's ear for talented songwriters led him to the label's first star. Singer Gene Pitney wrote two rock standards: Rick Nelson's hit "Hello Mary Lou" and the Crystals' "He's a Rebel." Vocally, Pitney's flair for intense drama came through on his first hit singles: "The Man Who Shot Liberty Valance" and "Only Love Can Break a Heart." When the British Invasion and changes in pop music left UA executives uncertain about Musicor's future, Art Talmadge jumped at the opportunity to run his own label. Talmadge Productions—Art and Pappy—purchased Musicor from Schroeder in 1964.

With Pitney still on the label and George and Melba added to the roster, Musicor's appeal could now expand into the country field. Pappy would take Jones to another level there, not always in a good way. George soon found himself over-recorded, with sessions mixing masterpieces and respectable material with mediocre and abysmal songs that had no purpose except to fill a steady stream of George Jones LPs. The figures speak for themselves. From 1965 through 1967, Musicor released five Jones LPs a year, some solo efforts, others duet albums pairing him with Pitney or Melba. They cut back to three a year in 1968 and 1969. Pappy grabbed songs from across the country spectrum but paid special attention to material published by his companies: Pappy Daily Music and Glad Music. Among their composers were three gifted ones: Leon Payne (who wrote "Lost Highway"), Dallas Frazier, and George's buddy and Melba's brother Peanutt Montgomery, who also toured with George and became one of his closest drinking and hell-raising buddies. He often played guitar behind George and his sister when they toured together.

George had no illusions about Pappy's intent. In 1996, he noted, "When I was at Musicor, I recorded an entire album in three hours, a practice that violated the Musicians Union's rules. I'd go through one take, Pappy Daily'd play back what I had done, and then he'd usually holler, 'Ship it!' It'd be at the pressing plant next day." It wasn't far from the truth. He'd recorded entire albums in a day at United Artists as well. Pappy, of course, had ample motivation to cut corners at both UA and Musicor. At UA, lower production expenses saved him money. At Musicor, where Pappy was part owner of the company itself, he had even greater incentive to put quantity ahead of quality.

Pig Robbins, who played piano on virtually all the Musicor dates, agreed. "Pappy always thought he ought to get five or six songs on a session, but Pappy didn't have the arrangements. He just wanted quantity instead of quality, I thought." George's effectiveness in the studio still depended on his alcohol intake, and too much inevitably led to problems for everyone present. "George, when he crossed that line, he would get belligerent," Robbins recalled. "He wouldn't listen to anybody, and by God, he was gonna do it his way or nothin'. That's just the way he was. Sometimes it went smooth and other times, he would get that way."

IT'S NOT CLEAR WHAT MOTIVATED ART TALMADGE TO TEAM PITNEY WITH George on records, but the younger singer agreed to give it a shot. Country and pop singers recorded together in the forties and fifties, when Ernest Tubb recorded best-selling duets with the Andrews Sisters, Red Foley did likewise with singer Evelyn Knight, and Tennessee Ernie Ford recorded successfully with Kay Starr, but it didn't happen that often in the sixties. No one in their right mind thought a Jones-Pitney pairing would entice Beatle-loving teens to buy Jones records, yet the chance Pitney might reach country fans was at least worth exploring.

Prior to the sessions, set for January 5 and 6, 1965, Pitney and George met at a Nashville motel to run down material, heavy on country standards like Moon Mullican's "Sweeter Than the Flowers," the Rusty and Doug Kershaw Cajun hit "Louisiana Man," Faron Young's "I've Got Five Dollars and It's Saturday Night," and Acuff's "Wreck on the Highway." Known for his own unique phrasing, Pitney saw he'd need to alter his own approach when he heard George. "I realized right then and there," he told interviewer Jim Liddane before his death, "that there was no way that he was gonna change one iota of his phrasing to suit mine—I was gonna have to change to suit his. And the beauty of it was that when we got in the studios and we started the very first song, everybody just stopped playing, just listening to the blend—a combination of the high sound that I have, and that beautiful low bass sound that he has—it just seemed to be like magic, and I had no problems with him whatsoever—it was just automatic."

The Jones-Pitney duets felt natural even if they didn't succeed on a scale with their respective solo singles. "I've Got Five Dollars and It's Saturday Night" broke the Top 20, and their spritely version of "Louisiana Man" made it to the Top 30. They appeared together on ABC television's prime-time *Jimmy Dean Show* prior to the release of "Five Dollars." Pappy wound up with two George and Gene albums: the 1965 album, inelegantly titled *For the First Time! Two Great Stars,* and the 1966 release *It's Country Time Again!* He'd also complete a solo set, *The Country Side of Gene Pitney,* and record an LP of his own duets with Melba. After those four albums, Pitney ended his country experiment. Aware of how the business worked, he had no issues with George or the music. But hearing industry gossip that he was planning a permanent move to country, Pitney chose to veer away from future Nashville collaborations and refocus on his pop career. Years later, he explained—correctly—that the Jones sessions happened "before you could cross over from pop to country and back again, as you can do nowadays."

GEORGE'S SOLO RECORDINGS INCLUDED ONE ACKNOWLEDGED MASTERPIECE: Leon Payne's brilliant lament "Things Have Gone to Pieces," a virtual punch list of misery including everyday mishaps and misfortunes. George's peerless approach elevated this simple ballad to a masterpiece that became his first solo hit on Musicor in the spring of 1965. Today it remains a high point of his six years with the label. One of his UA hits got new life in the pop market when crooner Jack Jones, known for his successful easy-listening fare like "Wives and Lovers," took "The Race Is On" to the pop Top 20 with an arrangement loosely based on what the Nashville musicians had created for George's single. It enhanced his stature enough that on May 13, Beaumont honored him with "George Jones Day."

At home, things with Shirley could go either way. She was raising the boys when he was touring, partying around Nashville, whoring, and boozing with his buddies. One stop at home led to one of the most notorious of all George Jones incidents. Seeing he was too drunk to drive, Shirley confiscated his car keys. Wanting to fill himself up, he looked out the window and saw his riding lawn mower. Cutting his lawn on a riding mower was one of his favorite avocations through most of his life. With no other transportation available, he hopped on the mower, drove eight miles to the nearest liquor store, and returned with the needed libations, a true story that only added to the Jones legend.

George's stature meant he worked with Nashville's best musicians, a group of players who went from session to session. Their talents, versatility, and instincts made them indispensable, since they worked together so frequently in the studio they could collectively put together polished and commercial arrangements quickly. Producers could work with them to create arrangements, or simply let them huddle with the singer to come up with ideas. They were known informally as the A-Team. Among the major players: pianists Floyd Cramer and Pig Robbins; tenor saxophonist Boots Randolph; guitarists Grady Martin, Fred Carter Jr., Pete Wade, Ray Edenton, Harold Bradley, Billy Sanford, and Jerry Reed. The fiddlers included Tommy Jackson, Buddy Spicher, and Shorty Lavender. Bob Moore, Lightnin' Chance, and Junior Huskey were the primary bass players, and Buddy Harman, Kenny

Buttrey, and Willie Ackerman the primary drummers. In-demand pedal steel guitarists included Pete Drake, Lloyd Green, Buddy Emmons, and Weldon Myrick. Charlie McCoy played harmonica, bass, and guitar.

Daily frequently called Bob Moore, the Nashville-born bassist who'd worked recording sessions, radio shows, and the Opry since the 1940s and had played bass in Owen Bradley's dance band. More often than not, Bob was George's session leader, the musician who led the band and did the actual production. At other times, fiddler Tommy Jackson handled the leader duties. Moore remembers George showing up drunk, but adds he wasn't the only one at the bottle.

"Pappy used to call me and we'd have a session at nine thirty in the morning and he'd call me at seven thirty drunk and tell me, 'I'll give you $250 if you go in there and supervise that session.' And I'd do it, but his name would go on the record as producer. I did a bunch of it. I had a deal with Musicor to produce whatever I wanted to. Well, it didn't turn out good, because [the label] didn't do shit after you gave it to them! I was more or less producin' George, and so was Tommy Jackson. Pappy . . . he'd maybe show up and maybe not. And half the time he did show up, he was drunk. I'm not puttin' Pappy down. In fact, I loved him. He was one of my favorite people. But he had all he could handle, you know. And so he was prone to the bottle anyway. And so was George. He'd be the one to get George drunk to start with!"

Moore hired Lloyd Green on quite a few Jones Musicor dates to handle the steel guitar. "Moore booked me on many of those Pappy Daily Musicor sessions, especially George Jones, between 1965 and 1970," Green recalls. "Bob was essentially the leader/producer always, with Daily being little more than the putative producer, in title only. The way we cut those records was always the design of Bob, in whom Daily entrusted the artistic, musical, and creative responsibilities." Jones had similar opinions about the Musicor days. To biographer Dolly Carlisle he praised the musicians, crediting them with the arrangements and adding, "There were good engineers on the sessions, but no one supervised the mixing. This is a big regret of mine . . . Those sessions sounded much better than they do on record." He firmly believed his voice wasn't prominent enough in the mixes. In many cases, he's correct. As usual, much of the blame for this lay at Pappy's feet. He was usually anxious to get back to Texas and rushed the sessions.

George spent a good bit of June 1965 in the studios, deferring to Pappy's sense of current trends. The hot Nashville act of the moment was George's pal and former writing partner, Roger Miller. After one hit single ("When Two Worlds Collide"), Miller became a hugely successful songwriter, but he still struggled to establish himself as a singer. To fund a move to Hollywood to try acting, Miller recorded a farewell album of his zany, off-the-wall novelty songs. It unexpectedly yielded two hits: the loopy "Dang Me" and then "Chug-A-Lug," followed by his 1965 "hip hobo" ditty "King of the Road," a chart-topping country single that reached the pop Top 5.

With Miller's unexpected success creating a niche for goofy songs, Pappy fed George novelties like "Love Bug," a ditty about domestic bliss, and Dallas Frazier's bizarre "I'm a People." Stranger than any of Miller's work, it centered on a monkey's loopy insistence he was human. George's exuberant, zany, and hyperactive treatments put both into the Top 10: "Love Bug" in 1965, "People" in 1966. Pappy had more for George to do that summer. He set up recording gear at Dance Town USA, a hall on Airline Drive in Houston, to record an entire show. Kicking off with "White Lightning," George seemed in good shape, as always, referring to himself in the first-person plural as he said, laughing, "We're glad to have the chance to be back with you, this time in a little better shape than with the . . . *flu* we had the last time." They performed a rich sampling of George's hits, yet the crowd shouted so many requests he had to ask them to hold it down. Responding to a request for a "fast" number, after noting he didn't normally perform rock, he flew into a hell-for-leather version of Larry Williams's "Bony Moronie."

George and Shirley threw a fiftieth-anniversary party for his parents in Vidor that August. A sober George was fully aware of the importance of the day, given his daddy's newfound sobriety. Family members who arrived hoping for a private concert of George's hits were to be disappointed. Deferring to the occasion and his mother's piety, he stuck to singing hymns, joined by Burl and Annie Stephen. Beyond the party, George was his usual self around home. On September 9, the *Port Arthur News* reported his arrest in Orange, Texas, the county seat east of Vidor, for a DUI. The article noted the "nationally known singer and entertainer" was apprehended by Highway Patrolman J.M. Burleyson and released on $500 bond.

While George caused most of his own problems on the road, on November 6 he and the Jones Boys faced a tribulation not of their making. With the bus out of commission, they temporarily moved to an oversize van. After rolling into Shelley's, a large dance hall in La Porte just outside Houston (later reinvented as the famous Gilley's), George met with Jackie Young, the former wife of singer Texas Bill Strength and the secretary of the George Jones Fan Club, about the wording of a Christmas card he wanted to send members. Young had some sort of intoxicant in her system and passed out in the front seat of the van, and was still there when George and the band went onstage. She was gone when they returned. Everyone took off to party before heading west for the next show.

Hours later, Young was found in her car, four miles from Shelley's, beaten and strangled to death. It was no surprise Houston police investigating the homicide wanted to talk to George—immediately. En route to perform in West Texas, no one knew anything was out of sorts until the bus radio picked up a local station broadcasting an urgent message for George to contact Houston police and let them know his location. When they stopped and one of the band members called Houston, advising where they were, local cops soon arrived. It was agreed they could play the scheduled concert, then head back to Houston immediately.

The local media detailed Young's connection to George, and their presence at Shelley's set off a frenzy as speculation grew as to whether he or the band was complicit. They submitted to polygraph tests conducted by police at a local motel, and everyone passed. Interviewing the women the boys partied with after the show bolstered their alibis. As time passed, official suspicion faded, but George and his musicians continued to endure the fallout. In January 1966, the *Houston Chronicle* ran an update declaring police had no new leads, further indications that George and his musicians were in the clear. He ruefully remembered seeing more cops than usual at shows and having to deal with hecklers shouting out questions about the murder. The stalled police investigation would resolve itself in the summer when a transient named Victor Eugene Miller II would confess to the killing. He would be sentenced to life in prison in September.

GEORGE KICKED OFF THE YEAR MUSICALLY WITH THE THOROUGHLY EFFECTIVE ballad "Take Me," bearing his and Leon Payne's names as cowriters, and it wouldn't be the last time he'd chart with the song. George's reputation for missing dates—"no-shows"—grew in the 1960s as he wandered off, blowing off shows or drinking himself into incoherence. Johnny Bush, however, recalled a very different situation during his two weeks as a temporary Jones Boy. Bush lived in Madison, Tennessee, in the spring of 1966. The former Cherokee Cowboy drummer had made his first records as a singer and toured with longtime Texas buddy Willie Nelson as his drummer. One day, members of the Jones Boys stopped by Bush's home. George, who'd fired his drummer, needed a replacement for a two-week Texas tour consisting of "makeup dates that George had screwed up on, either got drunk, didn't show, whatever." Since Willie wasn't touring during that time, there'd be no problem. George agreed to pay Bush fifty dollars a day at a time most stars paid sidemen twenty-five or thirty dollars.

Expecting two weeks of the usual bad behavior, Bush was amazed to discover that George "was a perfect gentleman the whole time. All those makeup dates, he made every one of them and sang his butt off. He was nice and polite as he could be. He even told Don [Adams], the bass player, 'Why don't you let John sing one before I come up?' He knew that I was tryin' to go out on my own, and Willie was trying to help me at that time. All those fourteen dates, makeup dates, he was sober and he was straight and he was a perfect gentleman. I told the band, 'Man, when I get back to Nashville, I'm gonna ruin his reputation because I never worked with a nicer guy in my life.' He was just a prince. The only problem we had, the band was more notorious than he was for trashin' motels. Every town we'd come to, we'd have to look two or three hours to find a place that would let us stay there because of the trips before."

George spent much of May in Nashville recording a gospel album, duets with Melba and other solo material. He continued to be reluctant to try songs Pappy pushed at him, one being "Walk

Through This World with Me," a Daily-published ballad by Arizona writers Sandra Seamons and Kay Savage. "I fought Pappy," he wrote in his autobiography, "telling him consistently I thought the song was weak. He kept pitching it to me, and I kept telling him no." When he agreed to do it, he made it clear he agreed only to shut the old man up. His performance was nondescript enough to end up slotted into an album as a filler track.

George also began getting songs from another Daily composer: Don Chapel, who'd recorded singles for Musicor. He was actually Lloyd Amburgey, the brother of country-gospel legend Martha Carson and Sun rockabilly vocalist Jean Chapel. He took Jean's stage surname of Chapel as his own. He worked as a desk clerk at Nashville's Anchor Motel and met George at one of his regular Nashville hangouts, the Biltmore Motel, to give him a song. George, in party mode, sitting on a bed with a hooker and a drink, paid little mind to the woman with Chapel: his girlfriend Virginia Wynette Byrd, an aspiring Alabama singer who'd come to town hoping to be discovered.

IN VIDOR, GEORGE HAD OTHER BUSINESS GOING ON. HE BOUGHT SIXTY ACRES OF land, constructed a new $100,000 home, and set up a ranch with Angus cattle, quarter horses, and Appaloosas. His ultimate goal seemed to be scaling back his touring by building an outdoor country music park where he could perform. Such seasonal venues were popular in both the North and South, especially after World War II, as Americans became more mobile. The parks offered a casual atmosphere, ample seating, refreshments, and most of all a steady stream of national country stars on weekends. A few, like Sunset Park in Chester County, Pennsylvania, west of Philadelphia, and New River Ranch near Rising Sun, Maryland, became iconic.

The George Jones Rhythm Ranch would be a dual-purpose showplace, able to stage concerts or rodeos with grandstand seating and a permanent stage. When home, George found great satisfaction doing some of the construction work himself. He didn't skimp on talent for the July 4, 1966, opening. George would headline, joined by his drinking buddy Lefty Frizzell and Merle Haggard, who'd come far from their first meeting in Bakersfield. His earliest hit, "(All My Friends Are Going to Be) Strangers," and his current single, "Swingin' Doors," set him apart. Tickets were required, but the place was soon inundated with fans and curiosity seekers, and as George remembered, "relatives, relatives and relatives and friends, and friends of friends." He shrugged and the gate crashers won the day. Nonetheless, he remembered the concert made money, even after expenses. He took off with Haggard after the show and didn't return home for a while. Opening day marked the first and final show ever held there, another of his impulse-driven projects turned sour.

THE FALL OF 1966 SAW GEORGE FEELING QUITE DIFFERENTLY ABOUT "WALK Through This World with Me," the tune he'd reluctantly recorded in May to quiet Pappy. Claiming he wasn't satisfied with his vocal, he asked the old man to let him take another run at it. At a November session, approaching the song in another key, his vocal became more focused and convincing as he injected understated hope, joy, and optimism into the lyrics, blissfully imagining a future of love and joy. This version, clearly worthy of release as a single, entered the charts in early 1967. By April it became his first No. 1 since "She

Thinks I Still Care" nearly five years earlier. George recorded his final sessions with Melba in late 1966. Their releases hadn't been selling the way they once had. She became involved with Jones Boys guitarist Jack Solomon: the couple would marry in 1968.

Pappy had other writers to pick from. Dallas Frazier was primarily known for writing novelty tunes like the Charlie Rich hit "Mohair Sam," but he gave Jones another stunner of a ballad: the intense "If My Heart Had Windows," a 1967 Top 10. Musicor would release an entire album of George singing Frazier songs in 1968. "Small Time Laboring Man," cowritten by George and Peanutt, had a powerful and evocative lyric summarizing and celebrating the pride of the working poor. Its success was marginal, yet it left a deep, lasting impression on another singer-songwriter: Bob Dylan, who singled out "Laboring Man" as his favorite song of the year in a 1968 *Rolling Stone* interview.

The Rhythm Ranch had been dismantled, the property sold, and the entire venture forgotten, but the messy situation at home didn't fade. Shirley had been dealing with George's drinking, absences, and the continued rumors about George and Melba and all the best she could. After more than a dozen years of marriage, in Houston, Beaumont, and Vidor, she was no more comfortable being a show-business spouse than she'd been at the start. Pursuing a lucrative career kept George's demons in a constant tug-of-war, and his self-absorbed, self-destructive lifestyle left his wife and children to their own devices. Between his first child, Susan, and his two sons, it was clear George, like other celebrities, fell short of the mark when it came to fatherhood.

Shirley later admitted her discontent was intensified by George's benign indifference to Bryan and Jeff. "Not that he was mean to 'em," she explained to *Texas Monthly* writer Pepi Plowman, "just that he didn't have any time or any love for 'em." Dub Scroggins admitted to Dolly Carlisle that given George's hijinks, "Shirley had a lot of room to feel hard towards George." But during the sixties, she'd made a new connection: Vidor resident John Clifton Arnold, known as J.C. A widower and longtime friend of George and Shirley's, he owned the building housing the Chuckwagon. With George on the road, J.C. provided needed solace, apparent to Shirley's friends and even to George's family.

At some point a story emerged that an enraged George discovered the couple together, pulled a shotgun, and filled Arnold's *gluteus maximus* with buckshot. Accounts of the incident vary. George's sister Helen had detailed memories when she spoke to Carlisle and said a local physician told her there was a shooting. George's propensity for violence while intoxicated was a matter of record, and his love of gunplay is well-known, even if he denied it later. George, Shirley, and Arnold nonetheless had a unified response: it never happened. George, who admitted to a confrontation, declared, "All of my wrath came out as words, not as buckshot." The veracity of the story remains a mystery. Was George capable of it? Yes. Could Arnold have refused to press charges? Quite possibly. Any definitive truth seems lost to the mists of history.

He and the Jones Boys were performing in Michigan on September 6, 1967, when he got an emergency call from Helen and Ruth. George W had suffered another, more severe stroke, one leaving him comatose and unlikely to pull through. In anguish, George caught a plane in Detroit and arrived home to join the death watch. His emotions ran the gamut as he pondered memories good and horrific. If it was any consolation, he had made his parents' golden anniversary, with his daddy sober and the couple's tranquility restored, a special occasion. The old man died the next day. Following services at Memorial Funeral Home in Vidor, George Washington Jones was interred at Restlawn Memorial

Park in a plot for two. A bronze marker, flush with the ground, would later be installed. There's no doubt the old man's health remained shaky despite his sobriety and recovery from the previous stroke. But external events may have played a role.

George carried a mortgage on the Vidor home he'd bought his parents. For some reason never quite clear, the mortgage payments weren't being made. No one—George included—seemed to be paying attention, and with him constantly on tour, the property somehow wound up in arrears. When Clara and George W were notified by Orange County deputies their home was to be repossessed, they were in a state of shock, George W in particular. After the earlier stroke, this stressor was the last thing the couple needed. In his autobiography, George blamed Shirley for failing to make the payments on time. Nallie's recollections of her handling the checkbook for George's band lends at least some credence to the notion. Even so, George deserves considerable blame for not making certain she'd taken care of that obligation. It was ultimately his responsibility. The inattention wasn't surprising given his steady stream of impulse purchases: buying, swapping, and selling cars and boats like they were baseball cards, often taking a loss. On a more responsible note, after his father's death he readily paid to add a room to the Scroggins home so Clara could live there, where the always reliable Helen and Dub could see to her needs.

The endless Musicor sessions continued, blending conventional ballads with screwball compositions like the Alex Zanetis novelty "The Poor Chinee," with its idiotic, pidgin-Chinese lyrics. Peanutt, too, was capable of both gems and oddities, like the bizarre "Unwanted Babies," a strange minor-key tune that's nothing less than sixties folk rock with an arrangement to match, a further reminder of the versatility of Nashville session players. As with "Rock It," Pappy agreed to release the single under a pseudonym, this time "Glen Patterson," an alias created by combining an alternate spelling of George's middle name with the maiden name of his mother, Clara Patterson Jones. At least one account survives of Ralph Emery playing the song when George visited his late-night show, and an upset George insisting, "It's not me, Ralph! It's not me!" The single stiffed. The song wound up (under George's name) on the Musicor album *If My Heart Had Windows,* issued in June 1968.

As 1967 drew to a close, one thing was abundantly clear: George and Shirley's long-troubled marriage was entering the End Times. Thirteen years of her misgivings and hostility to the showbiz life, his perpetual absences, and the boozing and hell-raising on the road and at times when he was home were just part of it. He'd not been there to see the boys grow up, saddling her with most of the responsibility. George's life was inexorably tied to Nashville, to the industry and his fans. The next move was anticlimactic. On April 11, 1968, Shirley Corley Jones filed for divorce from George Glenn Jones. The matter was so casual between them that one attorney represented both (widely discouraged in such matters). George gave her all she demanded, and that was plenty: property and homes around Vidor, his tour bus, musical gear, and, most significantly, half his songwriting royalties for all tunes he wrote and cowrote from the start of his career in 1954 up to 1968. That covered "Why Baby Why," "Just One More," "Life to Go," "Color of the Blues," "Window Up Above," and "Four Oh Thirty Three." The royalties, she felt, would be an annuity of sorts for the boys. A chapter had closed for everyone. Soon after, a tapped-out George and his road manager Billy Wilhite moved to Nashville.

CHAPTER 4

1968-1975

George left town so broke that Dub had to lend him $1,000. In Nashville, he and Wilhite set up a temporary base at the Executive Inn before George bought a new tour bus and a home on Brandywine Drive not far from Old Hickory Lake. Despite walking away from the Rhythm Ranch, George and Wilhite had a new venture on Lower Broadway. George Jones Possum Holler was a private club located upstairs at 412 Broadway, a building owned by Roy Acuff, whose museum, Roy Acuff Exhibits, occupied the ground floor, displaying rare fiddles and other things he collected in his travels. Tootsie's Orchid Lounge was five doors down, the Ernest Tubb Record Shop across the street, and the Ryman Auditorium, home of the Opry, a street away.

With its reasonable cover charge, Possum Holler became a sort of Tootsie's annex. The Jones Boys played there and George occasionally showed up to sing, as did many of his friends. Music business functionaries from Sixteenth Avenue South made it a regular watering hole. Even Acuff, despite his puritanical, sanctimonious public image, was a regular visitor who enjoyed a drink or two. Johnny Bush, enjoying his first successful singles for Nashville-based Stop Records, would also drop by. "I'd go into Nashville to record, I'd go up there to sing and have a few. In November, we'd have the disc jockey convention there. The place was packed and I'd go up and sing tenor behind George on 'White Lightning' and things like that. He said, 'I was tryin' to throw you and I couldn't.' I said, 'Man, I know your stuff as well as you do!'" Everyone carried on there to their heart's delight until the night a commode backed up, flooding Acuff's meticulously maintained downstairs museum. Surveying the damage, Acuff told an embarrassed, contrite George and Wilhite they'd have to close Possum Holler. Wilhite pleaded their case, but Acuff, despite his own regrets, stressed the business realities that affected him, declaring, "I can't have turds in my exhibits."

George remained friendly with Don Chapel, who'd given him a ballad titled "When the Grass Grows over Me." But he was far more interested in Chapel's wife, the woman who had accompanied him to George's motel room when Don was dropping off songs. Now known as Tammy Wynette, she was the hottest new female singer in the business, and George counted himself among her growing number of fans.

Virginia Wynette Pugh was born in rural Itawamba County, Mississippi, on May 5, 1942. The Pughs, a modest rural family, didn't live quite the hardscrabble life the Joneses had in the Thicket. Virginia's maternal grandfather was relatively well-off. Her father, sharecropper and amateur musician William Hollice Pugh, died of a brain tumor before his infant daughter was a year old. With World War II expanding job opportunities for poor rural southerners, Virginia's mother, Mildred, who'd worked a variety of jobs before the war, headed to Memphis to work in a factory. Virginia stayed on her grandparents' farm, working in the cotton fields, though accounts of how deeply she got into the actual labor tend to vary. Unlike the shy, solitary George, she was a highly popular student, admired by many of the girls and fascinated with men her own age and older.

Inspired by the father she never knew, she developed her own interest in music with a special affinity for gospel. She sang on local radio with two friends in a vocal trio known as Wynette, Linda and Imogene. When she went to Memphis to be with her mother, Mildred was working at a cleaning business alongside Scotty Moore, the owner's brother and a country guitarist. Moore and his friend, bass player Bill Black, were starting to work with an unknown Memphis singer named Elvis Presley. They rehearsed at the cleaners after it closed, Wynette able to hang out as they worked out songs. But country was her major love. After returning to Alabama to attend high school, where she remained popular, she began dreaming seriously of becoming a singer. She and her mother both loved country music, and like many others they considered George Jones among the greatest of the day.

In 1959 Wynette Pugh married Euple Byrd, a simple man who had difficulty finding work in rural Alabama. The couple had three daughters, Gwen, Jackie, and Tina, and to support them, Wynette took various jobs and studied hairdressing as her husband moved from job to job. His ups and downs caused considerable strain on the marriage since Byrd thought little of Wynette's musical aspirations. Wynette had her own emotional and physical issues. At one point she was hospitalized for depression and received electroshock treatments, the long-term effects of which weren't clear. She left Byrd and moved to Birmingham, working as a hairdresser to support her daughters. They resided in subsidized housing. Unwilling to settle for that lifestyle for long, she doubled down on her belief she could succeed as a singer.

A glimmer of hope came when she landed a spot singing on *The Country Boy Eddie Show,* a popular local TV program on WBRC. Entertainer Eddie Burns, the host, offered live, down-home music to the region and Wynette gained a following that led to local performing jobs. Dazzled by the possibilities and determined to see if she could succeed on a higher level, she began traveling to Nashville in 1965, hoping to find someone interested in her voice. Staying at the low-cost Anchor Motel, she met Chapel, who between performances worked there as a desk clerk. Mutual aspirations brought them together. Like most aspiring female vocalists who came to town desperate for fame, her visits to various labels large and small brought constant rejections and occasional casting-couch offers from producers who preyed on the desperation of the many young women hoping to be the next Kitty Wells, Patsy Cline, Loretta Lynn, or Connie Smith. Chapel, who had connections with Pappy, made him aware of Wynette's talents, but the old man decided to pass. Chapel proved supportive as she made the rounds. The couple began singing together. Frustrated with the rejection and ready to give up, she had nothing to lose when Chapel encouraged her to visit producer Billy Sherrill at Columbia Records, which had a large Nashville office and studio complex.

Even before George came into the picture, Sherrill's and Wynette's stories were intertwined. Born in 1936 in Phil Campbell, Alabama, Billy Norris Sherrill was the son of an evangelist. He played piano behind his father and later worked in R&B bands. Arriving in Nashville, he landed a job at the short-lived Nashville studio opened by Sun Records owner Sam Phillips. Sherrill's broader musical perspective gave him a contrarian view of most country music. Well versed in classical music, he also made no secret of his admiration for the work of wall-of-sound pop producer Phil Spector, who produced standards like the Crystals' "He's a Rebel" and the Ronettes' "Be My Baby." Spector was known for controlling every aspect of the music and surrounding vocalists with near-symphonic backing, a trait Sherrill would adapt to his own purposes.

He joined Epic Records, a longtime subsidiary label of Columbia, in 1964. Initially, he produced records by the Staple Singers and others. It was a time Don Law still ruled the roost at Columbia Nashville, but Law, who produced records by bluesman Robert Johnson in the thirties, was nearing the company's mandatory retirement age. With Law gradually stepping aside, the label brought in Bob Johnston from New York. Johnston, who coproduced Bob Dylan's *Highway 61 Revisited,* continued working with Dylan in Nashville and took on two of the label's other top country acts: Johnny Cash and bluegrass stars Lester Flatt and Earl Scruggs. Sherrill's first real country success came in 1966 producing Louisiana singer David Houston's hit ballad "Almost Persuaded," cowritten by Sherrill and Glenn Sutton. The single reached No. 1 and earned a Grammy that quickly enhanced Sherrill's stature around Nashville.

As Sherrill listened to the young woman, despite some initial skepticism, he heard enough potential to bring her into the studio to record a demo. When she told him her name, he looked at her blond hair and ponytail (the latter was a hairpiece) and, thinking of Debbie Reynolds in the film *Tammy,* suggested Byrd looked "more like a Tammy." Adding that to her middle name, Wynette, gave her a new identity. In September 1966, Sherrill produced her first single: the ballad "Apartment #9," cowritten by Johnny Paycheck. It reached the country Top 50 and impressed many, George among them. Billy teamed her with Houston to record "My Elusive Dreams," a ballad Sherrill cowrote with master composer Curly Putman, responsible for the timeless prison song "Green, Green Grass of Home."

As he did with his other artists, Sherrill refined the arrangements to frame Tammy's voice, apparent on her second solo single, "Your Good Girl's Gonna Go Bad," which peaked at No. 3 in the spring of 1967. She began touring with Chapel, whom she married in Ringgold, Georgia, in April 1967. Their bus identified the act as the "Don Chapel–Tammy Wynette Show." They were joined by Don's teenage daughter, singer Donna Chapel. That summer, "My Elusive Dreams" topped the country charts, giving Tammy's career a one-two punch, followed by "I Don't Wanna Play House," the Sherrill-Sutton ballad that became her first No. 1 and earned Sherrill his second Grammy. Tammy's success reversed the dynamic with Chapel, who hadn't really come close with his own efforts. She continued to rise with two more No. 1 singles: Sherrill and Sutton's "Take Me to Your World" and "D-I-V-O-R-C-E," a ballad about dealing with children amid a dying marriage. It, too, was a tune that George loved.

For the next decade or so, George would have a virtual merry-go-round of road managers. When Billy Wilhite departed for a time, George turned to a figure from his early career: Bill Starns, the son of Jack and Neva. As George crossed paths with Don and Tammy, he grew more attracted to her. For her part, she was thrilled by the attention from her favorite country singer. His efforts to encounter her whenever possible soon evolved into clandestine meetings. Starns did what he could to divert Don's attention when George wanted to hook up with Tammy. Sometimes when the Chapels were on a bill with George, she'd ride in his Cadillac instead of in the bus with her husband. Tammy made sure Bill told George that she and Don were playing a Jaycees benefit at the high school in Red Bay, Alabama, the town where she grew up, to raise money for the school's air-conditioning. George, not touring at that moment, arrived to hang out. Don introduced him from the stage and George sang a duet with Tammy. After the show, she kissed him on the cheek and said, "Love ya, George!"

Over time, Tammy's hairdressing experience led her to suggest George grow out his flattop haircut into a longer, slicked-down style. It made sense, since fashions were changing in the country field. Aside from Porter Wagoner, Little Jimmy Dickens, the Willis Brothers, and a few other holdouts, the rhinestone Nudie outfits George and other singers favored were giving way to more subtle, sophisticated western suits. George, too, would begin to abandon sequins in designing his show clothes.

Pappy had more material for him to record, but handled paperwork in the control room while bass player Bob Moore, the session leader, and his fellow musicians did the heavy lifting. As usual, when Moore wasn't available as leader, fiddler Tommy Jackson did the honors. A June 4 session turned out particularly well, with a daring Eddie Noack composition titled "Barbara Joy," the carefully crafted saga of a man convicted and condemned to death for raping his very willing, enthusiastic paramour after her husband caught them in the act. The standout, however, was Chapel's "When the Grass Grows over Me," an eloquent weeper about a man so deeply committed to a woman who's left him that he proclaims his love will end only with his death, a theme that would resurface in George's repertoire in a more profound manner later. Chapel's clear, unambiguous lyrics, articulating loss, pain, and undying passion, gave George the optimal framework to do what he did best, to probe—exhaustively—every emotional facet and deliver a compelling performance. The single topped out at No. 2 in early 1969.

Pappy teamed George with Brenda Carter, who'd recorded for his D Records label in Houston, for "Milwaukee Here I Come," a lightweight ditty by Hank Mills, who wrote the Del Reeves hit "Girl on the Billboard" and actor Robert Mitchum's 1967 one-shot hit country single "Little Ole Wine Drinker, Me." Despite being insubstantial, "Milwaukee" was engaging enough to reach the Top 20. George's tongue-in-cheek delivery put it over as he delivered lines about trading a Ford for an Oldsmobile, adding, "I might get all drunked up and trade it for a Rolls."

Drunked up indeed. George had liquor in his veins at most sessions. The musicians were rarely teetotalers, given their grueling (and very lucrative) schedules of several sessions a day. But as part of the A-Team, they followed union rules and a code. For them, or any musician, the notion of simply walking out of a session was unthinkable. Dealing with George, however, presented challenges they didn't face recording with Loretta Lynn or Eddy Arnold. When George's drinking went into the red zone at one session, Moore set his own line of demarcation. "I made a reputation for walkin' out on George Jones at two o'clock in the morning. We'd been workin' all day long, and I had a nine o'clock session the next morning, and it was quarter till two and we had worked our butts off on this one song. George kept gettin' drunker and drunker and finally got to where he couldn't even get through the first line. But he just raised hell with us and [would] say, 'Naw, I gotta do one more. I gotta do one more.' I said, 'I'm gonna give you this one more and if you don't get it, I'm gone!' And he didn't hardly get through the intro, and I picked it up and left. And Pappy was in the control room, he come runnin' out of the control room applauding, sayin', 'Thank *God*!'"

Once George and Bill Starns dropped by Don and Tammy's home to find "When the Grass Grows over Me" playing on the stereo. There was already stress in the house after a food-poisoning incident the night before put Tammy's three daughters in the emergency room. Tammy later claimed Chapel couldn't be found (his daughter Donna disagrees) and noted that George and Bill arrived at the hospital to help out. Don was home when George and Starns arrived. Liquor flowed as Tammy prepared to serve dinner. As everyone sat down, it became obvious Tammy and Don weren't in a great place. They began arguing, Chapel agitated enough to direct a torrent of verbal abuse, including the word *bitch,* at his wife. George quietly suggested Chapel shouldn't talk to her that way. "What business is it of yours? She's my wife!" Chapel angrily responded. That was all George needed to hear.

Drunk and outraged, he stood up, flipped the table over, and hotly responded, "Because I love her and she's in love with me, aren't ya, Tammy?" After a pregnant pause, a stunned Tammy found herself replying, "Yes, I am." George told her to collect Jackie, Gwen, and Tina before leaving. Well aware Don would call the police, he dropped Tammy and the girls at the Nashville Hilton. When authorities showed up at Brandywine Drive, he could honestly say Tammy and her daughters were not there. Tammy and Don planned a Mexican divorce.

In her autobiography, *Stand By Your Man,* Tammy recounted her first night with George in detail, the two in the massive four-poster bed in his lavish Spanish-themed bedroom. A bottle of whiskey sat on a table at his bedside as he watched his favorite movie, the tragic 1962 boxing drama *Requiem for a Heavyweight,* starring Anthony Quinn, Jackie Gleason, Mickey Rooney, and

Julie Harris. Written by future *Twilight Zone* creator Rod Serling, it told the tale of over-the-hill, honest Native American prizefighter Mountain Rivera (Quinn), afflicted with concussion-related dementia, facing blindness and ready to hang it up after losing his most recent bout in the seventh round. Maish Rennick, Rivera's unscrupulous manager, played by Gleason, had insisted Rivera would go down earlier in the bout, betting against his own fighter. Ma Greeny, a female bookie known for ruthless debt collection, expects Rennick to cover her losses of around $3,000.

Desperate to raise the cash, Rennick tries to keep Rivera working in a new guise: as a cartoonish wrestler in an Indian headdress. Army (Rooney), Rivera's first-aid man and the only one on Rivera's team truly concerned with his well-being, finds it all repellent. Seeking work through an unemployment agency, he's aided by social worker Grace Miller (Harris), who pitches the gentle boxer for a job as a children's camp counselor. After Rennick gets him drunk and Rivera embarrasses himself in front of the camp's owners, the job offer vanishes. Before his first scheduled wrestling bout, Rivera discovers Rennick had bet against him at that last boxing match. Furious, he's ready to walk until the bookie and her crew arrive to inflict extreme bodily harm on Rennick. Feeling perversely obligated, Rivera bitterly dons the headdress and returns to the ring as "Big Chief" Mountain Rivera to save his manager. A tearful, enraged Army stands by, barely able to watch his friend's self-humiliation.

Requiem touched an emotional chord in George, not unlike the way his own ballads affected fans. Tammy remembered, admiringly, that he had tears in his eyes as he drank and watched the film. What connection did he feel with *Requiem* that brought forth such a deep and emotional response? Was it merely a sad film that appealed to his simple, sentimental side and lifelong empathy for the underdog? Or did he identify with Rivera and the way his talents had been used and exploited beyond his control? The fighter was expected to perform on command, as George was, starting with those coerced performances for George Washington Jones in the Thicket. George, when drunk, may well have identified with the idea of rebelling, given his growing frustration with Pappy and Musicor and suspicions about Pappy's side deals. Did he see Pappy as his own Maish Rennick?

George and Tammy flew to Mexico in a day so she could divorce Chapel quickly. When they returned on August 22, Tammy, again stretching the truth, impulsively announced she and George had married. Once the lawyers jumped in, things took some surprising turns. Tammy, consulting with her attorney, discovered Tennessee didn't recognize Mexican divorces. Chapel filed against her for desertion and adultery, plus an alienation-of-affection suit against George. The intrigue continued when Bill Starns, visiting Alabama, talked informally to an attorney who advised him that Alabama law barred remarriage for a full year following a divorce unless a judge gave specific approval. Marrying Don ten months after divorcing Euple Byrd meant the marriage to Chapel was invalid and easily annulled. Tammy gave him a limo, a home she owned, and a bus. Devastated by the breakup, Chapel fulfilled bookings with daughter Donna singing in Tammy's place.

George and Tammy still toured separately, George making surprise appearances at her shows when he could. But conflicts surfaced amid their contentment. Although part of it stemmed from George's mood swings when he drank, a musical sticking point also surfaced. George, who'd loved Tammy's early hits, heard a dub of her as-yet-unreleased recording of "Stand By Your Man" and let her know he didn't care for it. It wasn't the message of marital fidelity that bothered him. Given his biases in favor of fiddle-and-steel honky-tonk, he found the Sherrill treatment too slick. A furious Tammy began having misgivings about the song until Billy calmed her down. The public had the final say. *Billboard* showed the single reaching No. 1 November 23. It stayed there three weeks and became her signature song.

They shared another milestone when George rejoined the Opry on January 6, 1969, the same night Tammy, Mel Tillis, and Dolly Parton became the show's newest members. With their solo engagements completed, the couple could begin touring together. The first joint appearance came at the Playroom, an Atlanta club, in mid-February. Things got off to a good start until Tammy got another sample of George at his impulsive worst. After briefly going back to Nashville for a bit of studio work, she returned to Atlanta to find George angry and drunk. At their next performance, he walked off after only one song and, driven by his desire to escape far away, flew to Las Vegas with the club's owner. Furious at the irresponsibility, she had to carry the show and wondered if there'd ever be a wedding. George returned a few days later, still surly. The next day, bright and upbeat, he told her to prepare for their wedding. The ceremony took place February 16 at the courthouse in Ringgold, Georgia, the same place where she'd married Chapel.

George had given Shirley nearly everything in the divorce, but he had held on to a Lakeland, Florida, getaway home the couple had owned. How much they ever used it isn't clear. George was renting it to friends in early 1969. The changes in his and Tammy's lives and a desire for a respite from Nashville's intrigues (not to mention overzealous fans and anxious songwriters) led them to move to Lakeland in March 1969. In spite of occasional blowups, they settled into a happy domesticity, hanging out with their neighbors, the Hyders. Cliff, a former navy man who suffered from

ALS—Lou Gehrig's disease—and his wife, Maxine, grew close to George and Tammy. George's compassion led him to work at getting Cliff, despondent over his debilitating affliction, into the world, be it on a fishing boat, dining out, or playing board games at home. Contented, even entranced, by their new environment, the couple decided to join the local business community. George purchased fifteen nearby acres for a trailer park, in part because Tammy wanted to move some of her family, including her mother, to the area. "Tammy's Courts" was the name of the facility. Billy Wilhite moved there to manage the place.

Musicor released "I'll Share My World with You" as a single in late March, smart timing since it appeared to be tied to the recent wedding, foreshadowing Sherrill's later strategy of tying the couple's solo and duet singles to whatever transpired in their marriage. The same applied to George's *I'll Share My World with You* LP, released in June. George and Tammy were on the cover. Today, country singers routinely do cameos, known as "vocal events," by appearing on records by other singers signed to different labels. That wasn't the case in 1969, when the practice was rare and largely forbidden by record companies. With Tammy contracted to Epic and George still tied up with Musicor, she couldn't openly record with her new husband, but that restriction didn't apply to an album-cover photo that served to remind fans of the connection. They could also sing together on television. A joint appearance on the syndicated *Wilburn Brothers Show* soon after their marriage demonstrated their musical compatibility as they tore into an aggressive, joyous "Milwaukee Here I Come" that left the Brenda Carter duet in the dust. The couple enjoyed themselves onstage so much that George began thinking beyond Pappy and Musicor, anxious to find a way he could partner with Tammy on records as well.

Closer to home, George had to deal with something more personal: a problem involving nude candid photos Chapel took of Tammy when they were married and swapped with other men. In this case, the truth is all but impossible to determine. In her 1979 autobiography *Stand By Your Man,* Tammy insisted a fan at a concert showed her a nude shot of herself, clearly taken when she and Chapel were married. George claimed Billy Wilhite bought and destroyed the negatives. Chapel told Jimmy McDonough, Tammy's biographer, the pictures were Polaroid instant photos with no negatives.

In Lakeland, her own family now living nearby, Tammy happily welcomed members of George's family from Vidor. Bryan and Jeffrey came in, as did Clara, then contending with cardiac issues. Tammy, who loved Clara, did all she could to make everyone comfortable, yet Clara was stunned by the lavish lifestyle George and her new daughter-in-law enjoyed, aeons from what she knew in the Thicket, Vidor, or anywhere else. Her steadfast religious beliefs made her averse to gambling, but she still enjoyed attending the local dog races when she visited. George and Tammy once took their mothers to a Polynesian restaurant in Tampa that George loved. The teetotaling Clara sipped champagne and in her usual direct manner, commented, "Glenn, that stuff tastes just like vinegar!" She was amazed that he left a $40 tip on the $150 dinner tab. She remained the one woman who could calm George when no one else could.

During that time, George's binges were fewer and his contentment, except for a few lapses, seemed higher than in the past. Along with touring, the couple made guest appearances on *Hee-Haw,* the new CBS prime-time country music/comedy show based on *Rowan & Martin's Laugh-In.* Their tour bus roamed the country, emblazoned with the billing MR. & MRS. COUNTRY MUSIC. They cowrote songs like "Never Grow Cold," a tune George recorded for Musicor on which Tammy sang prominent harmony. Pappy's desire to avoid problems with Epic Records may explain why he buried the song on an album.

Back in Nashville for the 1969 CMA Awards, Tammy was again nominated for Best Female Vocalist. When George returned to his old haunts, he started drinking again and, she claimed, knocked her against a wall. She attended the ceremony with makeup covering the bruise and won the award. As her star rose, George hadn't had a No. 1 single since "Walk Through This World with Me" two years earlier. Jerry Chesnut's ballad "A Good Year for the Roses" was the standout song at his February 1970 Musicor session. Behind spare, understated production, George gave the song a searing rendition, his passionate vocal making it among his most enduring efforts at Musicor. Released later that year, it fell just short of topping the country charts in early 1971. His continuing successes with the label didn't diminish his desire to record with Tammy and to finally free himself from Pappy.

George was delighted when Tammy discovered she was pregnant in early 1970, especially since she'd suffered a miscarriage the previous year. Around that time, he made his own discovery in Lakeland: a dilapidated seventy-year-old white-columned home. It was built in 1902 by H.B. Carter, who made his fortune in lumber, on the lake that occupies the center of Lakeland. Another owner moved the home several miles south to a five-acre lot. The couple purchased it for $100,000. Vast amounts of additional cash would be required to fully restore it. With his usual zeal, George set to the task, revealing an uncanny eye for color coordination and interior decorating, an unusual skill for a honky-tonk singer from the Thicket. Tammy marveled at his talents in this area, though one finishing touch wasn't so original: the estate's guitar-shaped swimming pool, not unlike the one Webb Pierce installed at his Nashville home years earlier.

Asked by *Country Music* magazine to interview George in 1980, five years after their divorce, Tammy questioned him about that skill. While he never explained how he developed it, he said if he had to make his living doing something else, decorating was "something that would probably be one of my favorite choices, to try to get into." He added, "When I used to decorate our houses a lot, back then [my taste] was Spanish . . . I have different tastes for a lot of different furniture now."

George actually had a plan to pay for all this spending involving another investment: buying more than thirty acres of land adjacent to his new home to build yet another outdoor music park. The Old Plantation Country Music Park would put the short-lived Rhythm Ranch to shame. His extravagance in overdrive, he imported exotic plants and palm trees and spared no expense for stars and the public. Unlike the shithole dressing rooms he and his fellow performers often encountered on the road, Old Plantation's would be classy and well appointed. There'd be bleacher seating for the public, with a roof later added to protect everyone against Florida's quick-changing weather. George supervised the workers and again did some of the labor himself. He also had to deal with local government, particularly zoning officials who insisted he follow regulations. Nearby residents feared the park would prove intrusive and cause them ample problems.

As Tammy neared her due date, George went on another bender that took him to Texas, but he was back and ready when their daughter was born on October 5, 1970. George drove Tammy to the hospital, doing everything he could to keep her calm. Ecstatic, he called his family, exclaiming, "Hot a-mighty!" When the couple's daughter was born, Tammy feared George would be disappointed it wasn't a boy. He wasn't, and the happy parents named her Tamala Georgette Jones. Two weeks later, they moved into the restored home as construction continued on the park, set to open that spring.

In 1954, Pappy had taken a young, unschooled, and ambitious George Jones under his wing. The two had made money together and, at least for a while, enjoyed a father-son relationship George had never had with his own daddy. When he was carrying on, ranting, raving, drunk, and dissolute, Pappy stood by him, no doubt motivated as much by his bankability as affection. But the George Jones and Pappy Daily of those early days were long gone. George may have been unsophisticated regarding business, but he'd seen enough to want to sever ties with Pappy and with Musicor. It would take time—and considerable cash. "I was still under contract to Musicor, and its executives wouldn't let me record with Tammy on her label, Epic, unless I bought out my contract," he wrote in his autobiography. "I paid $300,000 to get out of one contract so I could enter another. Had I not paid the money, there might never have been any duets by George Jones and Tammy Wynette."

He later took direct—largely accurate—aim at Pappy in comments to Nick Tosches, saying of his old mentor, "We were fairly close at one time. Then the truth comes out. He was pitchin' me around to different labels and I kinda got tired of that. Made deals on the side for extra money for hisself, which I never found out till later." The exact financial cost may never be known. A six-figure amount is certainly credible. George had to fulfill remaining obligations to Musicor as he became acclimated to Billy Sherrill, whose techniques were the inverse of Pappy's.

He got his feet wet with Billy by recording with Tammy for Epic in 1971 as he continued winding down his Musicor commitment with his final sessions. In the famous Quonset Hut, part of the Bradley studio complex Columbia had purchased from the Bradley brothers in 1962, the session was a different atmosphere given Billy's careful, hands-on control of every aspect of an arrangement and sound on the singles. And he favored A-Team musicians who gave him exactly what he wanted, including ideas he could adapt. Contrary to popular belief, Billy did not exclude the pedal steel, despite his more sophisticated approach to arrangements. The producer often used Pete Drake, who'd done some of George's Musicor dates. If Drake was unavailable, he often turned to another A-Teamer: Lloyd Green, who'd briefly toured with George and played steel on "Too Much Water" in 1957. One of the most cerebral and perceptive musicians from that era, Green, who worked with Nashville's greatest producers from the fifties into the eighties, explained Sherrill's technique from a session player's perspective.

"I always thought that Sherrill was the best producer in Nashville. I agree some of it was a little pretentious, but Billy Sherrill records were the only records that were created by Billy Sherrill. He literally choreographed the entire song, every song he did. He didn't tell you exactly how to play it, but he gave you the idea of how he wanted you to play it and it was always right."

Norro Wilson, the Kentucky-born singer, songwriter, and producer who wrote some of George's most enduring material at Epic, had listened to country and pop music in his youth and later sang in a gospel group before becoming a country vocalist. Even while recording for various labels, he became one of Sherrill's stable of writers along with Carmol Taylor, George Richey, Glenn Sutton, and Bobby Braddock. Among the hit compositions he cowrote for Tammy were "I'll See Him Through" and four No. 1s: "He Loves Me All the Way," "My Man (Understands)," "Another Lonely Song," and "(You Make Me Want to Be) a Mother."

Wilson became a keen student of Billy's production techniques, comparing them to those of his other hero: Decca producer Owen Bradley, responsible for Patsy Cline, Loretta Lynn, and Conway Twitty, who for years led a Nashville-based big band playing pop and swing music. "I learned more from [Billy] than anyone," Wilson said. "I learned all my production things from him. Billy's [use of] dynamics in making records changed the sound of Nashville music, I think. I got a lot of thoughts and ideas to emphasize something, play a little louder, play a little harder. That's color. Nobody made a record better than Billy. He played saxophone. He played really good piano. He's a learned guy. I don't know if he was as learned as Owen with musical knowledge because of [Bradley's] big band stuff, but he was damn close. He knew where he was all the time. He was also able to communicate with the players. . . . You won't talk to a player who won't tell you they had the utmost respect for Billy. His ears were marvelous."

Sherrill had a profoundly different vision for how to frame George musically, and, not surprisingly, lavished special attention on the songs he planned to release as singles. Beyond singles, however, many of George's Epic albums include numbers produced with the traditional accompaniment he always preferred. Jones told Jimmy McDonough as much when he said, "If Billy *believed* in the song, he was there every second. If it was an album cut—a good song, but it wouldn't make fire come out your butt, he wasn't interested." George added that Sherrill wasn't always present when he and the band recorded those numbers. He would have the proceedings in the studio piped into his office.

In Sherrill's heyday, smoother production style stirred intense debate between those who appreciated his work and those who felt his approach entirely too slick for country artists. My own views on his production have evolved. I've noted that he was a total control freak in the studio, far more hands-on than other renowned Nashville producers who gave the famous A-Team session players latitude in working out arrangements. He didn't always get the best results with some artists, yet he stopped at nothing to get the arrangement he envisioned for a given recording, carefully controlling his singers' delivery and calling the shots on material. He used a select group of A-Teamers whom he trusted to give him precisely the sound he desired, or who could develop original ideas he could adapt to the arrangement. But if the arrangements seemed slick, with strings and backup singers, George's vocals were far from smooth. Sherrill wisely convinced George to focus even more on his lower register much of the time. Maturing into middle age, George's voice still conveyed magnificent, unvarnished emotion, amplified and enhanced by Sherrill's arrangements and smoother production values. Instead of softening George's impact, the glossy background gave him even greater clarity and bite, the equivalent to displaying a beautiful, weathered piece of wood against a velvet or satin backdrop that accentuates its unpolished qualities.

For George and Tammy's first duet single at Epic, Sherrill remade George's 1968 Musicor hit "Take Me." Hearing it in the context of rock-based, twenty-first-century country, the performance seems nearly as hardcore as George and Melba singing "We Must Have Been Out of Our Minds." True background vocalists coexist alongside Pete Drake's pedal steel. Tammy begins, Drake adding graceful fills in between her pauses. George, in the lower register, handles himself ably, adding his trademark bends and cries. The song's traditional feel echoes his past, yet the smoother background heralds a new era in his musical development.

With local officials temporarily satisfied, Old Plantation Country Music Park, capacity ten thousand, opened on April 4, 1971, with a true all-star lineup. The couple headlined, as did two more of the era's hottest stars: Conway Twitty and surprise guest Charley Pride. Billy came in from Nashville for the opening. Twenty thousand people, twice the capacity, showed up, many turned away once the park was filled to overflow. Traffic was reportedly backed up six miles, confirming the concerns of many of the neighbors. For that day, the crowd was mesmerized, and so was George. This was no repeat of the Rhythm Ranch fiasco. He had a $20,000 electric sign built, declaring the venue the HOME OF COUNTRY MUSIC'S GEORGE JONES AND TAMMY WYNETTE. The grounds had carnival rides for the kids, food concessions and other amenities, and examples of George's continued free spending: a collection of expensive antique cars, one of them a vehicle used by Hitler's staff. George drove around in a Nudie-customized Pontiac Bonneville (as had Webb Pierce before him) with four thousand silver dollars embedded into the leather upholstery. The door handles were six-shooters. On the doors, signs touted OLD PLANTATION COUN-TRY MUSIC PARK, CENTRAL BARN RD. S540A, LAKELAND, FLORIDA. HOME OF GEORGE JONES & TAMMY WYNETTE.

For the moment, he was proud and enthusiastic. On the road, he was delighted with his wife and enchanted by his infant daughter. He relished meeting old friends. In San Francisco, he crossed paths with Beaumont honky-tonk partner Luther Nallie, now guitarist with the Sons of the Pioneers. They were performing in California for Bob Eubanks, who, along with hosting TV's *Newlywed Game,* promoted country concerts. Eubanks had booked George and Tammy for some West Coast appearances. In San Francisco, the Pioneers were on the same bill, and Nallie saw his old friend's contentment, albeit briefly. "The last time I saw George was not long after he married Tammy. The Pioneers were one of the first ones to go on, and when we got off, we got paid and went on home, well, just as we were walkin' out to our cars, George was walkin' in. That was the first I'd seen him in a long time. And we were glad to see each other and hugged and all that and he said, 'Look, I'm getting ready to go on,' and said, 'Come back to the bus for just one minute. I want you to meet my wife Tammy.'" Introductions were made and George headed for the stage.

But a two-week engagement at the Landmark Hotel in Vegas served as a reminder of how fast things could sour. Billy and his friend, music publisher Al Gallico (Billy was one of his writers), flew in for the show, but George went off on another bender, leaving Tammy alone to headline on her birthday, May 5, 1971. George's walkout exposed another problem that plagued him for decades: a malignant insecurity that made him feel unworthy of performing in higher-end places that welcomed such pop music giants as Sinatra, Streisand, or Presley. His absence affected Tammy's performance, but with the help of Jimmy Dean, who was in the audience, she got through it. When George finally arrived, he behaved for the rest of their stay, though he later disputed her claims he'd misbehaved playing blackjack in the casino. The disparity between Tammy's and George's memories on this and other issues would grow as time passed.

That was especially true in the case of one George explosion still debated more than forty years later. During his life, George was generally up-front about most of his dark side. Tammy was too, to a point, but her memories, including those in her autobiography, sometimes differ from the recollections of others, like the tale of George's alleged violent, drunken rampage through their newly renovated home. There's agreement that at some point, almost surely in 1971, a drunken George wound up being picked up for a ten-day stay at the Watson Clinic in Lakeland. After being discharged, he arrived home in a taxi to find everyone gone and the house looking like a tornado had hit the interior. Some accounts have George breaking down and crying, having realized what he'd done. While he was known for contrition after sobering up, George later disputed assertions he was responsible for the damage, noting his friend Cliff Hyder's speculation that Tammy may have ordered others to do the damage. The truth may never be known.

Regardless, he cleaned up the devastation, repaired the damage, and replaced what could not be fixed. Tammy returned to a home that looked much the way it did beforehand. She had her own issues involving her unexpected fame and wealth. She also had legitimate physical ailments that took a toll. Over time, her use of prescription medications caused her every bit as much personal and professional grief as George's drinking did for him.

Even if the facts and details are inconsistent, George was far from blameless, his antics often childish or simply absurd and impossible to fathom. When they returned to Nashville to do the Opry, he admitted being in a delusional, paranoid frenzy, thinking something was going on between Tammy and his longtime buddy Porter Wagoner. In the backstage restroom he came up behind Porter, dressed in one of his famous rhinestone Nudie suits and standing at a urinal. George declared, "I want to see what Tammy's so proud of," only to twist Porter's cock as he tried to take a piss. Porter, caught off guard, tried to pull away only to urinate all over his pricey rhinestone outfit. He couldn't go onstage until he donned a spare.

Back home, George and Tammy continued efforts to become part of the fabric of Lakeland. At one point, they taped a TV spot for the regional Badcock Home Furnishing Center chain—and for Old Plantation—that was a study in weird. Sitting at home, side by side on a garish yellow leather sofa, Tammy wore a white blouse, vest, and skirt with white go-go boots, while George sat smiling in a red shirt, gray pants, and shoes (not boots) complete with white socks. A small guitar sat between them and memorabilia was displayed behind them, as if to remind everyone who they were.

GEORGE: Tammy and I would like to tell you about some friends of ours—the folks at *Badcock Home Furnishing Centers*!

TAMMY: Here at our home at the Old Plantation Music Park in Lakeland, Florida, we count on Badcock for our furnishings!

GEORGE: You know, we're confident of quality merchandise from Badcock, and we also know that we'll receive the *best* in service!

TAMMY: Take it from us. Badcock will treat you right!

IN NASHVILLE, GEORGE RAN OUT THE MUSICOR CLOCK, RERECORDING MATERIAL from Mercury and UA, even remaking songs he'd previously recorded for Musicor and laying down covers of others' hits. Among them: Merle Haggard's "The Fightin' Side of Me," Billy "Crash" Craddock's "Knock Three Times," and Conway Twitty's "Hello, Darlin'." One October session brought the relationship to an end. Repeating the drill where he sold Starday to Don Pierce, Pappy sold his Musicor interests to Art Talmadge, who released one final compilation of George and Melba duets before finding another label willing to license George's Musicor material. The January 15, 1972, *Billboard* reported Talmadge turning over 230 released master recordings and 58 unreleased masters to RCA Victor for upcoming singles and releases in a three-year deal. Pappy was to select material, but by then was refocusing on his Texas music interests. Musicor would concentrate on other acts.

RCA released sixteen newly compiled Jones albums over the life of the contract. But in a market still flooded with recent Musicor releases, plus the new music George and Tammy were creating at Epic, the RCA material never made any significant dent, except to add some Jones to RCA's catalog for a few years.

Epic released the George and Tammy duet album *We Go Together* in November 1971. In early 1972, "Take Me" became their first Top 10 duet. George's first Epic solo single, "We Can Make It," by Sherrill and Glenn Sutton, was recorded in January. Released by Epic barely a month later, it entered the Top 10. The follow-up, "Loving You Could Never Be Better," written by Peanutt Montgomery, his wife, Charlene, and Betty Tate, gave George his greatest chart success (No. 2 on *Billboard*) since "A Good Year for the Roses" in 1970. Those songs, plus covers of Charley Pride's "Kiss an Angel Good Mornin'" and Rex Griffin's 1930's suicidal musing "The Last Letter," were included on George's first solo Epic album, simply titled *George Jones,* which arrived in May.

1972 was a presidential election year. For decades, country stars choosing to get involved in politics (except for staunch Republican Roy Acuff) took the Democratic side, the result of a firm belief that Franklin Delano Roosevelt's programs saved poor rural southerners during the Great Depression. One exception: Arizona-born Marty Robbins, an outspoken supporter of conservative Republican Arizona senator Barry Goldwater's 1964 presidential candidacy. The Democratic mind-set began changing in the sixties as rural white southerners and some blue-collar northerners grew angry at Democratic support of civil rights legislation. In 1963, Alabama governor George Wallace, Democrat and avowed segregationist, symbolically stood at the door of the University of Alabama to prevent admission of black students, defying federally mandated desegregation. After a carefully orchestrated face-off with a deputy US attorney general, Wallace stepped aside. Vilified as a blatant racist, Wallace let his feisty, banty-rooster style and colorful personality keep his profile high.

Wallace ran for president in 1968 under the banner of the American Independent Party. His flag-waving, raucous rallies were well attended by blue-collar workers in the South, and, to the surprise of many, in working-class cities of the North. Most of his rallies included a country band to warm things up. Opry stars Grandpa Jones and Hank Snow were among his early supporters. Tammy sang for politicians in 1966, when she and Don Chapel performed for Georgia Democrat Zell Miller's unsuccessful congressional campaign. When Wallace again ran for president in January 1972, this time as a Democrat, his Nashville support had grown. Various acts, George and Tammy included, stood in his corner. Not everyone followed. Merle Haggard, assumed Wallace-friendly thanks to his flag-waving anthem "Okie from Muskogee," refused to support the governor, who conducted an aggressive campaign until he was shot by Arthur Bremer at a Laurel, Maryland, campaign stop on May 15. Paralyzed from the waist down, Wallace vowed to press ahead. Dewey Smith, a Wallace organizer in Polk County, Florida, which included Lakeland, heard of an all-star fundraiser being held for liberal Democratic hopeful Senator George McGovern and decided the idea could work for Wallace. He dubbed it "Wallace's Woodstock." On June 10, George and Tammy hosted a fundraiser at Old Plantation joined by Ferlin Husky, Del Reeves, Melba, and the governor's son, George Wallace Jr., an aspiring country singer. Press reports indicated the event drew between seven and ten thousand.

In the studio, Billy doubled down on the mystique surrounding the couple's life as it gained greater buzz with fans and the media. With things seemingly going well at the moment, the next choice was "The Ceremony," originally titled "Until Death Do Us Part." Its composers were Jenny Strickland and Carmol Taylor. Billy made changes and became the third cowriter. While over-the-top in many ways, this fanciful, overly dramatized version of the Jones-Wynette nuptials scored when the couple performed it onstage and became a Top 10 single. It seemed that many singles Epic chose to release alluded, directly or indirectly, to the ups and downs of the couple's relationship. Norro Wilson didn't believe this was always a deliberate effort, calling the material "songs that fit their particular environment at that time. I think because it was a good song, you recorded it because it was bringing out things about them. But I don't know that we consciously or they consciously thought that."

As Tammy accrued three No. 1 singles in 1972 alone, George's next solo effort, the ballad "A Picture of Me (Without You)," became another of his earliest Epic masterpieces. Norro Wilson wrote it, based on an idea George Richey had jotted on a piece of paper he kept in his wallet. With a haunting, gospel-like melody and Sherrill's careful production work, it became Jones's third Top 10 solo single at Epic that fall. Wilson was proud of the final result, noting, "If you can come up with a good title, sometimes [the songs] will write themselves. Everybody loved the song, and then when he opened his mouth and started singin' it and the playing and especially the piano licks on 'Picture . . .'" It remains a powerful performance, revealing how Sherrill's fastidious arrangements continued to accentuate the grittiness in George's voice. Beginning with gentle vibes and piano, George starts his vocal as perfectly placed, dramatic, Spector-like percussion figures punctuate each verse beneath him. As he sings, backup singers join on the chorus, with strings and pedal steel blending flawlessly in the background. The song wasn't necessarily tied to his tempestuous relations with Tammy, but it bolstered his growing, deepening stature as the king of heartbreak.

Country began gaining ground in escaping its niche-market status. Albums like the best-selling and universally admired *Johnny Cash at Folsom Prison* and his follow-up album *At San Quentin* were only part of the trend. In the 1960s, *Rolling Stone* magazine, known for its literate and incisive chronicling of the rock scene, had provided some of the earliest intelligent profiles of Cash, Buck, and Haggard. George and Tammy began to attract more interest from the print media beyond country fan publications. A sign of that came with a 1972 *Rolling Stone* profile of Tammy. Author Patrick Thomas followed her (with George mostly in the background) around Old Plantation. George already had a degree of popularity among rock and folk musicians like Dylan, though it was Johnny Cash who truly captured the counterculture as early as the 1960s folk revival. Among the Jones fans was Gram Parsons, the Florida-born former folkie turned West Coast country rocker. A founding member of the pioneering California country-rock band the International Submarine Band, Parsons had joined the iconic folk-rock band the Byrds, of "Mr. Tambourine Man" fame, in 1968. The group recorded George's old Mercury single "You're Still on My Mind" on their groundbreaking country-rock album *Sweetheart of the Rodeo*.

Old Plantation had been a resounding success since its opening, but one problem persisted thanks to the huge crowds: local government and residents' concerns about traffic congestion, zoning, and other related matters. As the hassles continued and time passed, an old pattern repeated itself: George began losing interest. He found the park as much a chore as a potential revenue stream. With him and Tammy busier than ever with records and touring, the homestead that had been so much fun to create felt less important. As 1972 came to an end, they closed the park, put their Florida holdings on the market, and returned to Nashville. Since they already had a residence there, they naturally needed a second. The 1973 vanity purchase they made was a classy one. They paid $310,000 for Oaklawn, a sprawling estate near Spring Hill, Tennessee. Built in 1835 by Absalom Thompson, the house had been Confederate general John Bell Hood's headquarters for one night during the 1864 military campaign that led to the Battle of Franklin. George had no interest in creating another music park. Instead he purchased farm equipment and Angus cattle to occupy his time, placing the Nudie-embellished Bonneville in a barn, where it became fair game for pigeons and rodents. Eventually he resold it to Nudie.

George and Tammy's TV appearances were expanding beyond *Hee-Haw*. They appeared on the March 16, 1973, *Midnight Special*, NBC's Friday late-night music variety show built around live performances by current rock and pop acts. Tammy sang "Kids Say the Darnedest Things"; George sang his hit "What My Woman Can't Do," proof their growing visibility merited appearing on a show whose audience cared more about the Doobie Brothers and Carole King. "What My Woman Can't Do," cowritten by George and Peanutt with the usual adjustments by Billy, was straight-ahead traditional. Pig Robbins added piano trills in the right places, and the backup singers blended nicely with keening pedal steel in the background. The lyrics' allusions to Tammy were obvious enough.

The emotional roller coaster for the couple and for everyone around them continued, though, on occasion, it yielded some positive results. In one blowup during a 1972 tour, both Peanutt and his wife were on George and Tammy's bus and heard

Tammy declare, "We ain't gonna make it!" Without thinking, George responded, "We're just gonna have to hold on." Hearing those lines would light up the section of any gifted songwriter's brain, the area that can turn such offhand remarks into music. Tammy had been irritated with Peanutt for his ongoing partying with George. By the next day, Peanutt had written part of "We're Gonna Hold On." George and Tammy liked what they heard. George added some ideas, and Tammy was thrilled enough by the song to set aside her aggravation at its composer. They recorded it at Columbia in March 1973.

George's return to Nashville had pretty much knocked him off the wagon. Norro Wilson saw the drinking as others did: a facade. "He was shy in quite a few ways. He was just really an old country boy. When he'd get crazy and did a little drinkin' it gave him courage, and that's when he'd act up." Accompanied by Peanutt, George's longtime picking and drinking buddy, he'd take off from Nashville for parts unknown whenever he pleased. Sometimes it was George's doing. At other times, Tammy went berserk and got physical with him, or found her own excuse to take off. In August 1973, she had divorce papers drawn up hoping to scare him straight. To say the move backfired is putting it mildly. Receiving the papers set him into a towering rage that ended at Columbia's studios, where he ended up cutting his hand and arm after punching a window at the security desk. Metro police arrived, arrested him for public drunkenness, and took him to jail. Peanutt bailed him out. Tammy decided to withdraw the papers and hold on, at least for the moment.

Released late that summer, "We're Gonna Hold On" was a restrained, simple declaration of resiliency. Tammy takes the first verse, George picking up the next. Billy kept things interesting by changing keys as the song progressed. It became their first No. 1 duet.

George's next Top 10 was a frantic solo reading of Bobby Braddock's "Nothing Ever Hurt Me (Half as Bad as Losing You)," which felt rushed. It certainly didn't make the best use of his voice the way the next single did. Johnny Paycheck, then recording for Billy at Epic, wrote "Once You've Had the Best," a celebration of reconciliation, a ballad that seemed to symbolize the ongoing George-Tammy issues. It had the usual Sherrill production values: subtle piano, strings, carefully placed percussion, and a male vocal chorus in the background. George sang the gentle lyrics, bending notes in all the right places. It became his most successful Epic single yet.

The situation ebbed and flowed behind the scenes. Tammy, despite Peanutt's obvious friendship with George and his compositional talents, was not personally fond of the Montgomerys, who finally left Nashville for northern Alabama, a region to figure prominently in the next phase of George's life. The year 1974 brought an even greater worry for him: Clara's failing health. Born four years before the twentieth century began, she had started to have heart problems around 1968 (a year after George W died), leading George and Tammy to regularly rush to Texas when she became ill. In April, they were in London to play the International Country Music Festival at Wembley Stadium when they got an emergency overseas call from Helen. Clara was failing fast. A thoroughly supportive Tammy, who also loved Clara, joined George on a transatlantic flight, a connecting flight to Houston, and finally a long drive to her bedside. They arrived too late. Clara Patterson Jones, the loving, righteous mother who'd given her son his best and most noble instincts and much of his love for music, died peacefully on April 13, before they got there. The pain burned deeply as the family gathered for the funeral. She was interred next to her husband at Restlawn Memorial Park under the couple's bronze marker.

AMERICAN RECORD COMPANIES LARGE AND SMALL EMPLOYED STAFF TO PRO-
mote new releases to retailers and to radio, as they did in New
York and Los Angeles, with larger labels having more elaborate
staffs. The exploding sales of rock and pop led to a growing music
press in the wake of *Rolling Stone, Creem,* and other publications
along with mainstream newspapers devoting increased space to
informed coverage of rock and pop. Along with radio and sales
staff, most labels had separate offices dedicated to promoting artists and new releases to print media. Until 1974, Nashville had
no such thing. To oversee the Nashville office, Columbia Records
hired Dan Beck, who'd formerly written for the New York trade
publication *Record World,* once interviewing Sherrill, who was
impressed with the published story. When he arrived, Beck hired
Mary Ann McCready, just out of Vanderbilt University, as his
assistant. Columbia "had all of these big artists and with a lot
going on, headquarters in New York was noticing that Nashville
was growing from the red to the black," McCready recalled. "Billy
was very anxious to have some marketing support in Nashville
with what was then a promotion and studio operation."

Once Beck set up shop he connected with Tammy, who, despite
the unpredictable ups and downs of her marriage, presented the
best possible face to the label, as did George. "Tammy was really
excited and engaged in the whole idea of publicity," he said. "I
think that went back to her days as a beauty operator when she
was in Alabama. What was stardom and fame back then? It was
those magazines . . . in the beauty shops. Tammy just idolized
George as a singer. I know it was kind of a tumultuous time for
them, but when I saw them, she was extremely happy. She just
loved the whole idea of being married to George, loved what a
performer he was and the whole thing."

Beck saw the other side of George—his disappearing skills—in action that year when New York–based *Country Music* magazine wanted a major profile on him. Tammy helped Beck plan an interview and photo shoot at Columbia following a scheduled meeting she and George had with Sherrill. After the meeting she'd bring him to Beck and both would escort George to meet writer-photographer J.R. Young. They'd shoot the photos in Columbia Studio B, and directed George to a stool in the studio. "Oh, great! That's great," George replied, adding, "I just need to go to the men's room." "George goes out the studio door into the men's room," Beck remembered. "I literally see him go in the men's room. Tammy and J.R. and I talk for a few minutes and George isn't around. I go in the men's room and there's nobody there. I come back and I said George wasn't there. So Tammy said, 'He might have gone up to see a couple of people in the building.' We start looking around for him and we couldn't find him. I didn't see him for another six months."

As Beck's assistant, McCready got a course in George's music from Sherrill himself. "Billy spent time talking to me about George Jones and his feelings about George as a singer and an interpreter. When George was in his office, Billy would often call me up and we'd sit and talk." She became entranced by his music. "I really fell hard for George Jones. I was not raised on country music. I was raised on Motown music. George hit me like a ton of bricks. I couldn't get over how magnificent he was."

Epic was about to unleash George's most powerful solo performance to date in the summer of 1974. "The Grand Tour," another masterpiece by Richey, Carmol Taylor, and Norro Wilson, was a wall-to-wall showcase of heartache, the milieu where George did his best work. He began alone, singing, "Step right up—come on in," before the band chimed in behind him. With an unabashedly traditional melody, he sang of a desperately lonely, grieving man, abandoned by a wife who took their child, walking through the home, noting every good time, pining for what he'd lost. It was a study in abject anguish.

Norro Wilson had attended the session and was pleased with the results. But he had no idea if the song had any traction—until he visited the Opry on a night George was to sing it on the show. Having performed on the Opry in the past, it was old home week for Wilson, who arrived early to visit with friends, including the show's musicians. "No sooner I walked in the door everybody come runnin' up to me and said, 'Jesus *Christ*! Have you got a *monster* on your hands!' So this is the first I've heard about it. I knew it was done. I was there when he recorded it and all that, but no knowledge in front of anything. And man, I went ballistic! Everybody that I ran across that night said, 'That's just gonna be a monster.' It was a really, really, really good record." "The Grand Tour" became George's first solo No. 1 single since "Walk Through This World with Me" in 1967.

Artistically, the *Grand Tour* album, which included "Once You've Had the Best," was among his strongest at the label so far, though it charted no higher than No. 11. There were songs by Bobby Braddock ("She Told Me So"), by Peanutt and Jimmy Richards ("Mary Don't Go 'Round"), and "Our Private Life," a George-Tammy original that openly lampooned the media buzz about their every move, shrugging off coverage about his drinking, carefully avoiding the fact that those real-life events were shaping the material.

For all their offstage differences, the couple presented a solid front when Olivia Newton-John, a rising British-born pop singer raised in Australia, was named Female Vocalist of the Year at the 1974 CMA Awards based on her lightweight, country-flavored pop hits "Let Me Be There" and "If You Love Me, Let Me Know." The CMA's ongoing inferiority complex made it anxious to rid itself of the "hillbilly" stigma, even if it meant embracing acts who had little connection to the music most of its practitioners performed and recorded. No doubt the CMA electors making these choices sensed them as an attempt to widen the music's reach. Many veteran artists, white-hot with outrage, didn't see it that way, and moved swiftly to publicly voice their disapproval. George and Tammy hosted a meeting of their fellow stars at their home. Among those attending: Jean Shepard, Dolly Parton, Porter Wagoner, Billy Walker, fellow Epic artist Barbara Mandrell (produced by Billy), Bill Anderson, Conway Twitty, and Hank Snow. Anderson was elected chairman of a new organization. ACE, the Association of Country Entertainers, was conceived to protect country music's unique identity. It remained intact for a time before slowly fading away.

Despite their ongoing issues, George and Tammy purchased a new home on Franklin Pike in Nashville's Oak Hill section, their most lavish yet. The one-story home, built only four years earlier, sat on eight wooded acres and had every palatial appointment anyone would want, including a yard large enough that George could indulge one of his favorite pastimes: cutting the grass with his riding mower. In the studio, "The Door," another ballad from Billy and Norro Wilson, came complete with pained allusions to war, of "a thousand bombs exploding" in a relationship facing a death spiral. It became George's second No. 1 in a row at Epic. Tammy's continued admiration for her husband's artistry despite their problems was one constant. As Wilson explained, "Aside from the fact that they got married, was they had an admiration society goin' on between them that was remarkable. And when he'd sing, she'd just about go crazy. And when she'd sing, he was affected deeply. They were big fans of each other's professional ability." Dan Beck saw this side of the couple's relationship as he sat in the control room with Billy and Tammy as George worked on overdubs for "The Door."

"Tammy and Billy invited me back one night to the studio. George was gonna be doing some overdubbing at probably eight o'clock at night. And it was just George in a darkened Studio B, and in the control room was Lou Bradley, the engineer, and Billy and Tammy and me. I was sitting behind all them on a couch, and they were all at the board. And I'm just kind of a fly on the wall. They were doing the overdubs, George starts singing, and everybody's looking at each other like this guy—he's amazing. He's just tearin' this song up. It's just so great. And Tammy turned to Billy and said, 'That Jones—he's the only man who could make *war* a four-syllable word!' To me, that was George Jones. She nailed it on the spot. It was just a magic moment."

Beck sensed no turmoil when he visited Franklin Pike to drop off press clippings. "They never gave an indication of [problems] to anybody, you know. It was Shangri-la, as I saw it. I would go out to the house and the two of them would be in the kitchen area in the back and George would say hello—always quiet. It was great. Tammy and I would sit down and George, he'd go get on the lawn mower and mow the lawn, in three variations of plaid. He'd have on plaid shorts, a plaid shirt, and a plaid hat. He'd be out mowing that eight- or nine-acre place."

They were in the studio in December recording a surprising selection. "Near You" was a song born of the other side of Nashville music: the city's strong (if not nationally recognized) pop music scene. In the 1930s and 1940s, WSM, home of the Opry, had a first-rate group of staff musicians. Orchestras led by Beasley Smith, Owen Bradley, and Francis Craig played the

The young troubadour in downtown Beaumont, Texas, 1943. *Russell D. Barnard Collection at Southern Folklife Collection, University of North Carolina*

A publicity shot from the mid-1950s. *Russell D. Barnard Collection at Southern Folklife Collection, University of North Carolina*

Below, left to right: Booking agent Hal Smith, George, and Pappy Daily in 1956. *Elmer Williams/Country Music Hall of Fame and Museum/Getty Images*

Songwriter Darrell Edwards, George, and Galveston singer Fidio Eriksen in 1958. *Courtesy of Kevin Coffey*

Onstage with the Jones Boys in the mid-1960s. *Russell D. Barnard Collection at Southern Folklife Collection, University of North Carolina*

The George-Melba *Bluegrass Hootenanny* sessions, mid-January 1964. *Left to right:* Ray Walker, Pappy Daily, George (playing Melba's guitar), Tommy Jackson, unknown, Curtis McPeake (banjo), Pig Robbins (piano), Bob Moore (bass). *Russell D. Barnard Collection at Southern Folklife Collection, University of North Carolina*

George and Tammy with Little Richard, George's favorite rock 'n' roll singer, early 1970s. *Michael Ochs Archives/Getty Images*

Hangin' with Tammy and Nudie Cohn at Nudie's Rodeo Tailors in LA, May 26, 1973. *Michael Ochs Archives/Getty Images*

Mr. and Mrs. Country Music with Billy Sherrill, 1970s. *Russell D. Barnard Collection at Southern Folklife Collection, University of North Carolina*

Looking the worse for wear, George with Emmylou Harris backstage at the Palomino in LA, February 1981. *Jasper Dailey/Michael Ochs Archives/Getty Images*

Onstage at Harrah's Metropolis, Metropolis, Illinois, June 2002. *Wikimedia/Secisek*

Kennedy Center Honors, December 6, 2008. *Left to right, standing:* Roger Daltrey, Pete Townshend, George; *seated:* Twyla Tharp, Morgan Freeman, Barbra Streisand. *Ron Sachs-Pool/Getty Images*

George and Nancy at his eightieth birthday party, September 13, 2011.
Rick Diamond/Getty Images

The shrine at Woodlawn Memorial Park, Nashville. *Courtesy of George Fletcher*
Inset: The marker. *Courtesy of George Fletcher*

town's fancy nightspots and country clubs. Craig composed the melody; New York songwriter Kermit Goell supplied lyrics. Early in 1947, Craig's orchestra recorded the semi-swinging number, with a vocal by Bob Lamm, for the Nashville-based Bullet label. "Near You" spent several months as America's top pop song. The muted performance became the final song George and Tammy would record as a married couple, though it wasn't released for some time.

A day after the session, George went to help Shorty Lavender, his and Tammy's booking agent, remodel his agency's new offices and stuck around downtown. In his usual fashion, he hit the bars and clubs and wound up shit-faced. Knowing drunkenness was a red flag for Tammy, he didn't want to return home that way and got a hotel room to sleep it off. When he finally called home, Tammy exploded, telling him not to come back. He did not. Tammy Wynette filed for divorce from her husband of nearly six years on January 8, 1975. George, for his part, knew the marriage was through, but he was crushed nonetheless. They divided the property. She kept the Franklin Pike house and had custody of Georgette. George got the Tyne Boulevard home, the couple's houseboat, and debts owed Columbia for advances against royalties. He was ordered to pay $1,000 monthly child support for Georgette. Tammy kept the tour bus, and a number of the Jones Boys became the nucleus of her new band, the Country Gentlemen. The divorce was finalized March 12.

In interviews, Tammy claimed, overlooking her own issues, that her ex-husband was "one of those people who couldn't tolerate happiness." George, back in Nashville and drinking his way around town, had his own comments, feeling bitterness about her hostility to some of his longtime friends, including the Montgomerys. Tammy would visit many dark places in the next phase of her life. Nor were her interactions with George at an end. He was about to enter a phase of his own that would see artistic triumphs he could never have imagined, with honors that would satisfy many for life. Mixed with that were horrors, most of them self-inflicted, that more than once nearly sent him to the grave.

CHAPTER 5

. . . .

1975–1983

The home on Franklin Road had a circular driveway, and he would occasionally enter, drive around a few times, and then leave. After his two prior divorces, this one left George dealing with pain and remorse, harboring hopes of reconciliation. Clearly both parties were at fault in the marriage. George's drunken, irresponsible, and impulsive behavior cast a pall, as did Tammy's own issues—her legitimate health problems, need for pharmaceuticals, and obsessive focus on surgery, sometimes of questionable medical value. She tried to maintain a civil relationship with her ex for Georgette's sake and soon she was dating, first Tommy Neville of the New England Patriots, then Rudy Gatlin of the Gatlin Brothers.

George unloaded the Nashville home on Tyne Boulevard he'd received in the settlement and began to spend increasing time with the Montgomerys in northern Alabama, specifically the area around Muscle Shoals and Florence. For George it became a haven from Nashville. He, too, found a new companion: Charlene Montgomery's sister, Linda Welborn. The two met in 1974. Welborn's earthy country-girl simplicity, free of Tammy's ego, appealed to George the same way Melba's had. George and Linda began living together.

Billy Wilhite was handling George's Nashville business at this point. He was present when George met another pivotal figure in his career, one who generated greater and darker controversies than Pappy ever did: Alcy Benjamin Baggott, nicknamed Shug.

A longtime Nashville nightclub owner, Baggott ran a rock club in town, steering clear of anything country because he simply never cared for the music. His change of heart, he claimed, came after he saw George and Tammy's 1974 performance at the Opry House at a benefit for Ivory Joe Hunter, a veteran R&B singer ("Since I Met You Baby") pursuing a country music career in Nashville before he was stricken with cancer. Shug first encountered George and Wilhite at the Hall of Fame Motor Lounge at a time George was too blitzed to talk. When they finally connected, Baggott proposed reviving the Possum Holler club in a building he owned in Printer's Alley downtown. When the two visited the location, George's decorator mind-set kicked in and he began to visualize colors and layout. With little money, he'd have no ownership stake, but he was to receive a royalty from Baggott for the use of his name. The new George Jones Possum Holler opened on March 22, 1975, ten days after his divorce was final. George and the Jones Boys were present to entertain. At some point later on, during a night when George was too besotted to perform at the club, Shug introduced him to the substance that became his new best friend and worst enemy (aside from himself) over the next eight years: cocaine.

In April, Peanutt, after years of keeping pace with George in the boozing/partying department, became a born-again Christian, giving up his bad habits. He and Charlene remained close to George, though Peanutt's new sobriety and George's growing dissolution would alter the dynamics of their friendship, with George initially skeptical of his friend's conversion. That fall, George found a home in the nearby Sherwood Forest development in Florence. He also bought some lakeside property in the area.

CBS Nashville was anxious to keep the career momentum going for George and Tammy. The label worked a PR blitz as Tammy resumed her career with some high-visibility performances and magazine pieces reflecting more resiliency than she actually had. The label had more singles ready. Before the split with Tammy, George recorded another ballad the couple cowrote: "These Days (I Barely Get By)," his only Top 10 single that year. A chronicle of unfettered woe introduced by a heavily bowed fiddle, George inhabits the lyric about memories of walking home from work in the rain and returning to an empty house to find the bills "on the desk in the hall" with a layoff in the future.

In October, he joined Sherrill in the studio to record "The Battle" as his next single. Complete with martial drum rolls, lines about firing "the guns of anger once again," he sings of being defeated by a woman's tears. Norro Wilson cowrote it with Richey, based on an idea they got from Linda Kimball, a secretary for Al Gallico. Despite being less monumental than "The Grand Tour," "The Door," or "These Days," the record was nominated for a Grammy.

After their divorce, George and Tammy didn't record duets together for a while. That hiatus ended with a performance that became one of their finest. Written by Bobby Braddock and Rafe Van Hoy, "Golden Ring" cleverly recounted the life cycle of a modestly appointed wedding ring, purchased by a hopeful groom in a pawnshop, placed on the bride's finger that day, and later thrown away when the couple splits, winding up back in the pawnshop. Crisp and simple, its catchy arrangement framed by acoustic guitars, it was the strongest George-Tammy duet since "We're Gonna Hold On" reached No. 1 in mid-1976, and remains one of their finest recorded moments.

Outside the studio, George was far from over Tammy. In April, the *Nashville Banner* ran a story in which he claimed he'd finally quit drinking, an assertion he'd make on and off for the better part of the next decade. A month later, he gave her a red Ford Thunderbird and a new ring, allegedly for Mother's Day. In Alabama, he was anxious to become part of a community beyond Nashville, not unlike what he had when he and Tammy put down stakes in Lakeland. He would run the back roads, drink, and hang out. He would buy and lose homes there over the next several years. Meanwhile, he'd ditched the house in Sherwood Forest because he couldn't afford the mortgage, then borrowed money to build an A-frame for himself and Linda on the lakeside lot he owned. The rural areas of northern Alabama became his and Linda's favored hangout as they explored the backcountry and hung out with friends, many of them not involved in music at all, or at least not professionally. During their time together, she tried to keep him connected with his kids. Georgette, now five, visited the couple in Alabama, as did George's sons Bryan and Jeff.

In the meantime, some changes had been taking place in Nashville, instigated by two of George's friends and fellow Texans: Willie Nelson and Waylon Jennings, supported by Tompall Glaser, Jack Clement, and a handful of others. The producer-driven Nashville formula of producers picking songs, hiring musicians, and overseeing the process that began in the 1950s with Chet

Atkins and Owen Bradley and that had worked so well for George over the years had clearly failed Nelson and Jennings, both of whom recorded for RCA. Their recorded successes had been, for the most part, middling. Feeling they had a better sense of what their fans wanted than RCA did, both demanded creative control of their recordings. Waylon negotiated it at RCA in 1972; Willie did so with Atlantic Records in 1973 and at Columbia in 1975. Many in Nashville's establishment eagerly waited to see these heretics fail. Some older fans were put off by their long hair, blue jeans, and beards. It didn't matter. Both found success with their core following and expanded their fan bases far beyond the country audience.

George loved and admired them both, but he never aspired to produce himself. He might bitch about the occasional song or other aspects of a production record, but he had no interest in the detail work that governed that end of his career. Delighted over Willie's success as a renegade (though Sherrill openly scorned the stripped-down sound of Willie's *Red Headed Stranger* album when he heard it before its release), CBS sought a way to introduce George to the new hybrid youth-cowboy culture rising in Texas. George and the Jones Boys were invited to play at Willie's Fourth of July picnic—his third—to be held near Gonzales, Texas. The lineup mixed Waylon and his wife, Jessi Colter; David Allan Coe; Kris Kristofferson and Rita Coolidge; Roger Miller; Bobby Bare; and Leon Russell with his wife, Mary. The Austin contingent included Doug Sahm, Kinky Friedman, and Rusty Weir.

The notion of performing in front of what he considered an alien audience had George scared, a trait that would frequently arise if he was playing to an audience outside his comfort zone. Mary Ann McCready had traveled with him and his entourage. His stage outfit was a black leisure suit, a seventies fashion statement that involved a casual jacket and matching slacks, along with flashy white boots. In a crowd of eighty thousand rowdies, a veritable sea of blue jeans, T-shirts, and tank tops, he was scared shitless, McCready remembered. "Oh my God, was he nervous. He was a wreck. I was flying with him and he was with Walter Cronkite's daughter for some reason. She was with us in the car." Backstage, she recalled his terror. "He said, 'These are not my people.' I'm like, 'They are going to love you; just try it!' He was the weirdest." When McCready saw Coe, another Columbia artist, she brought him over to run interference as George was about to go on. He rose to the occasion. "George, you know what?" Coe said reassuringly. "Don't worry about it. Here, brother, I'll walk you down there."

Taking the stage, casting aside his misgivings, George delivered an edgy, burning set of some of his biggest hits to a crowd he found beyond enthusiastic, and encored with a rocker he always loved: Little Richard's "Long Tall Sally." "He got up in front of that hippie-crazy audience and they went nuts. George got up there and freaking killed it," McCready said. "That was one of my most profound moments with George. He was really happy. He was happy, and he wanted out of there." Willie biographer Joe Nick Patoski saw both the triumph and the anxiety, noting "his nervousness showed throughout his performance and a roaring encore."

After the show, George and his entourage, including McCready, headed for dinner. "He wanted to go get some Mexican food and some hot salsa and we all went out, God only knows where we were, and got salsa. George and I got into some kind of conversation about salsa and he said, 'Yeah, the hotter the better!' So we ended up telling the waiter, he wants it as hot as it can be. And he took a big slug of this really hot salsa and he's like *WOOOOOOOOOOO!* Right in the middle of the restaurant!"

Shug was managing George, working with a new booking agency and an investor in a lucrative deal guaranteeing him a specific amount of bookings a year. Again George was trusting nearly total strangers. With the naïveté that got him in trouble so often in the past, he relied on Shug and his associates for guidance and for getting him the cocaine he craved. Shug was not a popular figure around CBS Records. While he met with upper-level executives regarding George, McCready remembered, "Billy didn't like him at all. He signaled very clearly on that."

Epic released two albums in the fall of 1976. The *Golden Ring* album became the only George and Tammy album to reach No. 1 (aside from their hits packages). They began appearing onstage and on television, the relationship at least civil. *Alone Again,* George's solo album, included his most recent hit, Bobby Braddock's "Her Name Is . . . ," another teasing allusion to a devastating lost love, the Tammy connection obvious. The album included two of his stronger drinking ballads, "A Drunk Can't Be a Man" and "Stand on My Own Two Knees." The album received a glowing review in the *Village Voice* from Patrick Carr, a longtime Jones observer who called it "his best album in ten years." The year 1976 also saw the release of "Near You," recorded two years earlier. It became George and Tammy's final No. 1 duet.

In November, he showed up at a Nashville apartment occupied by Billy Wilhite and his wife, accompanied by two women. The partying got out of hand. The pair claimed a drunken George tried to embrace one of the women and make her drink, then hit her in the face. He was accused of throwing a "briefcase" at the other that hit her in the back of the head. No arrests were made, but on December 17 both sued, demanding $51,000 each. George claimed the women were drunk and belligerent at the time, that he was sober and told both to leave, but admitted throwing a shaving kit at one of them. The suit was settled out of court.

To friends, the coke factor, on top of George's boozing, was taking him down. Linda filed charges against him in Alabama relating to a domestic incident, but the two eventually reconciled. On the road, his unreliability worsened. In September, after George missed both a concert and a makeup date in Augusta County, Virginia, the promoter sued, and George missed a court hearing. The result: a $29,654 judgment against him, one of many to come his way over the next six years as his dark side gained full control. It prevented CBS Nashville from ongoing efforts to elevate George and his music to a different level—and audience. Mary Ann McCready came up with an idea during a trip to New York to meet with music journalists she knew, among them Texas-born Chet Flippo, an editor at *Rolling Stone* and their primary chronicler of the changing country scene; Flippo's wife, Martha Hume, a former managing editor of *Country Music* magazine; and former *Country Music* editor Patrick Carr.

McCready remembers, "I was in New York making the rounds, [seeing] Patrick, everybody, and having dinner with Chet and Martha in this funky restaurant. It was great. And that's where the idea—first country artist to headline the Bottom Line—that's where that came from. That whole idea happened at that dinner. I was effusive, and I kept saying to Chet and Martha, I felt like if the critics in New York could hear George, that was the door that would open everyone to an interest in country music. That was the idealism, it was, hey, let George kick the door down, let's let the critics fall in love with George and see if we can get somewhere with country music because country music was [seen as] a joke. The major music critics in New York didn't care. So how to make 'em care?"

I went back and asked Billy and he said, 'If you can get him to show up . . .' "

The Bottom Line, owned by Allan Pepper and Stanley Snadowsky, had opened in 1974 and earned a reputation as Manhattan's hippest music club. To Flippo, Hume, and the others McCready consulted in New York, this seemed the perfect venue to showcase George for a new audience. McCready, Flippo, and Hume came up with an invitation list; Sherrill added names, as did Sue Binford, McCready's assistant. Cincinnati-born Rick Blackburn, CBS Nashville's new vice president for marketing, was also involved in the planning. Originally a pop record promoter, he'd been general manager of Nashville-based Monument Records before joining CBS. For the next decade, Blackburn would be a major player in George's career.

The CBS Nashville team organized a two-night event for September 6 and 7, 1977, showcasing George at the Bottom Line. No country artist had headlined there. Hoping a new audience would discover George, the invitees included media giants from CBS including Walter Cronkite and Texas native Dan Rather, the *Saturday Night Live* cast, as well as reporters from the *New York Times* and major publications. The label would fly journalists in for the show. It seemed an optimal opportunity to build George's brand.

It was little surprise that George viewed it all differently, realizing he'd again be out of his comfort zone. It was one thing to play for country fans in Manhattan. This was something completely different. "I kept telling people I didn't want to do that show," he later explained. "I was shy because of my old booze and cocaine-laced paranoia." Blackburn remembered, "George excused himself from my office, left, and we didn't see him for three weeks." With one night gone and a second night booked, Shorty Lavender and Nashville attorney John Lentz traveled to Alabama, intent on finding him and getting him to New York to salvage the second night. No luck. Blackburn and McCready were mortified. "I was so absorbed in my pain and sadness that I don't even remember how I handled that," McCready said. "I was so, just, dumbstruck because we had put security on him to make sure he got there. I just remember the place emptied out and maybe twenty people stayed and the Jones Boys did a set." She sat drinking with Binford and Bottom Line co-owner Pepper, everyone certain any mainstream media buzz over George Jones would fade quickly.

To everyone's shock, his failure to appear actually boosted his mystique, defining him as a different type of Nashville outlaw. "The funny thing was, the next day there was this press [that] George Jones is a no-show," McCready said. "So he got this press. He got more press in New York than he'd ever gotten. It was ironic in a way." For all the frustration, McCready even understood why he'd bailed. "I think he was so insecure and so ill-prepared for any kind of fame or recognition. If you look at him, he was always movin' around, just like ready to get out, and I think he was just ill-prepared for fame. I think he wanted to go be George. He wanted to go to his comfort zone, and I think he was so far out of his comfort zone that he'd just run. I'm sure the thought of playing New York scared the shit out of him."

George's skills as a duet singer led Billy to engage a number of George's friends and a few artists beyond the country field to create an album of duets. One of the first involved a ballad, written in tribute to George, by one of his many admirers in the pop and rock field: James Taylor. Taylor wrote "Bartender's Blues" with a traditional country melody and lyric custom-tailored to George's approach, so elemental and authentic that it revealed Taylor was more than a casual listener. Taylor would later add harmony vocals, giving the song greater marketability without compromising it. Recorded in October, released a month later, it would reach No. 6 in early 1978. It was George's first duet with a pop singer since the Pitney recordings.

The album also featured collaborations with Waylon, the Staple Singers (whom Sherrill had produced earlier for Epic), Willie, Paycheck, Ray Sawyer and Dennis Locorriere of Dr. Hook, and Tammy (on "It Sure Was Good"). It took Billy two years to assemble, given George's issues and the coke's effects on his voice and stamina. Another longtime Jones fan from the rock field was London-born Elvis Costello, one of the major exponents of the punk and new wave movement. Costello had the punk ethos but was also a serious music scholar with deep interests in varying forms of music, and he had a special affection for George's music. He'd written and recorded "Stranger in the House," the melody and lyrics clearly inspired by George's style of ho..ky-tonk. Bonnie Garner, a music business veteran formerly employed by rock impresario Bill Graham, came to Nashville to help CBS establish a pop division, a short-lived notion. Garner, who handled much of the A&R bureaucracy for Sherrill, helped him engage and coordinate artists for the duets album and brought Costello into the project. Billy was to record George and Elvis singing "Stranger" together. Making it happen required some added effort on Garner's part.

"George didn't have a clue who Elvis Costello was. He didn't know who James Taylor was, either, but he kind of liked ['Bartender's Blues']. The whole thing is set up with Elvis. Elvis comes in. He's at the studio. Session's set up, musicians and everything else. And we're waiting, and we're waiting and we're waiting. No one can find George." Irritated, Garner got in touch with Pee Wee Johnson, George's assistant and buddy. "I called Pee Wee and I told him to tell George that his mama raised him better than that, and he was being rude and ill-mannered because Elvis Costello had come all the way from England to do him the honor of singing with him on this record and he sure as hell better show up. And he did. It took about an hour. I think the 'mama' and 'rude and ill-mannered' references [did the trick]. I just was so angry. And I usually would blow everything else off, like, 'Oh, that's George.' But this just set me the wrong way. But George came in and showed up and he did a great job. He was not in great shape when he finally got to the studio, but he did it. And Elvis was such a gentleman. And George was sweet to Elvis, apologizing and everything else. And Elvis didn't care if he had to sit there for twenty-four hours."

McCready witnessed the session itself as Jones and Costello recorded "Stranger" at the same microphone. "It was so funny watching them in the studio, because their downbeats were completely the opposite. I couldn't take my eyes off of their feet, because George would go down on the beat, and then Elvis would go down on the beat right after that. They were in complete opposite beat modes. I remember when Elvis started singing . . . that was unreal."

George wasn't terribly familiar with many younger fans of his music. Emmylou Harris was making a name for herself in the mid-1970s with solid, traditional country albums like *Pieces of the Sky, Elite Hotel,* and *Luxury Liner,* produced by her then husband Brian Ahern. A few years earlier, she'd become a George fan while harmonizing with Gram Parsons as a member of his band. Mary Martin, the Warner Bros. Records executive who'd signed Harris to the label, knew she wanted to meet George. Bonnie Garner did the honors at Possum Holler. The two sang together for the first time. "I was the one who introduced him to Emmylou Harris. She was a nervous wreck, and I don't think George had a clue who [she was] or anything else about her. And he introduced her as 'Emma-lou,' and that's what he called her from then on, and Emmy was not going to correct him. She said, 'That's George Jones. He can call me anything that he wants to.' So it was 'Emmalou.' But when she opened her mouth and sang with him, it was like, Whoa, okay. And I think George was impressed."

As the cocaine sent his behavior and outlook far into the stratosphere, he often brought forth two alter egos: the Duck, or Dedoodle, and the Old Man, the first based on Donald Duck, the second on Walter Brennan. He did both voices, the two constantly arguing. At times he'd argue with both of them. The pair emerged at various times—when he was hanging out, recording, being interviewed on radio, and even when he was onstage. But what seemed hilarious to him wasn't so amusing to friends. It merely proved that the combined booze and coke seemed to be loosening his grip on reality. After her fling with Burt Reynolds and a four-month 1976 train-wreck marriage to Florida real estate developer J. Michael Tomlin, a marriage George counseled her against (Tammy told him to mind his own business), Tammy found a husband in someone she already knew. George Richey, a former gospel sideman and onetime producer for Capitol Records, was part of Sherrill's inner circle at Epic as a writer. The couple married July 6, 1978. Over time, given Tammy's physical and emotional fragility, Richey, her husband until her death in 1998, turned out to be the most Machiavellian and toxic of all her spouses.

George's state of mind wasn't great when he received a new Bible his mother intended him to have that Tammy hadn't promptly turned over after their divorce. He found Clara's written message inside, desiring that "George Glenn" get this particular Bible and declaring, "I made a failure, but I hope we all meet in

Heaven." The message, given the place George was in, crushed him, but it didn't slow his recklessness. His coke use spiked as dealers did everything possible to keep him onstage, the better to earn more money to fund his habit. They physically forced him onstage in some cases and at times, he remembered, packed his nose with the powder. When he ducked shows, he became adept at eluding Shug's associates as they pursued him around the Muscle Shoals–Florence area. George, assisted by the Montgomerys, sometimes taunted his adversaries on the citizens band radios popular in so many vehicles during that time.

Amid these hide-and-seek games, he didn't seem to concern himself with his worsening finances. That side of things hit the fan on September 1, 1978, when Davidson County judge Hamilton Gayden issued arrest warrants for George. He had $86,000 of debt accrued over missed concert dates, and Tammy's lawyers sought $36,000 back child support for Georgette. Since George's residence was in Alabama and the civil judgments were in Nashville, he was subject to arrest if he set so much as a boot heel in Nashville or surrounding Davidson County. George's attorney Jack Norman claimed George was addicted to alcohol and had placed himself under psychiatric care. Shug told reporters the child support would be paid in full "by the end of next week."

Those psychotic episodes and paranoia led him to turn hostile to Peanutt, whose conversion to Christianity and decision to become a minister lit a fire in George's coke-addled mind. Peanutt's new beard became a target when the two met. George began referring to him mockingly as "Little Jesus" and repeatedly threatened to pluck the beard one hair at a time. Peanutt, who still loved George, tried to be philosophical about it as he watched his buddy and onetime boss continue flying beyond any level of reason. It came to a head between them on the night of September 15, 1978, near Florence, just off the Savannah Highway, on a pull-off next to Cypress Creek, a place George, living at the Georgetown Apartments on Chisholm Highway in Florence, sometimes went seeking solitude.

Peanutt had heard that George, who'd been spewing anti-Peanutt tirades all over the area, wanted to see him. He told George to meet him at the pull-off and found himself facing his longtime friend, enraged, irrational, and coked up. Peanutt, sitting in his Pontiac Trans-Am, realizing his friend was in a severely altered state of mind, tried to calm him, urging George to repent and see the Light. Clara could talk to him about such things. But Peanut was not Clara, and George was in no mood to be placated. He screamed, "All right, you son of a bitch! See if your God can save you now!" and fired his .38-caliber pistol toward Peanutt. Contemporary photos show Peanutt sitting in the vehicle, a bullet hole in the door just below the driver's-side window. After firing, George raved some more, jumped into his own vehicle, and took off, seemingly oblivious to what he'd done. In his 1996 memoir, George, again denying gunplay—as he had with Tammy during their Florida days—claimed he never fired a pistol at his friend.

Local law enforcement thought differently at the time. Concerned as he was about George, Peanutt saw this as a step too far. The next day he went to Lavern Tate, the Lauderdale County district attorney, and filed charges of Assault with Attempt to Commit Murder, insisting his main goal was to see George forced to get desperately needed professional help. On September 17, Lauderdale County sheriff's sergeant Milton Borden took George into custody at his apartment. He was freed on $2,500 bond. The charges were later dismissed, with the understanding they could be refiled if he acted up again.

Tammy had her own drama going in Nashville. On October 4 she told police she had been kidnapped and hinted that either George or Shug was involved. Local police found no evidence of a kidnapping, nothing to support claims of a beating or Tammy's account of being forced to drive eighty miles. When skeptical officials suggested she might take a polygraph, she refused, raising further doubts. Meanwhile, George was in court October 10 regarding back child support. With his attorney present, he asked the court for mercy, admitting he was "addicted to alcohol." He later claimed he had assumed Shug cut a check for Tammy, which apparently hadn't happened. Nashville lawmen remained ready to move if he showed up in town, which led to complications when Shorty Lavender, still booking George, called him about Mel Street.

Best known for his 1972 hits "Borrowed Angel" and "Smoky Mountain Rain," Street's vocal style was clearly modeled on George's. On the morning of October 21, his birthday, Street sat down to breakfast with his wife, brother, and sister-in-law, then left the table. Moments later, he walked upstairs and shot himself in the head, just as his father had done. Jim Prater, Street's manager, told the Associated Press the singer returned from a tour of Texas depressed and had failed to appear at a booking two days before his death. George, who deeply admired his talents, considered Street a friend. His grieving family wanted George to sing at the funeral. The services were to be held at the Cole & Garrett Funeral Home in Goodlettsville, a Nashville suburb straddling Davidson and Sumner Counties. The warrants for George's arrest in Davidson County made things dicey. Shorty Lavender arranged special dispensation so police would look the other way while George entered, sang, and departed.

Two days later, a disconsolate George appeared at the funeral home, where he shakily sang a pained, searing rendition of a gospel standard he no doubt learned in the Thicket: "Amazing Grace." He asked for a bit of time alone with the coffin; friends had to coax him to leave before local authorities lost their patience. He stated that when he left the funeral home, a local police car followed him to the county line.

Street was out of his misery, but George received another legal wallop early in November when the Third National Bank of Nashville sued him for $56,966.70 in unpaid loans. Regarding his finances, he had but one remaining option. On December 15, 1978, he filed for bankruptcy in Nashville, quoted by the *Nashville Banner* as saying he felt "rescued from death." At the time it was reported he had missed fifty-four concert dates in the past year.

It was a laundry list of financial irresponsibility involving the Third National Bank debt, $12,000 in credit cards, an unpaid $40,000 loan for a new tour bus, nearly $78,000 owed Columbia Records in advances against future royalties, $200,000 in attorney bills, and $300,000 in miscellaneous other judgments. There were, the filing stated, a total of forty-six creditors. George's assets were listed as $64,500, his liabilities at $1,400,000. George's explanation for the missed show dates was a memorable one. His attorney, S. Ralph Gordon, explained to the court that his client "didn't feel he was performing in such a way the fans were getting what they paid for." George didn't help his case (or his attorney's arguments) by blowing off court appearances where his presence was required—or he if did arrive, appeared obviously coked up. Holed up in Alabama, he continued to miss show dates. In November, Linda alleged he roughed her up. Johnny Cash and Waylon Jennings gave him a total of $64,000 in cash that he turned over to the court as a token payment. While the court denied his bankruptcy petition, he no longer faced arrest if he came back to Nashville.

George's deteriorating mind was a mass of contradictions. When the press asked him about the canceled shows that had earned him the both affectionate and derisive nickname of "No Show Jones," he continued claiming he wasn't up to performing and didn't want to give the fans less than his best, a line of bullshit given the less than pristine condition he was often in when he did appear. Early 1979 brought the release of the duets album *My Very Special Guests*. Solid as Billy's idea was, even with the success of "Bartender's Blues," George's vocals were subpar. Despite the mystique building around George, the album's sales were modest.

Shug had his own problems. The Tennessee Department of Revenue auctioned the contents of Possum Holler to satisfy back taxes on January 24, 1979. Baggott also filed for bankruptcy. Two days later, Shorty Lavender, one of the few during this time who actually seemed to give a damn about George himself, sued Baggott, claiming the manager had been in business for himself, booking George into venues in different places the same night. The financial issues took a turn for the better when new attorney Thomas Binkley took another run at a bankruptcy filing in a Tennessee District Court. This time, a new judge approved the petition, which had a flexible payment plan giving creditors twenty cents on the dollar. George would be repaying the debts into the 1980s, when he began to recover. To aid the repayment, songwriting and record royalties not tied with his previous divorces were applied to the debt, now at $1.5 million. A legal conservator would oversee his finances.

Even relieved of that pressure, George continued imploding. When visiting Nashville, he stayed at two hotels: either the Hall of Fame Motor Inn or Spence Manor Inn. He often hung around in the lobby, sometimes singing with his guitar like a common street busker. Unpaid room bills got him banned from both places. He moved to an apartment. His support system in town was shaky by then. In August it became even shakier when Shug was busted for selling two pounds of coke to an undercover federal agent, bringing his time with George to an abrupt end.

Simon & Schuster released Tammy's autobiography, *Stand By Your Man,* cowritten with Joan Dew, who was introduced to her by Dan Beck at Epic in 1979. Channeling Tammy's memories and viewpoints into a narrative, Dew later told Tammy biographer Jimmy McDonough, "I don't know if Tammy even read the book." It was optioned for a TV movie. Don Chapel was especially unhappy. In late October he filed a lawsuit under his legal name of Lloyd F. Amburgey, demanding $12 million in compensatory damages and another $12 million in punitive damages, citing harassment and humiliation from "fans, co-workers, peers, employers, agents and managers." At issue was Tammy's contention he didn't contribute financially or emotionally to their marriage, and her account of the infamous photos, which he insisted were taken with her permission. The suit was eventually dismissed.

In Alabama, George continued to dodge drug dealers and, he later claimed, cops friendly with said dealers. He rarely ate actual meals but indulged in sardines, beef jerky, and other junk food. The psychodramas with the Duck and the Old Man continued. Despite the shooting incident, Peanutt and Charlene Montgomery kept tabs on their friend and grew more alarmed seeing him heading for the abyss far faster than anyone could have expected. On December 10, 1979, Peanutt filed legal papers in Lauderdale County, seeking permission to commit George involuntarily to the Eliza Coffee Memorial Hospital in Muscle Shoals, to be treated for substance abuse. Probate Judge Ralph Duncan agreed. George was admitted on December 11. Four days later, he was transferred to Hillcrest Hospital in Birmingham, better equipped to deal with his drug issues and alcoholism. The hospital staff had a challenge. Peanutt later said George talked the ambulance driver into stopping en route to Birmingham to get him a pint of booze. After treatment he was discharged, and like George Washington Jones, he quickly fell back into old habits.

Things appeared to turn a corner in 1980. Relations with Tammy began to mend after she attended one of his recording sessions. He signed a deal with her agent, the most highly regarded country music booker of his time: Tulsa's Jim Halsey. Halsey was still attending college when he got his start booking and managing Oklahoma-based honky-tonk singer Hank Thompson in the fifties. Roy Clark later became another of his clients. Halsey expanded his agency, booking the Oak Ridge Boys, Mel Tillis, Don Williams, Tammy, and many other top-echelon acts. George's business affairs would be handled by Tammy's brother-in-law Paul Richey, George Richey's brother and part of Tammy's organization. Plans were made for George and Tammy to begin performing together and resuming their duets.

The media buzz was substantial. The couple was featured, George looking particularly bad, on the June 1980 cover of *Country Music* magazine, with the cover line "Tammy Interviews George Jones." Inside was a nine-page Q&A interview. The dialogue, while colorful in spots, sanitized George's issues as he talked of possibly returning to Nashville to live. Asked by Tammy about her book, he said he hadn't "been able to get a hold of a copy. I wasn't offered one." Tiptoeing around the truth, he insisted, "I believe you'd be fair," adding, "I don't shy away from the truth, as long as it's the truth." He called past problems "water under the bridge."

When she brought up the reason their marriage ended, he said, "We were smothering each other." Discussing the *Special Guests* album, he was more candid, admitting, "I did a bad performance of a lot of the things on there, but some of them came out good, and some of them came out bad. I wasn't in very good voice at all." Discussing his hospitalization, he spoke kindly of his treatment, saying the staff "really know how to work with you and take care of you, and get your thinking cap on right." As for missing concerts dates, he admitted it, adding, "The people I was involved with were booking me, a lot of times, for two or three shows on the same date." But he also added a telling bit of contrition when it came to the fans he'd let down, saying, "These fans, who might be walking a country mile with their children just to get to the show and they get there and . . . no George," adding, "It breaks my heart now that I realize this and think about it." For the most part the interview soft-pedaled the problems, trying to create a buzz about the couple's professional reconciliation, and both mentioned their next duet ("Two Story House") and George's single: "He Stopped Loving Her Today."

At Columbia, Rick Blackburn's stellar track record handling CBS Nashville's music finally elevated him to the top job: vice president and general manager of the whole Columbia-Epic Nashville operation. For some time, George and Sherrill had been sparring over "He Stopped Loving Her." Written by Bobby Braddock and Curly Putman, Johnny Russell had recorded it on an album, but Sherrill knew how he wanted it tailored for George and had the composers rewrite to get it as he wanted it: as an epic ballad, a sorrowful tale of unrequited love centered on a man who never stopped loving a woman who'd spurned him. His yearning for her ended only with his death.

Recording George during that time was complicated, Pig Robbins remembered. "When he started doin' that cocaine, he went down the drain. George'd be there a lot of times, but if we saw he wasn't gonna be able to get anything that day, we'd just lay the track down and move on to another song. We'd just make tracks and they'd put [his vocal] on later. They'd catch him halfway fit [to record]. The background singers were there with the rhythm section. [Billy] used the [vocal group] Nashville Edition on a lot of them."

In spite of his dissolute state, George's skepticism when it came to songs remained in force and, as before, he wasn't always correct. He'd initially blown off "She Thinks I Still Care" and "When the Grass Grows Over Me." He complained that the melody for "He Stopped Loving Her" too closely resembled Kris Kristofferson's "Help Me Make It Through the Night" and mockingly sang the song's lyrics to the Kristofferson melody to drive home the point to Billy, who would not relent. The final, Billy-approved rewrite of "He Stopped Loving Her" connected with George's situation at that moment. Braddock and Putman's final rewrite belied George's misgivings. The man being dead, "all dressed up to go away" and "over her for good," was in many ways a thematic and superior variation on the message of "When the Grass Grows over Me," one speaking to George's faltering condition at the time.

Sherrill insisted he had to record George's version bit by bit, that the singer's diminished physical state made it impossible to get a complete take out of him. He envisioned the song as a virtual drama in miniature, complete with symphonic strings and the flawless soprano voice of session vocalist Millie Kirkham, infusing the song with gravitas above and beyond his usual work with George. The drama was carefully constructed, complete with a feature rarely heard on the country records of that time: a spoken recitation in the middle as Kirkham's soprano soared above his words.

From the forties to the sixties, some country hits included vocals with recitations, like Red Sovine's "Little Rosa" and Jimmy Dean's "Big Bad John." Porter Wagoner made recitations an art form with songs like "The Carroll County Accident." A few, like T. Texas Tyler's "Deck of Cards" and Johnny Cash's "A Boy Named Sue," were totally spoken. The idea had largely fallen out of fashion, but George's performance revived it. The spoken interlude, despite Billy's uptown production, left no doubt it was a deep, emotional, and unabashedly *country* record. The final vocal revealed George totally at one with the lyrics, conveying all the pain and tragedy in a way that made his performance transcendent. It seemed as if he'd effectively summed up his entire career in one recording. Billy's arrangement became a foil for George's primal, passionate vocal, the culmination of the sound he'd first pursued on "Tender Years" nearly twenty years earlier. Still not convinced, George, insisting the song was too maudlin, bet Sherrill $100 nobody would buy it.

"Two Story House" entered the *Billboard* charts in March. It would reach No. 2. "He Stopped Loving Her Today" made its first chart appearance a month later, and on July 5 it knocked the Oak Ridge Boys' "Trying to Love Two Women" out of the No. 1 spot, remaining there just a week before it was knocked off the top slot by, ironically, Charley Pride's cover of Hank Williams's "You Win Again." The buzz around the song, however, did not die down. The many artists who revered George and everything about him were dazzled by it. One night Emmylou Harris and her Hot Band had pulled into a truck stop near Oklahoma City. "Hey," she told Tony Brown, her keyboard player and a former Elvis Presley sideman, "go to the jukebox and play 'He Stopped Loving Her Today.' It's gonna kill you!" Brown never forgot that moment.

As George's contract with Epic neared its end, CBS took note of the near-universal praise for "He Stopped Loving Her Today." That acclaim surprised George, who still perceived the song as the maudlin ballad he didn't much care for. During the summer,

Epic released the follow-up: his take on Tom T. Hall's ballad "I'm Not Ready Yet," about a man wanting to leave his woman but unable to actually do it. Nearly three years after ducking out on CBS's gala, George finally played the Bottom Line in September. During his performance he brought Linda Ronstadt, who was in the audience, onstage to sing "I Can't Help It" solo.

That fall, his personal life wasn't in any better shape than before. The buzz over "He Stopped Loving Her Today" continued, and the Richeys were overseeing his affairs. As for Shug, he was out of the picture. On September 29, the coke arrest landed him a three-year prison sentence. As the CMA Awards ceremonies approached, publicists went to work, spinning the illusion that George was on the mend. In October, prior to the awards telecast, the Associated Press ran a story detailing George's seeming recovery. "Less than a year after his life was devastated by alcoholism, sobered-up singer George Jones could become a major winner in tonight's nationally televised country music association awards show," it said, adding, "In fact, Jones has never won an award from the CMA." That night, he won two: Single of the Year for "He Stopped Loving Her Today" and Male Vocalist of the Year. Bobby Braddock and Curly Putman shared Song of the Year. It would have been a night of triumph for anyone. But given George's condition, he was barely able to savor it.

George's Nashville friends did what they could to get behind him. Late in the year they staged a special tribute at the Exit Inn titled "Nashville Loves George Jones." Some in town feared it might be the last time he'd be seen alive. He and the Jones Boys did occasional concerts with Tammy and her band, but his reliability continued to be a crapshoot. He missed a show in Columbus in February, the same month "He Stopped Loving Her Today" earned a Grammy for Best Male Country Vocal Performance.

The year 1981 began with Epic releasing another tune seemingly ripped from George's real life: "If Drinkin' Don't Kill Me (Her Memory Will)," "her" yet another allusion to you-know-who.

George remained philosophical about throwing in with Richey, telling *Chicago Tribune* writer Jack Hurst in a March 22, 1981, profile that "sometimes, in this business, you have to bend over backwards. And sometimes when you do, you find it wasn't that hard to do. Bein' friends is better 'n stayin' enemies." He also admitted, "All my life, I've been runnin' from somethin'. If I knew what it was, I could run the right direction. I know where I want to go, but I always seem to end up goin' the other way. I know there's nothin' down that way. I been down there too many times."

In March, the TV-movie adaptation of *Stand By Your Man* appeared with Annette O'Toole, at the time a young actress just starting her career, in the starring role. Character actor Tim McIntire, who portrayed pioneering rock disc jockey Alan Freed in the 1978 film *American Hot Wax,* was cast as George. O'Toole, who immersed herself in Tammy's records, did a respectable job approximating the star's vocals. But overall accuracy was not a top priority. The characters were dumbed down to simpleminded, one-dimensional caricatures. McIntire was miscast as George. Billy Sherrill, played by James Hampton, is shown not as a CBS Records executive but as an independent Nashville producer-manager, his screen personality worlds away from Sherrill's often acerbic cockiness. It was one more fictionalized, simplistic music biopic like the bizarre *Your Cheatin' Heart,* starring George Hamilton as Hank Williams, and barely rose above the crappy B or C country-music films shot around Nashville in the sixties, released to small-town southern theaters and rural drive-ins.

The buzz continued on April 30, 1981, when "He Stopped Loving Her Today" won three awards from the West Coast–based Academy of Country Music: the same three that came from the CMA, Male Vocalist and Single of the Year for George and Song of the Year for Braddock and Putman. The honors meant little to George at this point as the dissolution continued both off and on the road. With no concern over the consequences, oblivious to the havoc he wreaked on his own life and those of everyone in his hemisphere, he drank and rammed powder up his nose, or local coke dealers did the honors. He'd later claim situations where others filled him up, sometimes involuntarily, particularly among the Alabama drug dealers he seemed at odds with. His shaky stature didn't prevent the occasional cameo on others' recordings. His friend Barbara Mandrell recruited him to add a vocal on her single "I Was Country When Country Wasn't Cool," released that spring.

On the road, high and indifferent, he blew off a concert in Manassas, Virginia. Paul Richey wanted to charter a jet to take George and road manager Wayne Oliver to the next stop at Possum Holler Music Park in Logan, Ohio, southwest of Columbus, named in George's honor by owners Jim and Stellie Ryan. George said he preferred sleeping on the bus until he arrived. With the jet already chartered, Oliver flew ahead. George remained in his room on the bus boozing and coking. When the bus pulled into Possum Holler on May 24, as the Jones Boys began setting up, George, under no one's watchful gaze and thoroughly wasted, pulled yet another vanishing act, slipping off the bus. As Oliver began hunting for him, George walked into the small town of Logan, met two elderly women, and was soon sitting on a porch, talking. When a guitar was produced, he sang to them. George asked the women to call a cab. The driver agreed to chauffeur George back to Nashville, George offering a private concert the whole way down. He took the guitar, promising the women the cabbie would return it. Back at the park, all hell broke loose when the announcement was made that George wasn't performing. Some audience members rushed the stage, venting their anger on anyone seemingly tied to the show. The bus's tires were slashed; one of its windows was broken. As police moved in, a sheriff's deputy was seriously injured and seven people arrested. While in the past the mystique of No Show Jones was funny, even folksy to many, no one felt that way this time. George was so out of control he clearly didn't give a damn about any repercussions.

Barely a week later, the Ohio State Fair canceled his scheduled June 2 concert appearance. Fair manager John Evans told reporters, "We try to run a family affair. We can't take the chance of something happening." Possum Holler's owners filed a $10.1 million breach-of-contract lawsuit against George, Halsey, and Richey, seeking $1.1 million in compensatory damages and $9 million in punitive damages, claiming the plaintiffs suffered "adverse publicity which seriously damaged [their] reputations." Jim Halsey did not need this. He dropped George as a client. Finally, everyone agreed to a makeup date. George, unhappy to be playing gratis, was flown in by helicopter so he couldn't bolt.

He couldn't even hold it together for the folks back home. A subpar June 2 performance at the Palace near Beaumont disappointed local fans. By then, family members staged their own intervention, forcing him to enter Baptist Hospital. The public claim was he suffered from "exhaustion." Days later, he left and headed for Alabama. The death watch ramped up as the media began trying to track him down. On July 8, WNGE-TV, Nashville's ABC affiliate, found him at the barbershop run by his pal Jimmie Hills, a gentle man satisfied to be George's friend. George talked to the reporters, telling them he had a total of $237 in his bank account. Hills was hired, at George's request, as a sort of companion/hair stylist/chaperone, and found himself constantly challenged by George's ability to slip away.

For a time, getting George back to the more familiar atmosphere of Texas, away from Nashville and its pressures, seemed like a sensible idea. Legendary Texas A&M football star and businessman Billy Bob Barnett had opened Billy Bob's Texas in Fort Worth in April 1981. Billed as the "World's Largest Honky Tonk," it was designed to be a larger, more dazzling version of Gilley's, the massive Houston venue named for singer Mickey Gilley. Barnett and Paul Richey would manage George's affairs. A July 29 show at Pee Wee's, owned by George's pal Pee Wee Johnson, was billed as his official farewell to Nashville. The plan soon collapsed when George unexpectedly pulled out of the Texas deal. By then Paul Richey, too, was out of the picture.

George found a new manager close to his Alabama homestead. Gerald Murray, a Muscle Shoals businessman and owner of Factory Outlet Mobile Homes, was a friend of Hank Williams Jr. and his then-manager James "J.R." Smith. George's business operations were consolidated in Murray's facilities. George had a three-thousand-square-foot office in the building, with fancy leather furniture. An article about George's organization in the Muscle Shoals *Times-Daily* was titled "New Day for George Jones," even as his substance abuse rendered him cadaverous and seemingly near the end.

Murray, who'd known him for a while, got a good dose of George's erratic side when setting up George in a colorful office area complete with the titles of some of his hits painted on the wall. Another painting, Murray said, featured "a big possum sittin' back with a hat on and he was playin' the guitar and all this music was comin' out of the center of the guitar. He got up there one day and said, 'I don't like that possum up there!' George Richey had given him this beautiful black leather jacket with this possum on the back. George took it out there and put it in the dumpster. He said he didn't want anybody to call him 'Possum.' He had us paint over the possum right there. It was offensive to him at that particular time. And a week later, he was just the opposite."

A drunken September 20 show at Meadow Brook Music Festival in Rochester, Michigan, seemed to embody Jones in decline. *Toledo Blade* reviewer Bob Rose detailed a concert that began with the Jones Boys playing eight songs, the musicians looking to the side for signs of George before he finally stumbled onstage, so wasted he was slurring lyrics. Unable to recall words, he had to be constantly prompted by the band. Even a move into the Hank Williams songbook faltered. Rose detailed his taking audience requests and beginning "Your Cheatin' Heart" only to—again—forget the words. "He asked a Jones Boy how that one went," Rose commented. As the Jones Boys tried to get him to wrap things up, he blithely ignored them, grinning and telling the thinning and disgusted crowd, "We're gonna play till three or four in the morning, right?" By the time management turned up the house lights to get him to leave the stage, most of the audience had left. His pitiful final words from the stage: "Somebody's trying to embarrass us."

He had three CMA Awards nominations for 1981: an unusual second nomination for "He Stopped Loving Her Today" as Song of the Year, another for Male Vocalist, and, unbelievably, the third for Entertainer of the Year. Given the messes left behind in Logan, Beaumont, and other venues, his chances of winning in that last category were remote at best. This time, the entire country saw the mess on the televised 1981 awards. Neither the prelude nor the aftermath, Murray said, were pleasant. When George arrived at the Opry House, Murray recalled, "Ralph Emery said, 'George, I've got something for you that the Opry gave us.' He handed him a watch, and George took it out and it had diamonds around the thing and it had some engraving inside it about the Opry. Inside the top it was really neat. And George just took it and we walked maybe ten steps and there was one of those flip-top garbage cans right there and he just reached over and hit it with the back of his hand, and throwed the watch in the garbage." After the show ended he returned to his suite, broke some lamps in his hotel room, and apparently got rough with Linda. No one was surprised when he failed to appear at CBS Records' CMA Week Artist Showcase.

With the contrived stories about George on the mend rendered moot, much of Nashville began accepting the notion that the World's Greatest County Singer, driving around with Hank Williams cassettes in his car and a life-size cardboard figure of his early hero, was heading for a similar if not identical end. He stiffed everyone on a November 22 show in Roanoke, Virginia. The promoter sued for $25,000. It had long been a crapshoot with his fans, yet enough still loved him that they continued showing up despite his disrespecting them. "He just had one thing on his mind, and that was the drugs," said Gerald Murray.

With "Still Doin' Time," another bleak ballad about lost love and symbolic incarceration in a "honky-tonk prison," at No. 1, any doubts over George's status with CBS Records were put to an end when the label re-signed him in November. He flew to Los Angeles with Rick Blackburn and his own attorney, Tom Binkley, to sign the new deal with a half-million-dollar advance to be applied to his debts. George, however, was still George, and threw a wrench into the deal at the last minute by demanding $100,000 for himself. He got the money and bought a new car. Most of the remaining cash likely went up his nose.

George was in Shreveport, Louisiana, with Wayne Oliver, who had a girlfriend there. Since he and George were flying to New York, Wayne arranged for his girlfriend to accompany them and bring a friend for George: Nancy Sepulvado, a Shreveport divorcee, the mother of two daughters, who'd spent twenty years working in a factory assembling telephones. From the start, George and Nancy found a bond. They were captivated with each other, to the point that George flipped off some shows to visit her in Shreveport. She ended up leaving Shreveport with daughter Adina to join George on tour. His relationship with Linda, who had stuck by him despite abuse and the stress of watching him implode, began to unravel. The bad blood between Nancy and Linda, with Jones caught in the middle, upset everyone, and Linda finally had enough. Before 1981 ended, she and George parted for good.

The year 1982 began with a disappearing act before a January 6 concert with Johnny Paycheck, now one of the hottest singers in the business, and Donna Fargo. As George and Nancy set up housekeeping in Alabama, George's situation grew more dire. The coke dealers were abundant. Nancy knew he drank, but cocaine added a chilling dimension that could turn him physically abusive, even to her. Unlike other women in his past, she reacted to his behavior with a steely determination to do everything she could to pull him out of what were clearly the last gasps of both his career and existence. She didn't care if he never sang again. Her love was for the man, not the icon.

ONE DAY GERALD MURRAY'S PHONE RANG IN MUSCLE SHOALS. IT WAS WAYLON Jennings asking, "Can you come and get the Possum?"

George had visited Waylon and Jessi's home in Brentwood, south of Nashville. George ended up out of control. Waylon's ill-advised decision to give him a generous dose of whiskey, hoping to calm him down, backfired badly. He trashed furniture, then threw a photo in a metal frame at his host. When Jerry Gropp, Waylon's guitarist, tried to restrain George, he ended up with a busted thumb. Waylon held George down. When he thought George was finally tired, he let go. George, who'd been faking, sucker-punched the man who had given him tens of thousands of dollars to help him out of his financial morass. Waylon finally subdued and restrained his friend, then made the call to Murray.

Murray arrived to find a mess. "He broke all his lamps and everything." George sat on a piano bench. Waylon "had him tied, his pants pulled down around his knees and his belt around his ankles pulled up there. Jones jumps up and squirms around a little bit like nothing ever happened [and said], 'You gotta hear this!' He asked Jessi to sing something. Waylon looked at me and said, '*Boy!*'" Despite it all, Waylon hadn't lost any of his affection for the man he'd met in Lubbock more than twenty years earlier. He refused to take any money for the damages.

The no-shows continued, although on occasions when George was in better shape he could still surprise those closest to him. Murray remembered one northeastern tour that took them to Long Island. "He walked off, come back down off the side of the stage, and he said, 'Is that enough?' I said, 'George, I believe if you did fifteen more minutes, we'd be good.' He walked on down there in the dressin' room and pulled off his shirt. He [wore] an old striped T-shirt. And he walked back up there and said, 'You all care if I sing one more?' He left an hour and a half later." He also took control when a problem arose at a Wheeling, West Virginia, concert involving a revolving stage that malfunctioned and cut the electricity to the band's gear. According to Murray, "George said, 'Oh well, I can handle that.' He just got a bar stool and set down and got his guitar and did the rest by himself. When he wanted to, he could do what he wanted."

That included times when he just wanted to hang out in Muscle Shoals with friends like Jimmie Hills or Murray. When George was off the road, Murray would pick up the ringing phone and find George on the other end. "He'd say, 'Me—you—outside in front of the office in a few minutes. I'm pickin' you up in the motor home! We gonna [cook] green tomatoes and Shake 'n Bake in Colbert Park and play some ball.' We were out there one day and the first time we did the ball thing and I kicked it and it went flyin' out across there and it went in the Tennessee River, floatin' down the river, and George just stood there and watched it float off and said, 'Guess it's useless to ask if you brought another ball.' He liked just gettin' in the car and goin' there, if it was something he was interested in. He just looked for something to occupy his time."

George, Nancy, and Adina settled in Muscle Shoals, where Nancy began to survey the regulars in his inner circle with a jaundiced eye. The Montgomerys were around, and Peanutt was now pastoring his own church, but the relationship had changed between George and his old friends as he grew closer to Nancy. Elsewhere drug dealers hovered, and rumors flew of life-insurance policies taken out with the expectation that George would soon be history. Nancy claimed a car attempted to force her off a bridge when she was crossing the Tennessee River between Florence and Muscle Shoals. George was vulnerable wherever he went, and local hostility toward Nancy seemed to be mushrooming. Someone was going to get hurt or killed, and finally George, Nancy, and Adina decided to head for Texas.

They were in transit on March 29, Nancy at the wheel of George's Lincoln Town Car with the "POSSUM1" vanity plate as he snorted coke. With Nancy and Adina begging him to ditch his stash, he threw it out the window. But the powder in his bloodstream was still calling the shots. On the interstate near Jackson, Mississippi, George rambunctiously slid his foot over and tramped on the gas pedal, kicking their speed to ninety-one miles an hour. A local officer pulled them over. When he saw who it was, a drug dog was summoned. George was arrested for possession of cocaine. The stash might have been gone, but enough remained on the floor mats and, Murray said, on the toe of one of his boots. Charged and released on bond, George decided to return to Muscle Shoals and relied on booze to get him home.

He, Nancy, and Adina flew through northern Mississippi on March 30. With Nancy again driving and George drinking, he pulled the same tramp-on-the-gas-pedal routine that got him busted in Jackson. Nancy had enough. She pulled over and exited the car. Adina did likewise. Now alone behind the wheel, George sped north on Highway 45. After a couple of turns, he wound up on Grubb Springs Road, running off the road and flipping the car. When Monroe County sheriff's deputy Pete Shook arrived on the scene, he saw the license plate and reported back. Sheriff Pat Patterson, a longtime Jones fan, responded that he knew exactly who it was. George was transported to Aberdeen-Monroe Hospital. Patterson later said he was "so slobbering drunk, he wouldn't have known if he was Roy Acuff or Jesus Christ."

Meanwhile, unaware of what had happened, Nancy and Adina went to a nearby house and asked to use the phone, telling the woman who answered the door who they were. She replied that she'd been listening to her police scanner and heard George Jones had been in a wreck nearby. Nancy called Gerald Murray. After some confusion over whether she was in Hamilton, Mississippi, or Hamilton, Alabama, he sent someone to pick her up. Murray agreed that George needed some sort of immediate intervention. With the help of three of George's sisters, Murray had him transferred from Aberdeen to Hillcrest in Birmingham. He was there for fifteen days until the hospital released him after finding someone had slipped him cocaine.

The coke case, obviously more serious, would take considerable time to litigate. As for the DUI, it happened in an era when drunk-driving in America wasn't viewed as gravely as it would be in later decades. George was willing to pay fines. He pleaded guilty and wrote a check to the Monroe County sheriff's office—on what turned out to be a closed account. Sheriff Patterson insisted Jones stopped the payment. His situation grew worse in late April as he missed shows at the Opry House in Nashville, in Birmingham, and a May 1 show in Florence, for which he was later sued. He spent part of the month in Nashville recording with Haggard, who'd signed with Epic. *A Taste of Yesterday's Wine,* named for the Willie Nelson composition "Yesterday's Wine," was an impressive example of two old buddies simply going into the studio and singing. The other material included "C.C. Waterback," the album's hit single, and "No Show Jones," a self-deprecating ditty with an obvious theme.

George's 1982 trail of madness wasn't quite finished. Back in Tennessee on May 25, he was drunkenly speeding down I-65 south of Nashville when Tennessee highway patrolman Tommy Campsey pulled him over. In no time, a Nashville TV station had a crew on the scene as Campsey dealt with a belligerent, drunk, and argumentative George. As Campsey arrested George and moved to put him in the patrol car (without the usually required handcuffs), Jones pulled loose and tried to kick the TV cameraman. Across the country, millions saw the video, showing his body emaciated, his eyes flaring with the psychotic glare of a trapped, desperate man who had lost all hope.

Monroe County, Mississippi, issued an arrest warrant over the nonpayment of the DUI fine, and George received a letter from Sheriff Patterson. The county talked of extraditing him, an absurd idea since at that time the charges were misdemeanors. More illogical were comments from Shook, Patterson's chief deputy, who'd responded to the accident. He told the Associated Press, "We don't think it'll get that far," meaning extradition. "We don't think he could stand all the publicity." After the coke bust, the televised DUI arrest in Tennessee, and other recent headlines, it's a mystery why anyone would think more negative press would bother George. Pee Wee Johnson finally drove to Mississippi to personally pay the fine, now $737.50.

In mid-June, Associated Press reporter Joe Edwards filed a story about George's deterioration, one far more ominous than the optimistic stories of the previous year. He quoted Tammy saying, "I don't know where George is. I doubt if even George knows where George is." Murray told Edwards that his client "told me he wants to be another Hank Williams," adding, "If something doesn't happen, he won't be around much longer. He needs to go into a hospital on his own to get straightened out." That view was echoed by Dan Wojick of the Lavender Agency—Shorty Lavender had died in May—who said, "George has to want to help himself."

In Jackson, Hinds County prosecutors indicted him for the cocaine bust. George also incurred the wrath of *Jackson Daily News Ledger* columnist Orley Hood, who referred to the singer as "Godless and friendless, a moral pauper who is perpetually ashamed of himself." In Williamson County, Tennessee, where the televised May 25 DUI arrest took place, officials issued an arrest warrant on July 14 for failure to appear in court. He arrived at the courthouse in Franklin in his tour bus two days later and agreed to give a free concert for the Williamson County sheriff's office as "community service." Judge Jane Franks fined him fifty dollars plus $123 in court costs.

Pee Wee accompanied him to an August 6 show in Augusta, Georgia. George had his motorcycle with him. After a drunken, half-assed performance that ticked off the audience, he compounded the insult by refusing to sign autographs. Pee Wee, his dark hair styled much like the star's, went to protect the motorcycle only to be attacked by fans thinking he was George. In San Antonio on August 11, an audience of two thousand dwindled to six hundred as he stumbled through a set that included not one but two performances of Hank Sr.'s "I Can't Help It if I'm Still in Love with You." The bills continued coming due. When he appeared for an October 25 concert in Salem, Virginia, he was served with a judgment for a previous show he'd missed. To satisfy the court, the local sheriff took George's gold watch, diamond ring, and $10,000 in gate receipts. For one small radio station, the constant parade of George Jones headlines was too much. The station manager of WRIJ-AM in Humboldt, Tennessee, northwest of Jackson, cited Jones as a poor role model for his children and declared his records off their playlists.

Taken as a whole, 1982 seemed to have finally moved George to the precipice. As he wobbled there, the slightest wrong move would surely take him over the edge.

CHAPTER 6

1983–1990

He'd finally left—escaped Alabama, where the drama, the threats, and the dealers had gotten to be too much. Once his refuge, it had become his, Nancy's, and Adina's own private hell. So George, Nancy, and her daughter settled closer to her home turf: the town of Lafayette, Louisiana. The year 1983 began with him missing a January 19 court date in Jackson on the coke charge, rescheduled to February 10. On the road, he was a bit shaky. At a February 1 concert in his former hometown of Lakeland, Florida, he took the stage after a fifteen-minute delay. Reviewer Dave Stuckrath described him as "not at his best," but added the opinion that "he wasn't noticeably drunk. He seemed in good spirits and even joked about moving back to Lakeland." He sang just eight songs, seven hits and his current single, "Shine On," before leaving the stage. The reviewer was sympathetic and critical, declaring, "One can't help but wonder what this great singer could do if he had only taken care of himself."

February 10 brought the rescheduled court date in Jackson, set to convene at nine A.M. George didn't arrive until about 11:30. With twenty-five spectators present, he accepted a plea bargain agreed to by his attorney. Prosecutors required him to plead guilty to a single charge: possession of cocaine. Hinds County circuit judge Breland Hilburn then sentenced him to six months' probation and, in lieu of a $30,000 fine, ordered him to perform a concert "for some worthy agencies here in this area in some appropriate amount of time." The judge also addressed George's unexplained tardiness, fining him $100 for the infraction, warning, "That will be paid before you leave this courthouse." It was. The worst of his charges was now behind him.

Fifteen years had passed since George, newly divorced and nearly broke, left Vidor and East Texas. Now that region began to seem like a place of renewal. Helen and Dub lived not far from the town of Woodville in Tyler County. Dub remained a simple man of the soil, one of the many qualities that George truly revered. That region held plenty of history for George. Jasper, the town where he'd played music in bars and on the radio with Dalton Henderson in 1947, wasn't far to the east. Lufkin, his daddy's birthplace, sat to the north. Kountze, the Thicket town where young George Glenn and his family moved after leaving Saratoga, where he sang with Brother Burl and Sister Annie, wasn't far south. It was, in short, the optimal place for George and Nancy to take stock and reorganize, far in mileage and spirit from Nashville and northern Alabama.

On March 5, George Glenn Jones married Nancy Ford Sepulvado at Dub and Helen's home. The wedding dinner took place at the Burger King in Jasper, the town where he'd hung out with

Dalton Henderson over thirty-five years earlier. But later that same month, he canceled shows. John McMeen, his booking agent, claimed the singer was severely stressed and fatigued, "brought on by a heavy concert schedule." He added that since September 1982, George had performed eighty-eight shows as an attempt to restore good faith with his fans. A seven-show European tour set to begin March 30 was also canceled. Clearly, George was still in flux. A show at the Armadillo Palace in Athens, Georgia, went sour when the club owner claimed he did only twenty-nine minutes onstage, walking off as soon as his road manager was handed the $10,000 fee. That brought another lawsuit. He left the road again on May 11, citing problems with bronchitis, laryngitis, and a virus. Still a smoker, he was plagued by respiratory problems on and off for the rest of his life. He recuperated at home, and on June 2 fulfilled his obligations regarding the Nashville DUI by playing a benefit in Franklin, Tennessee.

Health problems aside, with Nancy's tireless support and growing role in his career, he seemed to be gradually halting—even reversing—his decline. Offstage, a desire older than cocaine again reared its head, one that first struck him seventeen years earlier in Vidor, then in Lakeland. He had his brother-in-law scout land for yet *another* outdoor music park, this one set up to accommodate recreational vehicles. Again he seemed bent on cutting back on tours, spending more time close to family, and bringing in friends from Nashville and Texas who would draw consistent crowds. To pay for it, George performed around Texas and Louisiana for the door receipts. He and Nancy scaled back their expenses in ways George hadn't seen since the days when his mother seized upon any way to save a few cents. They maintained a garden near their large modular home, which George had no inhibitions about calling a "trailer house." The couple's goal: raising money to buy land for the park. By the spring of 1983, they accumulated enough funds to purchase sixty-five acres near the town of Colmesneil.

Again he planned the facility and did much of the work, clearing the land and doing the construction himself, assisted by Dub, Helen, and their children. There was none of the lavish spending that characterized the park in Lakeland. George recalled, "We built an economical stage and put a sheet metal roof over it. We had electrical hookups for recreational vehicles and another area where folks could camp in tents. There was a concession stand and a restaurant too, and Nancy and I pretty much lived on the property after building the facility." Jones Country Music Park was ready that fall, slated for a formal opening in the spring of 1984.

On September 16, he performed an hour-and-a-half show in Jackson for an audience of six thousand, raising $18,000 for local charities. Onstage, he was solid and professional. A little over two weeks earlier, he'd appeared on *20/20,* the ABC news magazine, calling himself "a changed and happy man" since his marriage. He'd given up cocaine on his own, claiming he'd simply lost any interest or desire for it.

As for the drinking, it was now under control. Even so, George Jones had not, despite what anyone assumed, embraced total abstinence. He still drank, but with Nancy at his side overseeing things, he was better able to control his intake. Finding the self-discipline to avoid the binges of the past, he slowly regained a level of self-esteem that allowed him to handle his responsibilities, both personal and professional, with greater confidence and consistency than he had for over two decades. Occasional slips happened, and not all of George's no-shows involved alcohol. Past indiscretions, however, continued catching up with him. A few years earlier, George had been chartering planes to handle some of his shows, and the bills weren't being paid. Wake County sheriff's deputies were present when he and the Jones Boys rolled into the North Carolina State Fairgrounds near Greensboro to play Dorton Arena. Before the show, the authorities seized his Martin D-41 guitar to satisfy a judgment of $5,295 in favor of the aviation company. George was civil and courteous, but the guitar, valued at $4,000, didn't quite satisfy the debt.

He joined the platinum record club in late December when *I Am What I Am,* the Epic album containing "He Stopped Loving Her Today," earned him his first RIAA Platinum album for sales of a million. Billy had him back in the studio in early 1984 to record another duets collection, this one teaming him with female singers on Epic and other labels. *Ladies' Choice* teamed him with Brenda Lee, Loretta Lynn, Emmylou Harris, Lacy J. Dalton, Barbara Mandrell, Terri Gibbs, Janie Fricke, Leona Williams, and Deborah Allen. George kicked off the album with a solo performance of "She's My Rock," a 1972 single by country singer Stoney Edwards.

Jones Country Music Park officially opened on April 1, 1984, with Johnny and June Carter Cash headlining. Other stars would follow. Tyler County was a dry county, so no alcohol was permitted on the premises. On the road, George began to build a reputation for reliability, more often than not offering sober, good-natured shows. The couple built a large log home on their land. On occasion his bronchitis resurfaced, sometimes forcing him to cancel concerts during tours.

As he began putting the dark years behind him, however, he absurdly opted to retaliate against one of his critics. In July he filed a $30 million libel suit against columnist Orley Hood, claiming Hood's 1983 column about the cocaine incident impugned George's reputation and "generally exposed [Jones] to ridicule, contempt, disgrace, embarrassment and humiliation." Considering the years of media coverage of George's misdeeds, it's no surprise the suit was dismissed. George's attorney asked the Mississippi Supreme Court to reinstate the case, a futile effort. In his later autobiography, George all but admitted Hood cited facts everyone knew were true.

Texas remained home base as he and Nancy toured or traveled to Nashville for business or recording. In August, he played Pee Wee Johnson's Nashville Supper Club, joined by longtime friend and Opry veteran Connie Smith. Three days later, Epic released "She's My Rock" as a single. The lyrics clearly alluded to his new beginnings with Nancy. It reached No. 2. Speaking to Jack Hurst that fall, George spoke glowingly of his marriage, describing his wife as "down to earth. She ain't no phony. She's just a good ol' country girl. She cuts up a lot, got a good personality."

GEORGE'S NEW AMIABILITY HAD LIMITS. CABLE TV'S THREE-YEAR-OLD NASH-ville Network, TNN, was taping *Radio City Music Hall Welcomes the Nashville Network* in Manhattan in March 1985 for broadcast a month later. George was to host the event, showcasing Epic Nashville artists Mickey Gilley, Ricky Skaggs, Lacy J. Dalton, Charly McClain, Exile, and Mark Gray. While George was gaining strength, his insecurities and sensitivity to slights remained intact. A number of things about the event ticked him off. He objected to singing in front of the full orchestra booked for the show, and he was supposedly upset with the catering in his dressing room and his transportation from his hotel to Radio City and back. When he angrily walked out before the taping began, producers pressed Skaggs into service as the host.

At his lowest, George had traveled the back roads with a cardboard cutout of Hank Williams in his car. Sober, he was in a perfect position to record a song about past heroes that looked both forward and ahead. "Who's Gonna Fill Their Shoes," cowritten by Troy Seals and Max D. Barnes, was an elegiac number lamenting the passing of many legends, questioning the future of traditional country as the number of stars dwindled, and wondering who would succeed them all. The list was lengthy, encompassing Waylon, Willie, Twitty, Cash, Haggard, Carl Perkins, Charlie Rich, and Jerry Lee Lewis, with allusions to the departed Elvis, Marty Robbins, Hank Williams, and Lefty Frizzell.

The accompanying music video, the first ever produced for a George Jones record, centered around George's tour bus stopping at a decrepit rural gas station, where the elderly owner asks him to sign a guitar signed by other stars. What could have been trite and gimmicky turned out to be a powerful, moving performance, one that more than merited the CMA Video of the Year Award it won that October. Issued that summer, "Who's Gonna Fill Their Shoes" became George's first solo hit of 1985. He may have been nervous at Willie's Fourth of July Picnic nine years earlier, but he had no problems performing at Willie's inaugural Farm Aid concert in Champaign, Illinois, on September 22. A rock club like the Bottom Line might have spooked him at one time, but now he thought nothing of performing alongside the heaviest of heavy hitters: Willie, Bob Dylan, B.B. King, the Nitty Gritty Dirt Band, John Mellencamp, Neil Young, and Tom Petty.

A few days later, the Nashville law firm that represented George sued for $124,000 in back legal fees. At a time when George was pulling out of such problems, albeit slowly, he found himself in deeper by failing to appear at a November 1 court date in Nashville. Dan Alexander, Jones's lawyer, noted that George spent time at his East Texas home and in Nashville. Robert S. Brandt, the chancellor overseeing the hearing, wasn't appeased, chewing out Alexander over his client's failure to appear, stating he didn't know of "any other entertainer of any note" with a worse reputation for not "being where he's supposed to be when he's supposed to be here."

George's loyalty to longtime friends remained strong. On December 19, 1985, Johnny Paycheck walked into the North High Lounge in Hillsboro, Ohio. When a male fan started chatting him up at the bar, Paycheck begged off. When the guy persisted, Paycheck pulled his .22 and shot him in the face. The victim's injuries weren't severe, but the circumstances of the incident were not favorable to the singer. Paycheck, who contended the shooting was an accident, was found guilty of aggravated assault and tampering with evidence on May 17, 1986. He was sentenced to nine and a half years in a state prison, three of those years mandatory since he'd used a gun in a crime. George and Haggard put up $50,000 bond to get him out of prison as he appealed his sentence. When appeals were exhausted, Paycheck entered an Ohio penitentiary. Before Paycheck served even two years, Ohio governor Dick Celeste pardoned him.

Linda Welborn, calling herself Linda Welborn Jones, filed a lawsuit in Alabama that July asserting that she and George had a common-law marriage. The suit, filed in Colbert County Circuit Court, requested alimony payments and a property settlement. One of her attorneys, James Hunt, told Florence, Alabama, *Times-Daily* reporter David Palmer that "she didn't realize her rights until she talked to an attorney." One element cited to support her case: two life-insurance policies on George listing Linda as beneficiary. The suit stated that the two had parted ways on July 15, 1981.

George and other veteran country singers had despaired that in recent years, the music had ventured too far into a sound that was little more than easy-listening pop. During his worst years, even as "He Stopped Loving Her Today" took him to another level, the dominant artists embraced the so-called Urban Cowboy sound inspired by the Travolta film, a ballad-heavy style marked by dull, symphonic string arrangements and bland, subdued performances. The chief exponents were Kenny Rogers, Johnny Lee, Crystal Gayle (Loretta Lynn's younger sister), and even Dolly Parton, then hitting her stride as an A-list feature film star. With radio and fans embracing the smoother sound, it dominated the early 1980s.

Before long, however, these smoother sounds began to bore fans. Country radio dutifully played this bland, predictable music, but fewer people seemed to be listening or buying records, which left executives and record companies increasingly worried. A measure of how quickly the bottom fell out came in 1985 when the *New York Times* ran a page-one story by their respected music critic Robert Palmer. He reported, "Nashville's country music stars are really wailing the blues these days. Audiences are dwindling, sales of country records are plummeting and the fabled Nashville Sound, which defined country music for decades and made this comfortable, tree-shaded Tennessee city one of the world's leading recording centers, may soon sound as dated as the ukulele." In the story, veteran singer Bobby Bare noted, "Country records are getting plenty of radio airplay, but they all sound alike and nobody's buying them." Such listener fatigue scared the shit out of status quo advocates on Music Row. A quick shift in direction was the only strategy.

It involved a modernized, updated version of basic, bare-bones country: George's style, performed largely by baby boomers who'd also grown up with the Beatles and the rock music of their generation. Ricky Skaggs, John Anderson, and George Strait had already succeeded with such a sound. Others now emerged, signed by the major labels as part of a movement dubbed New Traditionalism. It spawned several new stars: Randy Travis, Dwight Yoakam, Vince

Gill, Keith Whitley (who'd played bluegrass with Ricky Skaggs in Ralph Stanley's band), Reba McEntire, and Patty Loveless. To most of these younger performers, George was the gold standard, just as he was to his peers in the business and his fans. Buck Owens, Merle Haggard, Lefty Frizzell, Loretta Lynn, and other veterans were the touchstones for this new breed. George clicked with these younger artists in a way that would slowly and deliberately elevate him to levels of prestige that seemed impossible just a few years earlier. On April 1, 1987, the Texas Legislature that in 1963 had honored him as an admiral in the Texas Navy proclaimed it George Jones Day.

Health issues occasionally forced a slowdown. At the end of July, after taking a break from a forty-seven-city tour, he entered the University of Alabama Medical Center to be treated for bronchitis, which was plaguing him with increasing frequency, complicated by prostate and kidney infections and exhaustion. He left a day later—his stubbornness did not diminish with his improved mental state—and returned a day after that, now also suffering from stomach issues. He was discharged August 8.

The New Traditionalist movement may have given him hope for the future of his own music. One reality, however, loomed over everything when it came to recording. The Top 10 and No. 1 singles that once came routinely were dwindling. In 1987, only "The Right Left Hand" reached the Top 10. Two other releases, "I Turn to You" and "The Bird," got no higher than the Top 30. Younger artists who drank deep from the Jones catalog were carrying on his style, but for George, it was a disheartening transition even if successful touring helped ease his debts, with Nancy taking a greater role in his management. Late in 1987, he settled with Linda Welborn. Despite the fact his hit records were trailing off, he continued redeeming himself on the road.

But he hit occasional speed bumps in his attempts to stay reliable. Sometimes they involved health problems. On other occasions he fell back into old, bad habits, as he did at a December 3 concert at the Charleston Civic Center in West Virginia. Obviously drunk, he remained onstage too long, singing so poorly that most of the audience cleared out in disgust. The fiasco was duly reported in an Associated Press story by Steven Herman including candid comments from Jones Boys drummer and road manager Bobby Birkhead, who called the performance the worst he'd seen in five years and noted the singer had been shaky since a show two weeks earlier in South Carolina. George didn't try to cover it, admitting he wasn't up to par. He told what was left of the audience he'd sing "The Bird"—"if I can remember the words." No less candid, longtime Jones Boys bassist-backup singer Ron Gaddis told the reporter, "[George] goes through periods of time where he's OK, but he just fell off the wagon."

In Iowa for a May 4, 1988, show, he felt so badly he pointed the bus toward Birmingham and the University of Alabama Medical Center. Admitted two days later, he was diagnosed with double pneumonia and released after four days. Set to perform in Tennessee in August, he canceled because of a headache and ringing ears and again headed for Birmingham. This time the diagnosis was a serious sinus infection. He remained several days before being discharged on August 19.

His singles continued to stall. "I'm a Survivor," cowritten by Jim McBride and singer-songwriter Keith Stegall, peaked at No. 52; "The Old Man Nobody Loves" halted its rise at No. 63. The song that returned him to the Top 10 was a familiar number, one of the hit covers he'd recorded under a pseudonym for Pappy in the mid-1950s: Johnny Horton's venerable "I'm a One Woman

Man." The record reveals George clearly enjoying himself, jaunty, laying on the twangy tenor and playfully swooping down into a lower register, the way he'd done on "You Gotta Be My Baby" over thirty years earlier. Billy Sherrill produced it with stripped-down instrumentation propelled by a straight-ahead Ray Price shuffle rhythm, the kind of sound heard on George's Epic albums but rarely on his earlier singles for the label. It had the feel of Dwight Yoakam's 1986 hit revival of Horton's "Honky Tonk Man." Another New Traditionalist scored with a Jones oldie when Patty Loveless achieved her first Top 10 by reviving "If My Heart Had Windows."

Offstage, George had other issues. In 1989 Georgette was engaged to one Billy Wayne Terrell, and she wanted her dad to give her away at the altar at the ceremony on March 5. But she claimed that she contacted George, who begged off, saying he'd be tired since he was doing a show the day before. It was the beginning of a complicated relationship between father and daughter that would last for years.

With his days at Epic working with Billy slowly coming to an end, George's follow-up to "One Woman Man" was an odd choice: the quirky, tongue-in-cheek Roger Ferris ditty "Ya Ba Da Ba Do (So Are You)," a surreal yet amusing description of a man lamenting his lost woman, who took nearly everything. Left were a Jim Beam whiskey decanter in the shape of Elvis Presley and a Flintstones jelly bean jar. As the lonely narrator drank whiskey from the jar, a conversation took place between all three. Clever as the song was, a legal problem surfaced when Hanna-Barbera productions, creators of *The Flintstones,* objected to the use of their trademarked "Ya Ba Da Ba Do," Fred Flintstone's signature exclamation. The song was retitled "The King Is Gone (So Are You)," but it never left the Top 30.

Epic would release two more singles. "Radio Lover," the final one, told the story, with vocals and spoken recitations, of a disc jockey deeply in love with his wife of one year, who takes advantage of his air time to cheat on him. Billy added his more elaborate production values to the recording. Despite the ups and downs, the Epic era defined much of George's legacy to the world. Mary Ann McCready, who'd left Columbia in 1988, agreed, saying, "Everything goes back to Epic Records." The healing that began when George and Nancy moved back to East Texas six years earlier had seemingly done its job. In May 1989, they closed down Jones Country, sold the Texas property, and returned to Nashville.

CHAPTER 7

1990-1999

There'd been no serious documentary made about George, but in the wake of his turnaround, producer Gregory Hall and Charlie Dick, Patsy Cline's husband and a longtime buddy of George's, secured George's and Nancy's cooperation and began assembling other stars and old friends, as well as new and vintage video and film clips, for the documentary *George Jones: Same Ole Me: The Authorized Video Biography*. It included new concert footage, comments by Loretta Lynn recounting George singing Buck Owens's entire show (she was present at the time), and George Riddle recalling his days touring with the Jones Boys. Johnny Cash, at the time in a creative funk of his own, declared that his answer to the question of his favorite country singer was always "You mean aside from George Jones." The film included scenes shot in desolate Saratoga and the infamous clip of Tommy Campsey putting a sputtering, drunken George in the police car after the traffic stop on I-65.

But as far as recording went, things were not so steady. Two years earlier, "One Woman Man" became his final Top 10 single. Subsequent singles barely broke the Top 40. His final Epic album, 1991's *Friends in High Places,* was actually made up of duets done years earlier with Emmylou Harris, Shelby Lynne, Charlie Daniels, Buck Owens, Ricky Van Shelton, Ricky Skaggs, Sweethearts of the Rodeo, and Randy Travis. The Travis performance, "A Few Ol' Country Boys," a Troy Seals–Mentor Williams composition, was the most significant. Travis's label, Warner Bros., had released it as a single that reached the Top 10 in the fall of 1990.

Figures from George's past were fading away. On February 20, 1991, Bryan and Jeffrey lost their mother when Shirley, happily married to J.C. Arnold until his death in 1985, died in Vidor. She was buried next to her husband in Restlawn, the final stop for so many Joneses.

Another New Traditional voice emerged with Alan Jackson, a Georgia native who'd worked around Nashville as a songwriter for Glen Campbell's publishing firm. Jackson wound up with Arista Records, his 1990 single "Here in the Real World" and the acclaimed album that followed epitomizing the continuing popularity of the New Traditional form. His producer was Keith Stegall, who'd written tunes for George. In April 1991, Jackson's label, Arista, released the single "Don't Rock the Jukebox," with its memorable line "Don't rock the jukebox/I wanna hear some Jones/My heart ain't ready for the Rollin' Stones." The catchy, twangy single stood as yet another homage to George, one he deeply appreciated. It would lead to a close friendship with Jackson that lasted until George's death. That same year Lorrie Morgan, George's former backup singer and the widow of Keith

Whitley, successfully revived "A Picture of Me (Without You)."

Another musical sea change was looming. A new breed of younger singers, younger than most of the New Traditionalists, had musical visions blending some aspects of country with larger influences from rock and pop. Garth Brooks, an Oklahoma native whose mother sang and recorded country for Capitol, emerged in 1989 with a debut album that did well. Equipped with a degree in advertising from Oklahoma State University, Brooks had a better handle on the business aspects of his career than many of his peers. His first two albums of the 1990s, *No Fences* and *Ropin' the Wind,* became successes beyond nearly anything the country music field had ever seen, taking the notion of crossing over from country to pop success to unheard-of levels. A highly visual performer who took his stage-presentation ideas from, among others, the rock band Kiss, Brooks inspired an entirely different school of country acts, less interested in preserving the twang of the past. Always savvy in the very political atmosphere of Nashville's Music Row, he frequently and publicly expressed his admiration for George's music even though his sound and rock-pop-flavored songs were the antithesis of both George's music and the New Traditional sound.

GEORGE WASN'T WITHOUT A RECORDING CONTRACT FOR LONG. AT MCA Records, executives Bruce Hinton and Tony Brown, the former keyboard player for Elvis Presley, Emmylou Harris, and Rodney Crowell, set their eyes on signing him. Hinton handled the business end. Brown, one of Nashville's most successful musician-producers since Billy Sherrill, Owen Bradley, or Chet Atkins, saw George as an important get for the label. "I think Epic lost interest and were lookin' for new blood, and somebody mentioned that we could sign George. I was thinkin', 'My God, why would we not do that?' Bruce felt the same way 'cause he was such an icon and he still had music left in him. He still could sing good. And I think he'd been sober for a while when he came to MCA and he was still singin' real good and showin' up for his concerts. We signed him because we thought there was still life in radio for George."

The first album would be *And Along Came Jones*, produced by Kyle Lehning, who'd produced Randy Travis's classic singles like "Diggin' Up Bones." MCA released three singles: "You Couldn't Get the Picture," in 1991, and "She Loved a Lot in Her Time" and "Honky Tonk Myself to Death" in 1992. None performed well on the charts, not a great beginning. *And Along Came Jones* went no higher than No. 22 while the Epic material continued to sell. In February 1992, the Epic singles collection *Super Hits* earned a gold album.

Behind the scenes, Country Music Hall of Fame electors, whose votes would determine the 1992 inductees, were at work. No one doubted George would someday be inducted, but when that would happen was anyone's guess. The CMA's byzantine selection system, always highly political, left many things to question. Worthy artists like Webb Pierce, who tramped on too many toes around Music Row despite monumental musical achievements that more than justified his induction, languished for years. Pierce died in 1991. George was viewed differently. Loved by nearly everyone at his worst, through years of screwing up, leaving friends in the lurch, and dragging himself through the mud, the man and his talents were still revered by friends even if they hated his bad behavior.

MCA created a ball buster of a vocal event, defined as a single performance featuring one or more additional stars and staged to generate both buzz and record sales. In this case, taking a cue from the Epic singles that seemed to parallel his life, George recorded "I Don't Need Your Rocking Chair," a defiant refusal to be worn down by age, custom written by Frank Dycus, Kerry Kurt Phillips, and Billy Yates. George, nearly sixty-one, would be joined on the record by fellow MCA artists Mark Chesnutt (a New Traditionalist newcomer from Beaumont), Vince Gill, and Patty Loveless. Added to that group were Garth Brooks, Clint Black, Pam Tillis, Travis Tritt, Alan Jackson, T. Graham Brown, and newcomer Joe Diffie. Tony Brown saw it as a gesture of defiance to anyone thinking Jones was a mere relic, calling it "one of those marketing ideas that was like a no-brainer. It was like [flipping the] bird to the critics." Released in September 1992, the single barely broke the Top 40, but it was the perfect lead-in for George's September 30 Hall of Fame induction, when George and BMI executive Frances Preston received the honors.

George suffered a major loss a month later when brother-in-law Dub Scroggins, his longtime mentor, died on June 1 in Woodville, Texas, at seventy-five. His health had been failing for some time, in part due to his years working with chemicals at a Beaumont concrete plant. Dub and Helen had lent unflinching support when George and Nancy returned to East Texas in 1983. He'd lived long enough to see George inducted into the Hall of Fame, but the loss deeply pained George as another of his touchstones fell away. He lost another mentor on November 23, when Roy Acuff died of pneumonia at eighty-nine after a long battle with congestive heart failure. A month before, Acuff left his bed at Nashville's Baptist Hospital, intent on one final Opry performance with his Smoky Mountain Boys. Standing on a stage he'd virtually owned for fifty-four years, he managed one final time in the spotlight. Per his instructions, he was buried within hours of his death.

November also brought a second traditional Jones album, *Walls Can Fall,* produced by Emory Gordy Jr., who'd worked with Tony Brown in the Hot Band. The Jones renaissance continued. The Academy of Country Music, originally a West Coast–based counterpart to the CMA, presented George with its Pioneer Award in May 1993. That fall, the CMA awarded "Rockin' Chair" its Vocal Event of the Year Award, an increasingly important award in an era defined more and more by studio collaborations, some of them worthy, others, regardless of the artist, little more than filler.

George remained busy touring, continuing to build a reputation for reliability, having fun singing "No Show Jones," and leaving audiences amply satisfied. When he was off the road, MCA kept him busy. His third MCA album, *High Tech Redneck,* was released in November 1993. With Norro Wilson producing George for the first time, the goal, given the high number of novelty tunes, seemed to be to give him a chance for more radio airplay. To some degree, it succeeded. Released as a single, the title song told the tale of a good ol' boy who'd embraced the fledgling digital technology of that era and became his best-selling MCA single to date. But the album charted lower than the other two.

Tony Brown had another concept album in mind: *Rhythm, Country and Blues,* a sincere if somewhat self-conscious effort to find common ground between country stars and R&B vocalists. George was teamed with blues icon B.B. King on what became the album's powerful closing number: "Patches," a dramatic song that had won a Grammy for R&B singer Clarence Carter in 1971. George added effective vocal touches, though King's voice and guitar dominated the performance. Released in March 1994 to general acclaim, by May the album had achieved platinum status, an increasing delineator of success in the Garth-dominated 1990s.

Brown decided to revisit the duet concept with George on an

album pairing him with a variety of singers at Bradley's Barn, a studio in Mount Juliet, east of Nashville. The original barn was on the property of Decca Records executive Owen Bradley, who'd opened a small demo studio in a barn in the sixties so his eldest son Jerry could do some recording work. When Columbia Records, who owned the original Bradley Studio complex and rented it to acts from any label, changed their policy and made the studios available only to Columbia artists, Bradley quickly upgraded the barn to a full-featured facility open to everyone. Loretta Lynn, Conway Twitty, Bob Wills, Webb Pierce, Ernest Tubb, Kitty Wells, and rock bands like the Beau Brummels recorded there. Eventually, the place gained a mystique not unlike the Quonset Hut. After a fire destroyed it in 1981, Bradley, long retired from Decca, rebuilt it.

To produce the duet collection, Brown enlisted Canadian-born producer Brian Ahern, ex-husband of Emmylou Harris, to handle what became *The Bradley Barn Sessions*. His work on the first three Harris albums led Brown to offer him the job. "I put [George] with Brian Ahern strictly because three of the greatest country records ever made, to me, were Emmylou's first three [Warner Bros.] records. And I just thought that Brian wasn't being used by anybody here in Nashville." On the album, George would revisit classics from the past with carefully selected guests, some of them former duet partners: Emmylou had already worked with George on the *Special Guests* album, and Vince Gill, Marty Stuart, and Mark Chesnutt were part of the "Rockin' Chair" single. His partners, in most cases, were given the option to pick a Jones classic to sing with him. Three hadn't recorded with him before: Dolly Parton, Trisha Yearwood— one of the new female voices in Nashville—and Rolling Stone Keith Richards, who became a fan after hearing George onstage thirty years earlier in San Antonio. The album included another significant voice: Tammy Wynette, who reprised "Golden Ring" with him.

Ahern brought his Enactron Truck to the sessions. This forty-two-foot mobile control room on wheels was something he devised in the 1970s and used on Harris's first three albums and many others, Willie Nelson's *Stardust* among them. That arrangement made making the album challenging, since George had issues with Ahern's entire approach to recording. In a 1995 interview, he complained in detail about the process. Unfamiliar with the Barn, where he'd never recorded, he was also uneasy with Ahern's mobile setup despite its stellar pedigree. Far more disconcerting for George were the rough mixes he received at the end of each session that he called "the worst, worst, *worst* mixes on take-home copies that I ever got in my life from any recording." He cited inaudible instruments and complained his voice was buried on some tracks. Pleas to Ahern, he said, brought no improvement, souring him on the entire process. Nevertheless, in the end he proclaimed himself quite satisfied with the result. His frustration, by his own admission, led to his approaching the ongoing sessions with wariness and plenty of attitude that threatened the relationship with Ahern.

Brown, who'd enlisted Ahern, saw George's frustration stemmed in part from his preference for the way Sherrill had recorded him. "Every producer records different," Brown explained. "Brian cuts the way that I record. He cuts a basic track and then he starts coloring the tracks with background singers and strings and whatever later on. I think George was used to having everything [recorded] live on the date, and [Sherrill's rough mixes] sounded like a record when he'd take it home to listen to it. Where Brian was like concentrating on making sure that the tracks were really good and probably didn't stick George's vocal out, so I bet Brian's approach to producing was a totally different thing for George and it probably threw him for a loop."

Only one person could keep George sufficiently focused, Brown said. "I remember Nancy calling me one time when George was really kind of getting frustrated with Brian's way of working. And she said, 'Now, why did you talk me into doing this record with Brian Ahern and George?' I said, 'Because I think he would take care of the music with kid gloves because he's such an artistic kind of producer, and I think if anybody is worthy of working with George Jones it would be Brian Ahern.' I did it thinking it was creatively a great idea, and the end result was good, but I think Nancy really had her hands full during the cutting of that record."

Brown relied on Nancy throughout the life of George's MCA contract. "She was the saving grace. She had his ear and she was just the factor that things would get done. 'Cause he would do it for her. She was the liaison that made the last few years of recording close to being somewhat easy with George, because at that point he was frustrated about radio not playing him. And so she would keep things on an even keel. I really give her credit, for anything that got done with George at MCA was because of her ability to talk him into it."

In July 1994, the City of Beaumont and Jefferson County, spearheaded by Beaumont's Chamber of Commerce, suggested renaming the Neches River Bridge that separated Beaumont and Jefferson County from Orange County in George's honor. The bridge carried Interstate 10. Texas law stipulated both counties had to concur for the state to approve renaming the structure. Beaumont and Jefferson County officials, citing George's local roots, fame, and triumph over adversity, voted to support the idea. Mayor David Moore pointed to letters and other gestures of support, noting that five hundred responders approved and seven did not. Jefferson County officials voted yes within days. The July 21 *Beaumont Enterprise* printed an entire section of letters supporting the idea, leading off with one from former president George H.W. Bush, a Houston resident and longtime country fan: "George has fought some tough battles in his life; but he has fought adversity with courage and, I am told, he is doing well in all respects. His music, of course, is legendary." Following that was a note from George himself, acknowledging the idea, expressing appreciation for the "show of faith," and thanking everyone "for remembering me."

The view couldn't have been more different across the Neches in Orange County. At a July 22 meeting, Orange County commissioners took the matter under advisement. The renaming generated not only a lack of enthusiasm, but some outright opposition. Residents who spoke against it cited the past George was still trying to live down. Three women involved with Mothers Against Drunk Driving claimed renaming the bridge for a notorious alcoholic would encourage drunk driving, one testifying her daughter suffered disabilities because of an accident involving an intoxicated driver. Another resident complained George had given nothing back to the county he called home for a decade. Citing the fact that George and Nancy located the Jones Country venue outside the county, she concluded that since he hadn't brought business to the area, he didn't warrant an honor. Another resident declared George "had no business being honored in this county" since he was well paid for his performances (an assertion that made no sense whatsoever). Commissioner Kell Bradford, who said he knew George in his Vidor days, supported the move, noting that "Elvis died as a pill head and they had a federal stamp to honor him; Janis Joplin also died a pill head and Port Arthur made a monument to honor her," adding, "If we don't support this, it looks as if we are turning our backs on one of our own.'"

Opponents clearly had the edge. Commissioner Marcelle Adams advocated naming something else for George, noting that retaining the existing name for the bridge would end the controversy. Orange County judge John McDonnell claimed his messages ran three to one in favor of retaining the existing name. In an interview in the *Enterprise,* George fondly remembered fishing along the Neches and declared Beaumont his hometown, reiterated his triumphs over his addictions, and hinted he might decide to retire to the Beaumont area. But he clearly lost little if any sleep over the matter, declaring it an honor to even be considered. None of it mattered. Bradford made a motion for the renaming. It died for lack of a second. The view seems small-minded but not surprising, given Orange County's ultraconservative nature. Memories of George's local behavior clearly remained: the drunk driving, the stories about the alleged gunplay involving J.C. Arnold, and similar issues. At best it was a minor blip. He was about to face his biggest personal hurdle since freeing himself from cocaine.

Late in August, he appeared at a two-day Nashville talent showcase at Opryland, designed to showcase acts available for concert promoters and booking agents. On the first night, George grew more and more frustrated with a sound system that, to him, seemed seriously out of kilter. Finally, he stormed over to the sound board and attacked his sound man. It was the sort of episode that might have happened in the seventies. The media were all over it, sparking speculation that he'd fallen off the wagon again. He returned the next night and played without incident.

Nancy threw him a lavish sixty-third birthday celebration at their home in Franklin, with three hundred friends present, including Little Jimmy Dickens, Connie Smith, and others. George, not feeling well, made a brief appearance, then retreated to his bedroom. On September 11, he visited a local hospital for tests. Some ominous readings sent him to Nashville's Baptist Hospital, where doctors found three blocked arteries requiring surgery. George, no fan of surgery, dismissed the idea until doctors explained he had no choice if he wanted to live, but he still had misgivings. Since Waylon and Cash both had similar procedures at nearly the same time in 1989, Nancy thought advice from a friend might help. She got a message to Waylon on the road. He called in from Vicksburg, Mississippi, and later remembered Nancy telling him, "George isn't going to stay in the hospital unless he talks to you." When George got on the phone, Waylon alerted him to the realities of the situation. George agreed to go ahead with the operation.

On September 12, his sixty-third birthday, George underwent triple bypass surgery. The hospital waiting area was filled with family, including his sister Helen, friends, and fans. Georgette, a registered nurse, had a level of expertise that helped everyone understand what was happening. A week later, he was home. Given a regimen of diet and exercise, he battled to regain strength and it returned slowly. Getting him to exercise proved challenging. Again Waylon, who'd been through the same thing, offered encouragement. George had been drug-free for a decade, but surgeons had cracked his chest and spread the ribs, which meant he had to deal with pain medications. After decades of running at the edge, he faced his own mortality in a way he never had before. In November, he battled through his first concert in Davenport, Iowa, and clearly needed more recovery time.

When MCA released *The Bradley Barn Sessions,* the album was not a huge seller despite the album's diverse blend of personalities. But the remake of "Golden Ring" with Tammy generated enough buzz to inspire another idea: a George and Tammy reunion album twenty years after the divorce, in an era when both watched the country music industry, to which they had dedicated their lives, pass them by as new voices emerged. Tammy faced her own severe health issues. Her recording career had taken a precipitous dive just as George's was tacking upward in the seventies and eighties. The couple had resolved their longstanding differences and entered into an easy friendship, so the idea of teaming up made solid commercial sense to them and to their respective spouses, Nancy and George Richey. After George recovered, they recorded *One*, a new duets album and their first since *Together Again* in 1980. With Tony Brown and Norro Wilson coproducing, the notion was to combine new material with a couple of oldies.

Brown explained the rationale for the album. Tammy's hits, he said, "had completely gone away, basically. And in a sense it made more sense for her to do this with George . . . But the two together were such a force to be reckoned with . . . And they agreed to do it. It wasn't a great record, and they weren't both at the top of their game. And the songs—we got some good songs, but we didn't get the best songs."

For Brown, who'd performed with Elvis, recording these two icons proved both exhilarating and daunting. "I was so intimidated by the fact I was workin' with George and Tammy. Thank God Norro was there, because he knew them both . . . There was a little bit of a rub going on . . . because I don't think their heart was in it as much as [MCA's] heart was in it. It came off a bit [for them] like, 'We've done this. Why are we doin' this again?' . . . But they gave it their all, I will give them that . . . I don't think they had near as much fun as I did trying to cut that record."

At the time, George was still dealing with aftereffects from his heart surgery, and Tammy's health was failing in general. "They were really frail, and . . . Tammy was like skin and bones and just real fragile, not only physically but I think even mentally. That's why it was so hard for me. I was in awe of them . . . There was a dichotomy of Norro, who was friends and had a working relationship [with both], and me being the new guy who sort of luckily got to slip in on the project because of Norro. They weren't at their best. You can hear it in their voices, too . . . They both were not at one hundred percent of their game, but I'm glad we did [the album], because it was at least one last documentation of the two together."

Wilson had similar sentiments, noting, "They'd been split up, of course—she'd been sick and he'd been sick. It was kind of a tough project. Tony and I had such respect for them, and I'd known them longer. I was a little bit of a comfort zone [for them]. We did better by recording the [backing] tracks and gettin' one at a time and puttin' them on the record. And for some of it we actually got 'em [together] in one day. We did everything in our power to make that project easy. There's some discomfort with people when they've been married and had this happenin' to them in their lives. You just have to be careful." With George and Tammy recording most of their vocal parts separately, hearing the other only through the headphones, Wilson saw the continued respect they had for each other's talents. "If we got him on first or her, the cool part of it was, when each of them would hear the other sing, even though they weren't there, that was a turn-on [for them]. Once again, it was that admiration society. They admired each other so very much. I'm really happy I got to work on that project."

Brown said the relationship between Nancy and Tammy was never an issue, but when Richey entered the picture, that dynamic changed. Richey "didn't hang around, but you could tell there was a little oil-and-water thing going on with George and him and Nancy and him. He was just the opposite kind of person as George. His presence—when he showed up, the air got a little bit stiff. George Richey was a flashy guy. And Billy Sherrill wasn't a flashy guy . . . and I think that went against the grain of George Jones."

MCA released the album on May 30. On June 6, 1995, George and Tammy performed together at Fan Fair, and a concert tour was announced. The couple did joint interviews, noting their new maturity. The album cover was carefully designed in an attempt to mask the frailty Brown and Wilson noted. George was white-haired and bespectacled, Tammy bewigged and heavily made-up. Masking their frailty proved more difficult onstage. The shows received a mixed reception. The *Hartford Courant*'s Roger Catlin noted an "uneven show" in Wallingford, Connecticut, mentioning the presence of teleprompters and the weakness of the new songs. Catlin criticized the entire premise of the show and the idea of two divorced people singing hits relevant only to the time when they were married. "Time has taken a toll on their voices," he commented. George got the better end of Catlin's review, which noted that his voice was far stronger than Tammy's and that his solo spot came off considerably better than hers did.

George had other problems. Terms of his divorce from Shirley required him to share 50 percent of his songwriting royalties from 1954 to 1968 with his ex-wife. Bryan and Jeffrey would split that money upon her death, which took place in 1991. The royalty payments ceased in 1992, with Broadcast Music, Inc. claiming the payments reverted fully back to George. On September 5, 1995, both sons filed a lawsuit to regain their half of the royalties.

Following the bridge-renaming debacle, Beaumont officials, still anxious to honor George, decided on something requiring no input from Orange County. On October 1, the 300 block of Fannin Street, in front of the Jefferson Theater, where George did some of his first street singing over half a century earlier, was renamed George Jones Place. George, Nancy, and Tammy were present for the ceremony.

After George's Hall of Fame induction, Nashville author Tom Carter began urging George and Nancy to consider writing an autobiography. At first reluctant to do one, George eventually entered into a collaboration with Carter, who'd worked on memoirs with Glen Campbell, Reba McEntire, and Ralph Emery. Jones talked freely about his ups and downs and seemingly drilled deep into his drunken behavior from the start. He had no inhibitions about relating tales decidedly unflattering, like the incident with Porter Wagoner in the Opry restroom. *I Lived to Tell It All* was released in May 1996. Carter did his own research and interviews. Reviews were mixed. Jack Hurst, who had traveled with and interviewed Jones during the bad times, verified many of the stories, including those about Dedoodle and the Old Man. Others were less charitable. Candice Russell of Florida's *Sun-Sentinel* concluded, "The self-condemnatory writing gets old upon repetition. Even diehard Jones fans are likely to tire of the umpteenth remembrance of another blown show date, another rash of firings of band members and managers, another self-pitying binge."

Russ Corey of the *Times-Daily* in Florence, Alabama, wrote an article addressing the stories in the book regarding drug dealers, in collusion with local lawmen, forcing George to snort cocaine. Peanutt Montgomery, asked to comment, begged off, noting, "Some things are best left alone," and adding, "A lot of people have been killed around George." Billy Wilhite went on record as noting some Alabama cops were friendly with George and had brought him beer confiscated at the Tennessee state line. Lavern Tate, the former Lauderdale County district attorney who had charged him for shooting at Peanutt but later dropped the charges, claimed he'd never heard of George partying and doing coke around local cops.

Rick Singleton, then Florence's acting police chief, expressed "serious doubts" about the stories. A particularly scathing review came from Alanna Nash in *Entertainment Weekly*, who noted the lack of serious discussion about his music and declared, "Throughout these tales of self-destruction, and eventual sobriety, Jones comes across as alternatively despicable and selfish—walking offstage and causing riots, leaving his family stranded by a rural roadside and more wasted and pathetic than he ever let on."

Another hero of George's youth went down that fall when Bill Monroe, who'd suffered a stroke that ended his performing career, passed away in a nursing home. Ties with other old friends deepened as time passed. Since the nineties, George and Buck Owens had been laughing about their onetime rivalry. Like George, Buck was born into rural Texas poverty, yet his career had been the inverse of George's. Sober, reliable, and professional onstage and in the studio, he developed formidable business skills. He amassed wealth not only through records and concerts, but by owning a successful song publishing company and several radio stations. Still based in Bakersfield, in 1996 he opened Buck Owens' Crystal Palace, a supper club, performing venue, and museum. He had nine statues created to grace the club: himself, Johnny Cash, Garth Brooks, Merle Haggard, Willie Nelson, George Strait, Hank Williams, Bob Wills, and George, who played the Crystal Palace a number of times.

In the meantime, George and Nancy were involved in another commercial venture, summed up with a thirty-second TV spot titled "George Jones Talks about His Greatest Lines." He cited "He Stopped Loving Her Today" and "The Race Is On," adding, "They're all good! That's why they're hits, but I'm about to come up with the greatest line I ever had." That line turned out to be George Jones Country Gold Dog Food, in three varieties: milk coated, bite size, and gravy style. (He'd lend his name to Country Gold Cat Food as well.) The ad ended with him smiling, holding two puppies, and saying, "You thought I was talkin' about a new song, didn't ya?"

George would do two more MCA albums, both with Norro Wilson. *I Lived to Tell It All,* in 1997, was clearly named for the book. Buddy Cannon joined Wilson to produce *It Don't Get Any Better Than This,* recorded in 1997 and released in 1998. Wilson remembered the sessions as easygoing, even as the reality was clear that George would never again dominate either record sales or radio. He quickly figured out how to determine George's feelings about a given tune. "If you played him a song, you knew when he didn't like it. He'd start suckin' his teeth. It was hilarious. And you'd say, 'Okay, I know where we are on that one!' He asked me, 'How do you know?' And I said, ''Cause you suck on your danged teeth!' "

As he admitted in his autobiography, George had never totally quit drinking. He insisted he would have a beer or two here and there, and with Nancy around he was able to better regulate things than he had in earlier times. That applied to recording sessions as well. Wilson recalled one of the sessions he produced when Pee Wee Johnson was still working for George. "I remember bumpin' up against Pee Wee. I went to get a drink of water and he's comin' out of the bathroom. I bumped him by accident, not hard, but he clanged. It was little bottles of vodka in both [his] pockets. We'd be in the control room and George'd be doin' something and he'd say, 'Where's Pee Wee, Norro?' And I'd say, 'He's right here. What you need?' He'd say, 'Tell him to bring me some water!' So Pee Wee'd go out, go to the water [fountain], get a little [water], pour a miniature in there, and that'd be it."

The year 1997 was a quiet one. He toured and sang with Patty

Loveless on her Top 20 single "You Don't Seem to Miss Me." But *It Don't Get Any Better Than This* became George's final MCA effort. It was impossible for his singles to get airplay on radio. The growing emphasis on image consultants to build a facade around young stars continued to disgust him. Without a recording contract for the first time since 1954, he felt the loss as a painful blow to his self-esteem despite all the honors he'd been enjoying. He knew the changes in the business were to blame, and he began to feel cast off, even as he continued to deliver professional performances on the road. It gnawed at him that the country sounds that defined his era were a thing of the past. And it scandalized him that so many of the younger acts following Garth seemed less about singing and emotion, more about dazzling audiences by setting off smoke bombs as they performed music full of rock clichés from the seventies. "It was too late," Wilson concluded. "You're dealing with that wall of new leadership from radio."

The Nashville Network, however, saw the potential to give George a broader audience when it launched production on *The George Jones Show,* a musical program where he'd feature various artists, many of them good friends from several generations: Marty Stuart, Stonewall Jackson, Connie, Dickens, Loretta, Haggard, his ex-backup singer Lorrie Morgan, Loveless, Trace Adkins, and so on. It wouldn't resemble *Nashville Now,* the *Tonight Show*–based format Ralph Emery had used with a desk, couch, and live band. This version would be more intimate.

The show debuted February 17, 1998. Aware George lacked the hosting skills of a Cash or Glen Campbell, producers came up with a more amenable setting. George would sit in a comfortable living room set talking and joking to his guests, reminiscing with singers of his generation, like Haggard and Loretta, and chatting with the younger acts. It was never going to be a ratings blockbuster, but it put George in a carefully framed setting where he could relax and be himself.

ON APRIL 6, 1998, GEORGETTE WAS CALLED FROM WORK TO HEAR HER MOTHER had died after lying down at her Nashville home. Tammy's body lay for hours on the couch where she drew her last breath. Instead of a local physician pronouncing her dead, her personal physician flew in from Pittsburgh to handle the task, an unusual move. George was there for their daughter and—given the rapprochement of the past few years—he was devastated by Tammy's unexpected passing. In a time of unsettling transition, and despite the negative comments he'd made in his book, his public words were eloquent. In a prepared statement, he said, "I am just very glad we were able to work together and tour together again. It was very important to us to be able to close the chapter on everything we had been through. Life is too short. In the end, we were very close friends. And now I have lost that friend. I couldn't be sadder." He attended the April 9 funeral with Nancy, but he neither sang nor spoke.

The past fifteen years had been a time of rescue, redemption, honors, and growth as George, despite occasional ambivalence, settled into the role of Elder Statesman. But Tammy's death and his disgust at the changes in the industry he loved, including the loss of his MCA deal, gnawed at him. Nancy was dealing with some health issues as well. It all took a toll. George found himself falling into depression. He began drinking more steadily. Realizing the reputation he and Nancy had rebuilt brick by brick could collapse, he did it in secret. Instead of fifths of whiskey, he stuck to vodka in easily concealed pint bottles. This relapse, however, scared the hell out of him. Knowing what was at stake, he walked into the yard behind his home and prayed for guidance. "I said, 'Lord, I don't care what it takes. Make me straighten up once and for all and get my life together.' I said, 'Hit me in the head with a sledgehammer if you have to.'"

The recording situation was soon on the upswing, resolving with the help of friend and veteran Nashville publicist Evelyn Shriver, who was working for Asylum Records. Asylum became George's new label. He was soon back in the studio recording an album that became *Cold Hard Truth* with Alan Jackson's producer Keith Stegall. The material was impressive, particularly "Choices," a powerful autobiographical ballad written by Billy Yates and Mike Curtis. It was a subdued effort, but one that showed George both restrained and introspective.

He continued to drink in secret, as he was likely doing on the afternoon of March 6, 1999. Driving on State Route 94 not far from the entrance to his estate and horse farm, known as Country Gold Estate, in Franklin, he stopped to assist a motorist. With that finished, he returned to the wheel. Back on the road, delighted with the rough mixes of the album on cassette in his black Lexus LX 470 SUV, he was so excited that he spoke to Shriver on his cell phone, wanting to play her some of the songs. He couldn't get the cassette player to work. He called home, spoke to Adina, and let her know he wasn't far away.

Then she heard him scream, *"Oh my God!"*

The time was 1:30 P.M.

CHAPTER 8

1999–2013

The Lexus slammed into the concrete bridge abutment over the creek. George wasn't wearing a seat belt. It took first responders two hours to extricate him, unconscious, from the wreckage. He arrived at Vanderbilt Medical Center in Nashville by helicopter in critical condition, unconscious, suffering from a collapsed right lung, ruptured liver, and, not surprisingly, internal bleeding. Doctors decided to keep him under heavy sedation in the ICU. He was placed on a ventilator. Nancy arrived, and when she held his hand, he squeezed. Within a day he improved to the point that doctors indicated he might be removed from the ventilator.

On March 9, he seemed to be improving. Not only did he sing some gospel numbers, he asked to see gospel vocalist Vestal Goodman of the Happy Goodman Family, whom he'd met just a few months earlier. A day later, he was sitting up in his room, a dramatic improvement. It turned out to be a bit too fast. Diagnosed with double pneumonia, which he'd suffered some years earlier, George required a respirator and meds to reverse what could have been a serious situation. He later claimed that when the breathing tube was pushed down his throat, a vocal cord was bruised, which had long-term repercussions for his voice. The crisis eventually passed. On March 19, he was discharged and returned to the farm. At the family's request, there was no announcement, which allowed him to depart quietly. An irregular heartbeat brought him back to Vanderbilt April 8, with dehydration blamed as a possible factor. He returned home a day later.

Accident investigators, meanwhile, were busy. On March 11, Tennessee Public Safety officials revealed they found a half-empty pint bottle of vodka in the vehicle. They also alluded to his being on the cell phone and fumbling with the cassette. The investigating trooper expressed a view that alcohol was not a factor, and initially there was no evidence George was intoxicated, despite the vodka. George also didn't seem impaired to the motorist he had assisted just before the crash, nor to EMS personnel on the scene. The Tennessee Department of Transportation later billed him $2,492.44 for repairs to the bridge he hit.

Enough uncertainty remained for the accident investigation to be turned over to a Williamson County grand jury. District Attorney Ronald Davis announced his intention to subpoena George's medical records and call witnesses. Speaking on behalf of the family, Shriver initially insisted they would resist subpoenas, a vow that eventually evaporated. As George's condition improved, media interest grew. When Nashville station WKDF had interviewed him, he claimed he had no memory of the crash, citing the amount of pharmaceuticals doctors had pumped into his system while treating him, insisting he woke up in the hospital with no idea of how he got there. That was certainly plausible, and it became apparent everything was in a gray area. There was little doubt he'd been nipping at the vodka, but his exact level of intoxication was not clear. The drinking surely contributed to his inattentive driving, as did using a cell phone and fiddling with the cassette player. There was enough wiggle room for prosecutors and George's lawyers to negotiate.

On May 12, a plea agreement was announced. George would plead guilty to driving while impaired, reckless driving, and violating the state's open-container law in Williamson County Court. The reckless-driving charge would be discharged in a year pending completion of an alcohol treatment program and good behavior in the interim. George, who arrived wearing a purple short-sleeved shirt, was fined $550. In court, he admitted to presiding judge Donald Harris that he remembered little about the accident, but he assured Judge Harris, "There will be no more problems at all out of me." He made no attempt to sugarcoat his lapses. "I do know I was drinking and obviously my driving was impaired," adding, "I did wrong and I take full responsibility for what happened" and promised to "get my mind straight." "Truthfully," he added, "the struggle never ends, and I will get treatment to help me cope better." He'd admitted in his autobiography that he still drank and had not embraced total abstinence. But he clearly had lost the control he'd had for sixteen years, leading to two weeks in alcohol rehab.

He returned to the stage June 5 at the Kiwanis Community Center in Andalusia, Alabama, an area Hank Williams Sr. played in his early days. *Cold Hard Truth* was released June 22, and "Choices," the first single, would make it to No. 30, a modest success surely fueled by his brush with death. Mike Martinovich, a veteran of Columbia Records in New York who moved to Nashville in the 1980s after George had stabilized, had known George and Nancy quite a while. Doing consulting for Anderson Merchandisers, a huge corporation that handled music marketing for Walmart, he proposed a release-day idea to Nancy. "There was a big Walmart Supercenter on Franklin Road here in Nashville. I asked Nancy if Jones would do a CD signing on the day of release of that album. She said, 'Well, only if you can guarantee us a crowd.' I said, 'I don't think it's gonna be a problem.' It was on the heels of all the press about the accident, plus he's George Jones, plus he has a single on the radio."

When George arrived, he found a line snaking around the outside of the store.

Martinovich marveled at Nancy's approach to handling the fans. "They had a system whereby Jones would just sign his name, one of Nancy's daughters would customize it [with the] person's first name, and Nancy would take a picture at the same time. And this happened all in a matter of maybe five seconds. It was a machine like I'd never seen before. And he sold over a thousand albums that day. Just that one store enabled the album to debut in the Top 20 on the *Billboard* album charts." The experience was satisfying and Martinovich was delighted. Jones, on the other hand, was restless. "On the way out, I escort them back to their car, and I said, 'George, why don't you and I just go down on Second and Broadway and have a couple of beers together?' He couldn't *wait* to get out of there. He couldn't wait to get back to his television. He says, 'Are you *goofy?*' " Ultimately, *Cold Hard Truth* would reach No. 5, George's biggest album success since the *Wine Colored Roses* album on Epic thirteen years earlier.

At his 1999 Fan Fair performance, he thanked everyone for their prayers. An Associated Press account noted he appeared thin and "had trouble hitting low notes," likely due to the bruised vocal cord. He also admitted three factors leading to the relapse: Tammy's death after the two had finally reestablished mutual respect, MCA dropping him, and Nancy's health issues. He'd drunk half a pint of vodka and its effects hit him hard since he hadn't been gulping down booze that way in a while. Another story also noted him as "thin and frail," not all that surprising. The incident, which would have produced a shrug and another bender had it happened in 1980, had deeply shaken him. Still depressed, he spent time talking to Vestal Goodman about himself, his life, and his brush with mortality. That September, they did a video singing the gospel tune "Angel Band." One segment features George, wearing a pink shirt, standing on the very bridge where he nearly met Jesus firsthand. The video would be nominated for a 2000 Dove Award.

The *George Jones Show* came to an end, but the tours continued. That George had been scared straight seemed clear. "I like to died two or three times," he admitted. "And it put the fear of God in me. I knew I wasn't no spring chicken anymore. I quit smokin', I quit drinkin'. I even quit drinkin' coffee. All I carry with me now is a bottle of water. I'm clean cut anymore and I want to enjoy my final days and know what life's all about for a change. I'm tired of being in a foggy jungle." Interviewed by the Christian Broadcasting Network, he described his dark period as a "twilight zone." The saga wasn't quite over, however. In June, the demolished Lexus that nearly became his death car had its own run of stardom, offered for sale by a local salvage company for $22,000. A local physician purchased it as part of a campaign against drunk driving. It was suspended one hundred feet in the air from a crane with a warning to drive safely over the upcoming July 4 weekend.

George's anger in his drinking and coke days remained the stuff of legend, but his temper could flare when he was sober or in control of his imbibing, too, as it had at the Radio City Music

Hall TNN concert in 1985. Still disgusted with the state of modern country, he was pleased when he was slated to sing "Choices" on the September 22, 2000, broadcast. Nominated for the CMA Single of the Year award, it only made sense for him to perform the song in its entirety. The idiots running the broadcast, however, had a change of heart. The show's producers, clearly ignorant or indifferent to the song's and George's recent history, told him to drastically shorten the performance, citing "time constraints." He wasn't having it. Outraged and justifiably infuriated, George packed up and left.

Alan Jackson would settle the matter on national TV. Set to perform Jim Ed Brown's 1967 hit "Pop a Top," from Jackson's recent album of classic country covers, in the midst of the song, the band in on the protest, Jackson defiantly flipped into an entire verse of "Choices," bringing applause from an audience aware of the slight. George, at home in Franklin, watched with tearful delight. One of many disgusted by the slight, Ricky Skaggs later commented, correctly, that "Country music doesn't honor its elders." "Choices" won a Grammy for Best Male Country Performance. *Cold Hard Truth* earned a gold record.

Fed up trying to find major labels to sign George, he, Nancy, Shriver, and former Warner Bros. publicist Susan Nadler decided to form Bandit Records. From then on they would produce and release all of George's new albums, starting with his next one, to be titled *The Rock: Stone Cold Country 2001,* an inelegant title by half. The album had three producers: Keith Stegall, Emory Gordy Jr., and Allen Reynolds. Garth Brooks approached George about a duet. Why he bothered is anyone's guess. On July 30, 2001, the media reported George and Garth would record "Beer Run," a weak, gimmicky song worthy of neither and questionable in the wake of George's recent problems. His voice issues seemed to have resolved themselves enough that he could go back into the studio. In September, discussing his vocal control, he told the AP's Jim Patterson, "I'm finally right now getting it back. I've had to learn almost over again to control my voice and not go sharp or flat. I'm getting back to the old George Jones, I guess."

George got along with some of the Opry's Young Turks who used traditional country as a jumping-off point. His contempt for the continued watering down of the music he loved, however, did not abate. In a November 2001 interview I did with him, he continued to inveigh against the rock-and-pop-derived country movement even though it was, for better or worse, part of the music's ongoing evolution. Asked about his disdain for younger country singers of the past decade, he replied, "It's really not their fault. I talk to so many of them that would have loved to record a country album, traditional country. And the label people, the money people don't want that. They can't make enough money to satisfy 'em.

"You can't enjoy what you're not raised on and what you're used to feeling and singing, and I don't know how—there's some great country singers out there. It's just that their voice isn't being put to good traditional country music like they want to be, their own self. They have no say-so like we used to have. If they thought we could sing and make 'em any money, we had a long rope. We could do 'bout whatever we wanted to do. It's all money. It's all people who want to make money and make more of it. And they tried to change the record sales by [creating country styles like] crossover, middle of the road, and all that, and they take away the basics and that's why it's sounding like it is today. You don't hardly hear any good traditional anymore except Alan Jackson and George Strait. Other than that, you got pop music. They should be in the pop field and get the hell out of country, let us get back to doin' our thing."

George rarely sang songs about wars, except domestic ones. *The Rock* included Jamie O'Hara's ballad about the Vietnam Memorial titled "50,000 Names," a song that seemed right for the post-9/11 era. He declared, "People are a lot more patriotic today than they seem to have been in the past. We might have had a good wake-up call. I think it's bringin' the people a lot more and we're not hating quite as much. I think we need to clean our lives up, what I'm talkin' 'bout is the filthy films you have to watch on TV and all these things. I think we need to get our morals back."

In the interview, his opinions about rock musicians and their ties to country had clearly changed as he realized the depth of admiration went beyond Keith Richards and Elvis Costello. "The only rock-type music that I've ever liked at all was in the fifties: Chuck Berry and Little Richard. Little Richard was my favorite. That's all we had to listen to back in the fifties. You had to listen to what you could hear. That rock was three-chord stuff like country music, and if you stop and analyze it a little bit it reminds you of country with a beat, really. You take Fats Domino, he didn't sing nothin' but country music. They get their ideas and styles from different places."

At the same time, he was flattered by the admiration he received from later generations of rockers. "So many of 'em that love country music, the traditional. That is really something to make note of because it's amazing how they love traditional country music. Keith Richards, you can name 'em. Mick Jagger, he came to the hotel when I was in England wanting to meet me. I didn't even know about it. You'd be surprised at the people I talk to like Elvis Costello who say, 'I can't sing it, or that's what I'd be singin'.'" His belief in the future and integrity of traditional country music was unshakable. In February 2002 he joined other veteran entertainers protesting a pending format change that would convert

WSM-AM to sports talk, ending the classic country format the station had adopted in the 1990s. In the end, classic country won out.

Johnny Paycheck died broke on February 9, 2003. Following his release from prison, he'd attempted a comeback and even joined the Opry, but decades of hard living eventually left him with his own breathing problems in the form of emphysema, confining him to a nursing home. George purchased a burial plot for his ex-sideman and roaring partner and helped with the funeral expenses. On March 6, 2003, George and Smokey Robinson were each recognized with a National Medal of the Arts at the White House, presented by longtime Jones fan President George W. Bush, yet another validation of George's stature.

A month later, Bandit released *The Gospel Collection*, a double-CD set of sacred tunes that reunited George with the now-retired Billy Sherrill, who at Nancy's request agreed to rejoin George (as a favor to her) in the studio. The twenty-four tunes were gospel standards like "Lonesome Valley" and "I'll Fly Away," with cameos from Patti Page and Vestal Goodman. The arrangements were based on Sherrill's classic work at Epic, down to the backup singers and pedal steel. Johnny Cash died on September 12, George's seventy-second birthday; his wife, June Carter Cash, had died in May. George and Cash had first met in the Hayride days. Dressed in a gray suit and blue-and-white-checked shirt, George, with Nancy, attended the September 16 funeral and the November 10 Johnny Cash Memorial Tribute in Nashville.

He also had yet another commercial venture, this one following in the footsteps of Jimmy Dean. It came complete with a new TV ad featuring George and Nancy in their spacious kitchen with their grandchildren sitting nearby. "I'm George Jones, and just like you folks, I think breakfast is the most important meal of the day," he says. "My wife Nancy here, she serves only the best to the grandkids: George Jones Country Sausage!" In the next shot, holding a guitar, he sings (in a clear, strong voice) a bit of "Once You've Had the Best." In the final shot, of the product itself, George's voiceover says it all: "George Jones Country Sausage! Pure pork—no possum!"

George had two presidential fans named Bush. Former president George H.W. Bush had endorsed renaming the Neches River Bridge for George in 1995. But despite the honor the younger Bush bestowed on him in 2003, George didn't join Music Row's overwhelming migration to the Republican Party, which had begun long before the controversy over the Dixie Chicks' comments about Bush and the Iraq War. George had not openly endorsed a presidential candidate since he and Tammy performed for Wallace in 1972. But in February 2004, as Bush 43 sought reelection in an increasingly divided nation, George, his White House visit notwithstanding, backed a different man in a different party: retired general Wesley Clark, former NATO commander and a Democrat. George even recorded a campaign spot for Clark:

Hi, this is George Jones. You know, I've never done anything like this before, but I feel so strongly about where our country is headed, that I want to share with you why I'm supporting General Wes Clark for president. Wes Clark has dedicated his whole life to three principles: duty, honor, and country. And he shares the same values that you and I share here in Tennessee. Wes Clark knows what it means to put his life and career on the line for this country, and he'll put the nation's interests first—not the Washington special interests. I'm George Jones. Like Wes Clark, I'm no career politician, but I know a leader when

I see one, and that's why I'm asking you to vote for Wes Clark for president on Tuesday.

In releasing the script, the Clark campaign erroneously referred to George as a "lifelong Tennessean," which would surely surprise the state of Texas. Clark's candidacy was short-lived, but George's support stood out in a Music Row increasingly trending Republican. Given Clark's stature, no Dixie Chicks–style backlash ensued over George's endorsement.

HALF A CENTURY HAD PASSED SINCE THE GANGLY YOUNG SINGER STOOD AT THE mike in Jack Starns's living room and waited for the light switch to flip before singing "No Money in This Deal." Now 2004 became a year of celebrating his fiftieth anniversary in the business, even though he'd actually started in the late forties. To commemorate the occasion, Bandit Records offered *George Jones—50 Years of Hits,* a three-CD retrospective starting with "Why Baby Why" and ending with "Amazing Grace" from the gospel album. PBS offered a companion event: a special two-hour version of their *Soundstage* music showcase, also titled *50 Years of Hits,* to be broadcast Thanksgiving night.

The performers spanned forty years, from the sixties to the present day. Hosting was Reba McEntire, who'd gone from New Traditionalist to country-pop chanteuse to star of her own sitcom. Joining George were Lorrie Morgan, Kenny Chesney, Trick Pony, Amy Grant, Trace Adkins, Vince Gill, Randy Travis, Tanya Tucker, Wynonna, Aaron Neville, Connie Smith, Emmylou Harris, Harry Connick Jr., Alan Jackson, and rapper Uncle Kracker.

Most performances were first-rate, but a few stood out, like Jackson's boogie-driven "One Woman Man" and Neville reprising his sensitive, nuanced 1993 interpretation of "The Grand Tour." At the piano, Connick injected gospel blues into "She Thinks I Still Care." When George joined Travis to reprise "A Few Old Country Boys," his breathing problems made it hard to finish his lines. He sang a number of duets, with Connie Smith, Shelby Lynne, Amy Grant, and Tanya Tucker. Martina McBride went all the way back to Starday to reprise his hit 1956 drinking ballad "Just One More." Chesney, who'd opened for George and Tammy on their final tour, talked of George's kindnesses back then before singing "I Always Get Lucky with You" and "Tennessee Whiskey." Harris sang "One of These Days," which she'd discovered as a B-side of George's hit single "We Can Make It." After several participants reflected on "He Stopped Loving Her Today," George gamely closed the show with it. The special revealed much about how George was perceived by younger generations, enhancing his stature as an enduring fountainhead and influence, even though his style was verboten in the increasingly corporate world of contemporary radio. The presence of Connick and Neville spoke to his impact beyond country.

Behind the scenes, Bonnie Garner, who'd had her own Nashville management firm, helped Shriver and Nadler. "It was a tribute to George, and he was so nice and everyone was a nervous wreck singing with him. I told Evelyn and Susan that I'd help talent-wrangle. I can remember even Aaron Neville being nervous about singin' in front of George. I was proud of Kenny Chesney because he stood up there and sang. He was professional and I called [RCA Nashville executive] Joe Galante afterward and told him he should be proud of his kid. He made those songs his, he didn't try to be George."

For his next album, George and Keith Stegall went into the studio to do something George hadn't done since his United

Artists days: an entire album of others' hits, plus a new (and superfluous) reprise of "He Stopped Loving Her Today." The hits were inspired choices, standards like "Detroit City," the sixties Henson Cargill hit "Skip a Rope," Alan Jackson's "Here in the Real World," Willie Nelson's "Funny How Time Slips Away," and Merle Haggard's "Today I Started Loving You Again." Bandit issued it in 2005 as *Hits I Missed . . . and One I Didn't.* It became his final solo album. A year later, Haggard and George teamed up for *Kickin' Out the Footlights . . . Again,* where the two friends would record four duets and sing each other's favorites. While a well-considered idea, George's vocal issues on the 2006 album were also apparent. They left his voice rougher; the breath control, once rock solid, was less consistent, affecting his ability to project as he sang. His spirit and desire, however, remained unaffected.

GEORGE AND NANCY LOVED THE FARM, AND AS ALWAYS HE TOOK SPECIAL pleasure in working outside, riding his lawn mower, watching TV reruns on a flat-screen, and decorating for Christmas. Given those stark, minimal boyhood Christmases in the Thicket, he had fun creating elaborate holiday displays. Each December, he and Nancy invited fans to view the elaborate lighting setup, with illuminated angels, a train and reindeer, lavishly decorated trees, a seven-foot lighted rocking-chair model, figures of Santa and Mrs. Claus, and much more. Not even thefts (a pilfered golden eagle statue, returned three days later) could deter him. He used the occasion to raise money for local charities.

More old friends and associates were passing from the scene. George was a pallbearer when Don Pierce died in April 2005. In July 2005 he joined young, tradition-minded Dierks Bentley to record another version of "Murder on Music Row." The song, an angry lament over traditional country's declining relevancy in the new, youth-oriented Nashville, had been recorded in 2000 by Alan Jackson and George Strait. Despite the disgust the lyrics conveyed ("someone killed country music, cut out its heart and soul"), the song would change no one's mind about the way things were going in the industry. Recording it with Bentley no doubt made George feel better, especially since the final verse included the line "They even told the Possum to pack up and go home." Late that month he finally met James Taylor—the man whose admiration for George's singing led him to write "Bartender's Blues" for him nearly thirty years earlier—when he attended Taylor's July 31 concert at Nashville's Starwood Amphitheater. The exhibit *The Grand Tour: George Jones Country* opened at the Country Music Hall of Fame in December 2005. In March 2006 another honor came his way in Beaumont when his name (and boot prints) were added to the Walk of Fame, surrounding the Ford Park event center, convention, and exhibition hall, where George and Haggard were performing. Other locals made good, Edgar Winter, Tracy Byrd, Janis Joplin (from nearby Port Arthur), and Clay Walker, had all been previously honored. George happily put his boot prints into a block of wet cement.

Amid the honors, he continued to deal with health issues. On March 30, 2006, he returned to Baptist Hospital suffering from pneumonia, to be discharged two days later. He celebrated year seventy-five on September 12 by performing at the Opry on a Tuesday night. He was at Keith Stegall's Nashville studio on October 20 when a fall broke his wrist, resulting in more postponed shows. The next week, he underwent surgery at Baptist Hospital but made it to a Carnegie Hall concert with Kris Kristofferson four days later, using a hand mike and not his guitar. George participated in *God's Country: George Jones and Friends*, another all-star tribute effort with some of his younger admirers. He recorded the title song; Pam Tillis, Tracy Lawrence, Mark Chesnutt, Tanya Tucker, Sammy Kershaw, and others reprised Jones favorites.

"He Stopped Loving Her Today" entered the Grammy Hall of Fame on January 10, 2007.

George's life was increasingly becoming a blend of downtime at home, brief tours, and honors from the industry and friends. His seventy-sixth birthday generated a surprise party in Franklin attended by Billy Sherrill, Tom T. Hall, Dierks Bentley, Sonny James, Trace Adkins, Mark Chesnutt, Little Jimmy Dickens, and Tracy Lawrence.

When Porter Wagoner died of lung cancer in October 2007, George was at the Ryman to sing "I Saw the Light." The fact that George's music was transcending its hard country roots became clear when the acclaimed cable TV drama *Mad Men,* a complex story of personalities in a 1960s New York advertising firm, ended an episode with the Mercury recording of "Cup of Loneliness," Brother Burl's poem that George put to music over forty years before.

The success of Branson, Missouri, as a resort that made live music its focus led many country and pop acts to perform there regularly or even start their own theaters. The notion of a Branson-like spot closer to Nashville always appealed to country artists, and an Alabama entrepreneur named Ronnie Gilley had such a project in mind near Dothan, not far from where George had hung out in the foggy jungle of Lauderdale County. Gilley's Country Crossing resort would be a performing venue with tourist-oriented restaurants associated with country stars, accommodations, and, hopefully, a casino. George agreed to involve himself, participating in the October groundbreaking ceremony.

When George recorded the *Bradley's Barn Sessions* album, some performances were omitted from the final release. Bandit Records issued this material and some later duets on the album *Burn Your Playhouse Down—The Unreleased Duets* in the summer of 2008. Another duet with Keith Richards, on George's old Mercury stomper "Burn Your Playhouse Down," was one of the standouts. The album also included duets with Tammy, Mark Knopfler, Marty Stuart ("You're Still on My Mind"), Leon Russell, Vince Gill, Mark Chesnutt, and Dolly Parton. His duet with Georgette on the ballad "You and Me and Time" gave the album a personal quality.

Late in 2008 he achieved the ultimate accolade alongside his Hall of Fame membership when he received the annual Kennedy Center Honors celebrating luminaries of the arts. Acuff had been the first country artist to be named, followed by Cash, Willie, and Dolly. Barbra Streisand, actor Morgan Freeman, choreographer Twyla Tharp, and the Who's Pete Townshend and Roger Daltrey received the honors along with George, who attended the Washington ceremony with Nancy. First Lady Laura Bush introduced a film tribute, recalling her love of "The Race Is On" and Sinatra calling George "the second-best singer in America." The film moved through his career, the early years, the Tammy phase, the dark years afterward, and the final redemption. It ended with the words "Still country, still king." He waved as the audience gave him a standing ovation. In tribute, Brad Paisley sang "Bartender's Blues," Randy Travis following with "One Woman Man." Alan Jackson summed it up with "He Stopped Loving Her Today," a prescient choice.

George remained involved with the Country Crossing project, along with Travis Tritt, actor Jamie Foxx, Marty Stuart, Darryl Worley, and the band Alabama's leader Randy Owen. One of the new businesses was to be yet another Possum Holler: the George Jones Possum Holler Bed and Breakfast. He and the other artists also lobbied Alabama legislators to approve electronic bingo, but the venture's success would be short-lived and amount to little. The entire idea later imploded after Ronnie Gilley was tried for conspiring to bribe Alabama politicians to support the pro-casino legislation. Any chance of expanding gambling died in the Alabama House of Representatives. Gilley pleaded guilty in 2011 and was sentenced to over six years in federal prison.

The connection with Gilley wasn't a positive one for George or any of the others involved, but George's past achievements continued earning acclaim. His signature song, "He Stopped Loving Her Today," received another honor in June when it was added to the Library of Congress National Recording Registry. At Christmas, singer Ronnie McDowell, also a painter, delivered a painting Nancy commissioned: an updated study of the famous riding lawn mower incident that happened in Vidor in the sixties, showing the George of 2009 riding a modern John Deere from the liquor store, a police car following. His old hometown of Vidor, where many staunchly opposed renaming the Neches River Bridge for him, finally offered a token honor by adding his name to the Walk of Fame in front of its new City Hall on August 21, 2010.

As George continued to face the realities of advancing age and failing health, the notion of slowing down loomed larger. The farm, with all the work it required, was getting harder to handle given his growing physical decline. On April 6, 2011, he and Nancy put it up for sale with the asking price of $11 million. George was able to head back on the road, to play another rare political function when he did a July 2 benefit in Ocean Springs, Mississippi, for Republican gubernatorial candidate Phil Bryant, who went on to win the election in the fall.

There was another birthday celebration, at the Opry on September 13, a day after his eightieth birthday. Perhaps in recognition of his Hayride days, George received another induction on October 3, into the Louisiana Music Hall of Fame, and received the key to the city of Baton Rouge. In December, he performed at Itawamba County Community College in Mississippi for a project relating to Tammy. Another national honor came February 11, 2012, when he received the Grammy Merit Award in Hollywood with the Memphis Horns, New Orleans R&B bandleader Dave Bartholomew, and Diana Ross. Also present: Glen Campbell, whose battle against Alzheimer's disease had become public the previous year. With teleprompters and a band largely made up of family members, Campbell was still able to sing and play guitar.

Set to play Peoria, Illinois, on March 24, George endured a newspaper interview with *Pantagraph* reporter Dan Craft. Asked about retirement, George replied, "If I retire, what am I going to retire to? What would I do with my time?" The engagement never happened, the result of a chest cold that proved difficult to shake. In mid-April, his publicist announced upcoming shows, including a Canadian tour, were being postponed due to an upper respiratory infection. The idea was for him to resume performing May 20.

His return to the road never happened. On May 21, he returned to the hospital with additional respiratory problems, all part of the condition known as COPD, that began to assert itself after he came out of the cocaine haze thirty years earlier, almost surely aggravated by decades of smoking. He was discharged May 26, but it became clear his voice was failing, and his breathing problems grew more acute. The man who lived to sing, content in his life with the woman who loved and saved him, was losing the very thing that set him apart. He canceled additional concerts throughout the summer. Even his daily mowing had to end. The pollen and allergies made it impossible, a painful sacrifice he even mentioned in interviews.

Georgette's 2011 memoir of her parents, *The Three of Us: Growing Up with Tammy and George*, raised little controversy. Father-daughter issues, however, flared in April 2012. In an Associated Press story, George complained of comments he said Georgette, now married to musician Jamie Lennon, made about him on social media, including Facebook. Money, he insisted, was at the heart of the dispute, declaring, "I have gave and gave till I can no longer give. I will never let her go hungry, but I am tired of putting out, and I am not the person they claim I am." Defending herself, Georgette denied his accusations, saying others had misinformed him, adding he was upset that she'd reconnected with his sons Bryan and Jeff, who were long estranged from their dad. The final straw, she added, involved another wedding snub. She recalled asking George to give her away at her wedding to Lennon, received no response, and later discovered he was booked for a show that day (her twin sons did the honors).

With Glen Campbell touring the country, performing despite his affliction, and George's vocal skills faltering, the idea of a final victory lap made sense. On August 14, 2012, George and Nancy announced a series of concerts, carefully spaced apart to allow him to rest, that would constitute the "Final Grand Tour" and mark the conclusion of his performing career. The finale would be a gala all-star November 22, 2013, show at Nashville's Bridgestone Arena downtown. Things got off to a rocky start as he canceled September shows in West Virginia and South Carolina due to illness, and a makeup October 31 show in Minnesota had to be canceled again. Audiences at his concerts seemed torn as the Jones Boys and his backup singers had to frequently jump in when he couldn't finish a vocal line, a painful spectacle for those who saw him at the peak of his vocal powers. Some fans were in tears, upset to see him struggling. Others shrugged off his ragged performances, happy to see their hero for what would surely be the last time.

It became clear from the occasional dates—and the growing difficulty he had delivering even partial performances as his lungs deteriorated and the medications weren't able to improve things—that it was unlikely he'd be able to complete the tour. On April 6, 2013, he and the band performed at the Knoxville Coliseum. He struggled mightily to get through "He Stopped Loving Her Today." What it cost to deliver even that is impossible to determine, but when he left the stage, he said he knew that was his final show, adding, "I gave 'em hell." He headed back to Franklin, still struggling, only to rebound around April 13, feeling better and with enough energy that he and Nancy would ride around the countryside and have dinner around four P.M. After that, they'd settle in so George could watch DVDs of what became his favorite TV show: *Matlock,* starring Andy Griffith as a rumpled but shrewd elderly lawyer.

When he relapsed, suffering intense pain on April 18, Nancy called an ambulance. George was taken to Vanderbilt Medical Center. He improved there, but as Nancy told an interviewer, he finally asked his doctors the big question: "Am I dying?" Told that he was, George broke into tears. The man who had beaten death almost as many times as he'd charted a record, ever since that night he got slashed at Lola's and Shorty's, had to confront his mortality, this time knowing it was final. With the courage of a man who had beaten so much in the past, he asked only for pain medication, saw his minister, and told Nancy everything that needed doing.

Remaining alert as long as possible for the time he had left was his sole priority. Alan Jackson came to visit. George wrote letters to his grandchildren and even to great-grandchildren not yet born. Nancy recalled in an interview that when she broke into tears, George, as confident in his future in the afterlife as Clara would have been, said, "What are you cryin' about? I've had eighty-one good years. Some of 'em I messed up, paid for 'em. Now, I'm goin' to heaven. I've had eighty-one good years, so don't cry, honey." He told grandson Carlos, "You're the man of the house." On April 26, George and Nancy talked until he lapsed into a coma. About six hours later, George Glenn Jones, the Greatest Living Country Singer, drew his final breath. Just before the end, Nancy recalled his final words, certain he was introducing himself to God.

"Hiya. I've been looking for you. I'm George Jones."

When friends and the media found out, the reaction was not unlike the public response to Johnny Cash's passing. The entire music industry—country, pop, and beyond—stopped to pay tribute. The Opry reworked its Friday-night show to become a George Jones memorial, everyone singing his songs. The Saturday-night Opry continued the tribute. The arrangements were announced, and the May 1 viewing at Woodlawn-Roesch-Patton Funeral Home brought a raft of friends and fellow performers including Alan Jackson, perhaps his closest friend among the young traditionalists, Randy Travis, Ralph Stanley, Steve Wariner, and Joe Diffie. He would be buried in the Woodlawn Memorial Park in Nashville's Berry Hill section, where, years earlier, George and Nancy had purchased a large family burial plot.

Even the Ryman, where George had first performed nearly fifty-seven years before, wouldn't do as a site for the funeral. The Celebration of Life took place at the Opry House on May 2, 2013.

Garth Brooks and his wife, Trisha Yearwood, sat with Nancy and her family. The cast of nonmusic dignitaries was impressive and included former Arkansas governor Mike Huckabee, Laura Bush, and occasional country singer and CBS *Face the Nation* host Bob Schieffer, a lifelong fan. In his eulogy, Schieffer said, "We all wanted to sing—everybody wanted to sing—like George Jones," he said. "But nobody could sing like George Jones, unless you *were* George Jones. You couldn't—because you hadn't been through what *he* had been through." Laura Bush thought back to the early years. "A hot-tempered father who was made mean by too much to drink, and a kind and long-suffering mother. Pain and love. George Jones spoke of them both whenever he sang a note. He sang from his heart and his soul. He sang for his supper in clubs and bars around Beaumont. And it was only a few short years from the streets of Beaumont to recording contracts, the radio, and the bright lights of the Grand Ole Opry."

The music matched the occasion. Opry stalwarts Vince Gill and Patty Loveless, both close to George, teamed for "Go Rest High on That Mountain," the ballad Gill began writing after fellow singer Keith Whitley died and finished after the death of his own brother. Overcome with emotion, Gill had serious trouble maintaining his composure as he sang, Loveless patting his shoulder as he strummed his acoustic guitar. Long known as a formidable instrumentalist, he began a solo that said nearly as much as his vocals. Charlie Daniels eulogized George and then sang a song George no doubt heard when he was a boy: the traditional hymn "Softly and Tenderly." "With young singers who tried to emulate George Jones it was an affectation, while with George it was a God-given natural talent," he said. He marveled at the way his friend would "hold on to a word, teasin' it, turnin' it, and make you wonder where he could possibly go with it. But then just at the right second he'd turn it loose and you'd just kinda smile, and admire . . . He sang for us all." The always outspoken Daniels also took a shot at "cookie cutter sameness" that brought applause.

Travis Tritt sang an acoustic rendition of Kris Kristofferson's "Why Me, Lord?" He recalled being on a movie set in Spain when he heard of Tammy's death, marveling at the fact that George outlived Tammy (not all that much a surprise considering her own health issues). Alan Jackson, not surprisingly, reprised "He Stopped Loving Her Today." The two had been close to the end, George never forgetting the way Jackson had stepped in to settle the score at the 1999 CMA awards. Amid all the traditionalists, Jackson seemed to have absorbed the most. Although at times Jackson's voice seemed shaky, his rendition conveyed the essence of what George and Billy Sherrill had done through all the hard moments, and he managed to capture the true essence of the original down to the little bends and breaks that were George's trademark. The applause exploded at the end. George was buried in the family plot at Woodlawn.

Seeing her youngest son falter so often during her lifetime, George's mother, Clara, feared that she'd "made a failure." In her time, it may have seemed that way. But in the end, the kid from the Thicket had realized all his hopes and dreams, battled and conquered his demons, and finally departed the stage in triumph. The voice that moved tens of millions over several generations had finally been stilled, and yet it was everywhere.

2013-2015

The modest bronze plaque marking his final resting place at Woodlawn Memorial Park was strictly temporary. Soon an artist's rendering of the permanent memorial would be erected behind George's grave. He wouldn't rest for eternity in a crypt in an indoor mausoleum like Tammy's, also at Woodlawn, or in a stand-alone edifice like the one Buck Owens built in Bakersfield, raffishly dubbed "Buck's Place." His grave site wouldn't be a large, sedate affair like Roy Acuff's at Nashville's Spring Hill Cemetery or Bill Monroe's in Kentucky. Acting on ideas she said George began formulating before he died, Nancy unveiled the plaque to a crowd assembled at the site on November 18, four days before the concert at the Bridgestone Arena. Billy Sherrill was among the attendees.

Topping the massive, elaborate stone memorial was an arch with the name JONES carved into it. HE STOPPED LOVING HER TODAY was inscribed into a section beneath the name. A large left pillar included an engraved portrait with homilies about his musical gifts. In the middle was a guitar sculpture, the inscription THE POSSUM, and an engraved photo of George and Nancy. Identical carved stone vases sat at the foot of the monument. His grave, a full-length bronze marker, featured four etchings taken from photos, one showing the adolescent Glenn with his guitar on the streets in Beaumont. Another shot from the darker years depicted him in aviator shades. Two others were lion-in-winter shots from later in life. An adjacent space was reserved for Nancy, and two benches flanked the graves. It was, in some ways, a more modern variation on the elaborate Hank and Audrey Williams grave in Montgomery, Alabama.

At the event, Nancy also announced the creation of the George Jones Memorial Scholarship at Middle Tennessee State University, available to financially challenged students in the school's well-regarded Department of Recording Industry, which also offered a course in George's life and music. The list of requirements noted that "Preference will also be given to letters that express some knowledge of or interest in country music, such as that of George Jones." He would like that.

The November 22 Bridgestone Arena concert, titled "Playin' Possum: The Final No-Show," was revised into an all-star memorial show. The title alone reflected how time had softened the once-sour memories of George's bad behavior into an affectionate part of country folklore, like Cash's wildness, Hank's tragic Lost Highway, Willie's pot smoking, and Patsy's hell-raising. With the concert sold out, an outdoor video setup projected the show to a crowd outside the downtown Nashville venue. The lineup was a generation-spanning Nashville who's who encompassing, among others, Brad Paisley, Charlie Daniels, Garth Brooks, Lorrie Morgan, Montgomery Gentry, Eric Church, Ray Stevens, Blake Shelton, Miranda Lambert, Larry Gatlin, and two of George's oldest Opry friends, Little Jimmy Dickens and Jimmy C. Newman. The show included a surprise or two, including Jamey Johnson with the metal band Megadeth, not exactly perceived as George Jones fans.

The outpouring of love and admiration for George would not alter the direction of the music itself. Taylor Swift had finally established the youth market that country producers had tried and failed to create for decades even as she was about to pivot to more mainstream pop. The formulaic nonsense George had long hated continued to proliferate in the form of "bro-country." This successful but intensely controversial formula centered around male singers singing vapid ditties about hot girls, partying, boozing, pickup trucks, and related areas. Most of these acts seemed incapable of infusing these throwaway songs with any degree of emotion or nuance. Others, even George's friend Kenny Chesney, focused on tunes heavy on beach themes, a sound Jimmy Buffett made popular decades earlier. Creativity in Nashville came from a few individualists like Eric Church or Jamey Johnson, who refused to follow the formulas. Also unwilling to play the game: earthier female stars like Miranda Lambert and Lee Ann Womack and newcomer Kacey Musgraves. Traditionalists and younger, edgier acts would continue to draw deeply from George's sound.

Meanwhile, the Nashville of his peak years literally became a museum piece. The Country Music Hall of Fame occupies a massive new high-tech facility on Demonbreun Street downtown with a new Omni Hotel in its rear. RCA's famous Studio A, where so many Nashville Sound classics were recorded, lives on as a working studio, a unit of the Hall of Fame. The Columbia studios where George recorded from the fifties on were repurposed as offices and storage after the label quit maintaining studios in 1982, ending the days of Studio A and Studio B, the famous Quonset Hut where George and Billy did much of their greatest work. Both were eventually resurrected as studios. Belmont University restored the Quonset Hut with funding from the Curb Family Foundation, established by Curb Records owner Mike Curb. Studio A followed in 2015. Both are part of Belmont's Curb College of Entertainment and Music Business, whose many alumni include Brad Paisley, Steven Curtis Chapman, and Trisha Yearwood.

George, who'd had his first museum in his Chuckwagon Cafe in the sixties, was thinking along those terms again before he died. Nancy set to making that a reality. On April 24, 2015, the George Jones Museum opened at 128 Second Avenue North in Nashville, a couple doors down from the Wild Horse Saloon and only three blocks from the Ryman, Tootsie's, and the site of George's original Possum Holler. The Johnny Cash Museum is a couple blocks away. In a four-story, 44,000-square-foot space, exhibits cover George's entire life, his boyhood in the Thicket, his years on the radio and in the clubs. His many awards, old Nudie outfits including the "White Lightning" suit, a coat from his marine days, and even the jacket cut off him after the 1999 crash are prominently displayed. Visitors can gaze on a mid-sixties John Deere riding mower much like the model he rode to the liquor store in Vidor and examine a pair of the "Possum Panties" sold at the second, Baggott-owned Possum Holler. There's the usual gift shop, a theater and event space, even a rooftop bar with a prime view of the Cumberland River. An interactive booth allows visitors to sing along with videos of George singing his hits.

Served and sold on site: George Jones White Lightning Moonshine, manufactured by Silver Trail Distillery, already earning praise for its quality. The notion of a museum selling moonshine to celebrate the life of a man nearly destroyed by liquor startled many who knew of George's demons and caused them to wonder if he'd have approved such a thing. Apparently so. The rear label, an early-sixties photo (actually the same cover shot from the album *George Jones Sings Like the Dickens!*), features a 2012 quote from George: "Alcohol has owned me and controlled me much of my life. Now is my time to own it."

Time would claim more of his contemporaries and friends. Ray Price, the Hank Williams protégé and Texas honky-tonk innovator with whom George wrote "You Done Me Wrong," passed in late 2013 after battling pancreatic cancer. Known for his stubbornness, he recorded a final album after his diagnosis and performed as long as he could. Jimmy C. Newman passed away in mid-2014. George's longtime buddy Little Jimmy Dickens, "Tater," who came to his aid at his first Opry appearance and partied with him on the road, died the second day of 2015 at ninety-four. Opry veteran Jim Ed Brown died in June 2015.

Whatever country becomes as the twenty-first century progresses, the legacies of past greats remain embedded in the music's DNA, whether future stars and fans remember or not. It's inevitable veteran acts will fade as time passes. A small, slowly expanding group, however, some still living at this time, will endure. Jimmie, Acuff, Monroe, Hank Sr., Cash, Patsy, Dolly, Loretta, Buck, Glen Campbell, Tammy, Marty Robbins, Waylon, Willie, and Haggard all remain touchstones, their music and narratives powerful reminders of what the music, despite the fad du jour, was and is supposed to embody.

George Jones stands in the forefront of that group, his stature secure even as his mystique and historical place continues to evolve. Beyond the demons and the triumphs, the legends and stories true and false, his music remains his most powerful monument. What began at that slam-bang 1954 session in Jack Starns's Beaumont home and stretched over six decades, issued on vinyl 78s, 45s, and LPs, then on compact disc, endures even as technologies change. Now that natural, unfettered emotion flows digitally through wired and wireless conduits, via Apple Music, iTunes, Spotify, Amazon, Pandora, and similar music services of today and into the future, to be discovered and savored by current generations and those to come.

ACKNOWLEDGMENTS

One doesn't embark on a book like this without enormous help from a number of individuals, some of whom I met during my research and others I've known over my four decades in this business.

Patrick Carr gave me the chance to write for *Country Music* magazine in 1973, a year after the publication launched. Over the next twenty-four years, editors Michael Bane, Nick Tosches, Rochelle Friedman, Helen Barnard, and George Fletcher and longtime editor-publisher Russ Barnard were supportive as we covered, celebrated, and critiqued the goings-on of the moment. The inspiration of gifted writers like Tosches, Carr, Joe Nick Patoski, John Morthland, and Peter Guralnick enhanced the experience. Russ allowed me to explore the music's history to my heart's content, one of the paths that brought me here.

I'm also grateful to those who helped connect me with some of my interview subjects for this book, John Morthland and Gregg Geller in particular. Texas music authorities Kevin Coffey and Andrew Brown, who've forgotten more about the honky-tonk scene than I'll ever know, were enormously helpful. Andy kindly shared some of his relevant interview material and insights with me. Terry Maillet-Jones, librarian at the *Beaumont Enterprise,* and Angelika Kane at the *Pittsburgh Post-Gazette* were also helpful in tracking down rare clippings relating to George. Other friends at the *Post-Gazette,* some still there, others retired, who proved supportive were Allan Walton, Scott Mervis, Adrian McCoy, Matt Kennedy, Mary Leonard, and Tony Norman.

Other friends whose supportive insights made things easier include Alanna Nash, one of the pioneers of quality country journalism; Peter Cooper, one who continued that level of excellence; music historian Dave Samuelson; Dr. Travis Stimeling; Steve Weiss of the University of North Carolina's Southern Folklife Center; and Mark Yacovone.

I'd like to acknowledge the work of the first two George Jones biographers: Bob Allen and Dolly Carlisle, who were there thirty years ago and whose pioneering research offered insights and context, as did George's own autobiography.

At Dey Street Books, I have a number of editors to thank. The first is Cal Morgan, who initially suggested George as an idea, and Mark Chait, who took over when Cal shifted from Dey Street to other high-level editorial duties at HarperCollins. When Mark moved on, Carrie Thornton filled the slot, and when she became editorial director at Dey Street, Rob Kirkpatrick took over her duties. At the end, Sean Newcott very capably stepped in to handle the final phase.

My agent, David Dunton of the Harvey Klinger Agency,

deserves special thanks. A musician himself, Dave understands music and music journalism on the highest level. He has been a pillar of support throughout, offering suggestions, direction, advice, and wise counsel when it was most needed. It is a pleasure and an honor to be associated with Dave.

Other friends, including Helen and Mary Adisey, Karen Hutchinson, and Jim and Michelle Albert, offered conversation about things other than music when the project seemed overwhelming.

Finally, I'd like to thank my late parents, Dick and Nootie Kienzle, who didn't think the idea of writing about country music was a totally crazy idea.

SELECTED LISTENING

There are hundreds of George Jones anthologies out there, so this is only a select list of what's in print. Some titles are available only on CD but others are also available digitally on iTunes, Amazon, or other streaming services. Many older CDs and LPs can be found on eBay. I annotated a number of the Bear Family, Universal, and Legacy collections listed here.

Starday: *22 Early Starday Recordings* (Gusto) surveys his first two years with the label, encompassing "Why Baby Why," his original recording of "Ragged But Right," "Taggin' Along," and some Mercury material, including a remake of "No Money in This Deal," "Too Much Water," and both sides of the infamous Thumper Jones single. *Early Hits: The Starday Recordings* (Time Life) includes the two outtakes from his 1954 debut session in Jack Starns's living room, where his vocals channeled Lefty Frizzell on "For Sale Or For Lease" and Hank Williams on "You're in My Heart." *20 Original Classics* (Gusto) assembles other Starday-era tunes, adding duets with Virginia Spurlock and Jeannette Hicks. *Heartbreak Hotel* (Bear Family) consists of thirty-five upbeat and rocking tracks from Starday and Mercury.

Mercury: *Definitive Collection 1955–1962* (Universal) is a two-disc compilation built around essential Mercury recordings. *20th Century*

Masters: The Millennium Collection compiles the most important of these, plus a 1960 Nashville rerecording of "Why Baby Why."

United Artists: *The Complete United Artists Solo Singles* (Omnivore) assembles both sides of his sixteen single releases from 1962–1965. *She Thinks I Still Care: The Complete United Artists Recordings 1962– 1964* (Bear Family) compiles everything he recorded for the label on four CDs. *Vintage Collections: George Jones & Melba Montgomery* (Capitol Nashville) assembles twenty United Artists duets, including hits and a few tracks from the *Bluegrass Hootenanny* album.

Musicor: *The Great Lost Hits* (Time-Life Music) This two-disc, thirty-four-track overview includes "Milwaukee, Here I Come" with Brenda Carter. *George Jones and Gene Pitney* (Gusto) samples ten of their duets. Bear Family's identically titled CD *George Jones and Gene Pitney* offers the complete Pitney-Jones Musicor collaborations as well as Pitney's solo album *The Country Side of Gene Pitney*. Gusto, owners of the Musicor catalog, rereleased some original Jones albums on CD and digital, among them *Walk Through This World With Me, New Country Hits, 4033, If My Heart Had Windows*, and *Party Pickin'* (with Melba). Bear Family's *Walk Through This World with Me* is the first of two box sets exploring George's complete Musicor output. The first five-disc box covers 1965–1967, including George's duets with Melba but excluding the Pitney material. The four-disc *A Good Year for the Roses* picks up where the first left off, covering 1968–1971.

Epic: A good many classic albums with Billy Sherrill remain available in physical and digital form. **Solo**: *George Jones, Nothing Ever Hurt Me, A Picture Of Me (Without You), I Am What I Am, Bartender's Blues, The Grand Tour, Still the Same Ole Me, Alone Again, Shine On, Wine Colored Roses, One Woman Man,* and *Friends in High Places*. **With Tammy:** *We Go Together, Let's Build a World Together, We're Gonna Hold On, We Love to Sing About Jesus, Golden Ring,* and *Together Again*. **Other duets:** *My Very Special Guests*, with Elvis Costello, Linda Ronstadt, Emmylou Harris, James Taylor, and others. An expanded 2005 CD version by Legacy Recordings adds twenty-nine duets. *A Taste of Yesterday's Wine* with Merle Haggard and *Double Trouble* with Johnny Paycheck can be found on CD. *Yesterday's Wine* is also available digitally.

Anthologies: *The Essential George Jones: The Spirit of Country* (Legacy Recordings) surveys high points from Starday, Mercury, United Artists, Musicor, and Epic on two CDs starting with the original 1954 *No Money in This Deal*. Legacy's later two-disc compilation, *The Essential George Jones*, focuses on solo material, omitting Musicor material but adding recordings not on the *Spirit of Country* collection.

MCA: Much of his material here, some of it of uneven quality, can still be found: *And Along Came Jones, Walls Can Fall, High-Tech Redneck, I Lived to Tell It All, It Don't Get Any Better Than This* all remain available. So do *The Bradley Barn Sessions* and *One*, his 1995 reunion with Tammy. *The George Jones Collection* is a sampler from this era.

Asylum: *Cold Hard Truth* released after his 1999 car crash. It features "Choices."

Bandit: Several releases on George's label remain available, among them *Hits I Missed (And One I Didn't)* and *Burn Your Playhouse Down: The Unreleased Duets. Kickin' Out the Footlights . . . Again* (with Merle Haggard) can be found on CD. The two-disc *Gospel Collection* produced by Billy Sherrill is out of print, but *Amazing Grace*, a single-disc sampler, is available.

SOURCES

AUTHOR INTERVIEWS

Russ Barnard: July 2014

Dan Beck: June 18, 2014

Bobby Black: July 13, 2013

Tony Brown: May 29, 2015

Slim Bryant: October 2003

Johnny Bush: April 24, 2015

Bonnie Garner: April 23, 2015

Gregg Geller: March 17, 2014

Lloyd Green: July 2007

George Jones: October 2001

R.C. Martin: March 21, 2014

Mike Martinovich: August 14, 2014

Mary Ann McCready: April 14, 2015

Frankie Miller: October 1, 2013

Melba Montgomery: 1995

Bob Moore: September 2008

Gerald Murray: April 4, 2015

Luther Nallie: October 30, 2013

Buck Owens: Fall 1988

Pig Robbins: July 8, 2014

Bob Sullivan: September 26, 2013

Mychael John Thomas: September 8, 2014

Norro Wilson: June 5, 2015

Interviews by Andrew Brown

Arlie Duff: June 9, 1996

Patsy Elshire: July 1, 2000

Freddie Frank: July 10, 1999

George Ogg: April 6, 2000

BOOKS

Albert, George, and Frank Hoffmann. *The Cash Box Country Singles Charts: 1958–1982* (Scarecrow Press, 1984).

Allen, Bob. *George Jones: The Saga of an American Singer* (Doubleday Dolphin, 1984).

Bonney, Lorraine G. *The Big Thicket Guidebook: Exploring the Backroads and History of Southeast Texas* (Big Thicket Association & University of North Texas Press, 2011).

Brown, Maxine. *Looking Back to See: A Country Music Memoir* (University of Arkansas Press, 2009).

Carlisle, Dolly. *Ragged but Right: The Life and Times of George Jones* (Contemporary, 1984).

Cash, Johnny, with Patrick Carr. *Cash: The Autobiography* (HarperCollins, 1997).

Dawidoff, Nicholas. *In the Country of Country* (Pantheon, 1997).

Diekman, Diane. *Live Fast, Love Hard: The Faron Young Story* (University of Illinois Press, 2007).

Gibson, Nathan D., with Don Pierce. *The Starday Story: The House That Country Music Built* (University Press of Mississippi, 2011).

Hoffmann, Frank, and George Albert. *The Cash Box Country Album Charts: 1964-1988* (Scarecrow Press, 1989).

Isenhour, Jack. *He Stopped Loving Her Today: George Jones, Billy Sherrill, and the Pretty-Much-Totally True Story of the Making of the Greatest Country Record of All Time* (University Press of Mississippi, 2011).

Jackson, Stonewall, with Billy Henson. *From the Bottom Up: The Stonewall Jackson Story as Told in His Own Words* (L.C. Parsons, 1991).

Jennings, Waylon, with Lenny Kaye. *Waylon: An Autobiography* (Warner Books, 1996).

Jones, George, with Tom Carter. *I Lived to Tell It All* (Villard, 1996).

Jones, Georgette, with Patsi Bale Cox. *The Three of Us: Growing Up with Tammy and George* (Atria, 2011).

Jones, Margaret. *Patsy: The Life and Times of Patsy Cline* (HarperCollins, 1994).

Kingsbury, Paul, Michael McCall, and John Rumble, eds. *The Encyclopedia of Country Music: Compiled by the Staff of the Country Music Hall of Fame and Museum* (Oxford University Press, 2012).

Kingsbury, Paul, and Alanna Nash, eds. *Will the Circle Be Unbroken: Country Music in America* (DK Publishing, 2006).

Mandrell, Barbara, with George Vecsey. *Get to the Heart: My Story* (Bantam, 1990).

McDonough, Jimmy. *Tammy Wynette: Tragic Country Queen* (Penguin, 2010).

Montgomery, Charlene. *The Legend of George Jones: His Life and Death* (Heritage Builders Publishing, 2014).

Nash, Alanna. *Behind Closed Doors: Talking with the Legends of Country Music* (Knopf, 1988).

Patoski, Joe Nick. *Willie Nelson: An Epic Life* (Little, Brown, 2008).

Richards, Keith. *Life* (Little, Brown, 2010).

Russell, Tony. *Country Music Records: A Discography: 1921–1942* (Oxford University Press, 2004).

Texas Medicine Volume 8 (1912).

Tosches, Nick. *The Nick Tosches Reader* (DaCapo, 2000).

Whitburn, Joel. *Top Country Albums: 1964 to 1997* (Record Research, 1997).

———. *Top Country Songs: 1944 to 2005* (Record Research, 2005).

White, Howard. *Every Highway Out of Nashville* (JP Productions, 1990).

Wyman, Bill. *Stone Alone* (Penguin, 1990).

Wynette, Tammy, with Joan Dew. *Stand By Your Man: An Autobiography* (Simon & Schuster, 1979).

NEWSPAPER ARTICLES

Allen, Sherhonda. "George Jones Makes Pitch for Country Sausage." Florence, AL, *Times-Daily* (July 23, 2003): 1B, 4B.

"Angry Fans Walk Out of George Jones Show." *Ocala Star-Banner* (December 5, 1987): 2A.

Brewer, Steve, and Rebecca Shockley. "Bridge Idea Plays Possum." *Beaumont Enterprise* (August 2, 1994): 1A, 3A.

Buck, Jerry. "Actress Plays Tammy Wynette in TV Film." *Spokane Daily Chronicle* (March 27, 1981): 11.

Carr, Patrick. "George Jones Sings His Brains Out." *Village Voice* (November 8, 1976): 65.

Catlin, Roger. "George Jones, Tammy Wynette Give Fans an Uneven Show." *Hartford Courant* (July 7, 1995).

Cooper, Peter. "George Jones, Country Music Hall of Famer and Master of Sad Ballads, Dies at Age 81." *Nashville Tennessean* (April 26, 2013).

————. "George Jones Knew He Would Be a No-Show Tonight." *Nashville Tennessean* (November 22, 2013).

————. "George Jones: Remembering the Friend, Father, Husband." *Nashville Tennessean* (May 1, 2013).

"Country Artists Protest." *Gadsden Times* (November 26, 1974).

"Country Legend to Teach Music Business Fundamentals." Associated Press (January 18, 2007).

"Country Music Couple to Record." *Sarasota Herald-Tribune* (April 17, 1976): 10A.

"Country Music Singer Is Granted a Divorce." *Journal* (March 13, 1975).

"Country Singer Jones Faces January 19 Cocaine Trial." *Ocala Star-Banner* (December 12, 1982): C1.

Croft, Lynne. "Tammy Wynette–George Jones Relived in TV-Movie." *Lakeland Ledger* (March 31, 1981): 6C.

Edwards, Joe. "Marriage Gave George Jones a New Life." *Lawrence Journal-World* (March 14, 1984).

————. "They Don't Joke about George Jones Anymore." *Lewiston Journal* (June 19, 1982): 13.

————. "Year Long Battle Pays Off for Country Music Singer." *Prescott Courier* (October 10, 1980): 17.

"Fans Bolt Jones' Concert." *Gainesville Sun* (December 6, 1987): 2A.

"Farmers Receive Concert Tickets." *Rome News-Tribune* (May 28, 1987): 12.

Fausset, Richard. "Mower Meets Moonshine at a Museum for Country Star George Jones." *New York Times* (May 23, 2015).

"George Jones." *Kentucky New Era* (September 18, 1978): 10.

"George Jones Arrested in Tennessee." *Gadsden Times* (May 26, 1982): 2.

"George Jones Arrested on Drunk Driving Charge." Florence, AL, *Times-Daily* (March 30, 1982): 5.

"George Jones Behind in Child Support." *Sarasota Herald-Tribune* (September 22, 1978): 13A.

"George Jones Climbs One More Mountain." *Toledo Blade* (December 9, 1984): G3.

"George Jones Cocaine Possession Trial Delayed until Next Month." *Ocala Star-Banner* (January 19, 1983): 9A.

"George Jones Fan Backs Up His Admiration with $737 in Cash." *Ocala Star-Banner* (July 9, 1982): 5A.

"George Jones Files Bankruptcy." *Daytona Beach Morning Journal* (December 16, 1978): 2A.

"George Jones Files Libel Suit." *St. Petersburg Independent* (July 25, 1984): 2A.

"George Jones Grabs the Cash and Leaves in the Middle of Concert." *Lakeland Ledger* (May 7, 1983): 2.

"George Jones Hits the Road Again—Ahead of Schedule." *Lewiston Daily Sun* (May 7, 1983): 23.

"George Jones Hospitalized." *Rome News Tribune* (October 23, 1990): 12.

"George Jones Hospitalized." *Tuscaloosa News* (August 1, 1987): 4.

"George Jones Out of Hospital." *Wilmington Morning Star* (October 27, 1990): 2A.

"George Jones Pleads Guilty to Drug Charges." Florence, AL, *Times-Daily* (February 11, 1983): 13.

"George Jones Released from Hospital." Associated Press (March 19, 1999).

"George Jones' Check to Cover Fine Bounces." *Ocala Star-Banner* (June 11, 1982): 7A.

"George Jones' Two Sons Sue Over Royalties." *Wilmington Morning Star* (September 9, 1995): 2A.

Goodwin, Jim. "Young Vidor Singer Heads for Big Time." *Beaumont Enterprise* (January 15, 1965).

"Grand Jury to Investigate George Jones Crash." *Reading Eagle* (March 31, 1999): D10.

Gray, Ann. "Just Water Under the Bridge: George Jones Claims He's Put Past behind Him." *Beaumont Enterprise* (July 24, 1994).

"Halts Concert Tours." *Southeast Missourian* (March 27, 1983): 2.

"Her Kidnapping Is a Mystery to Tammy Wynette." *Sarasota Herald-Tribune* (October 6, 1978): 2A.

Hurst, Jack. "George Jones Puts New Loves into His Life." *Milwaukee Journal* (October 27, 1983): 1–2.

———. "Greatness, Grief and George Jones." *Chicago Tribune Magazine* (March 22, 1981): 12–14, 16, 18, 20–22, 26, 28–30, 34.

"It's More Than a Song Now." *Sarasota Herald-Tribune* (January 9, 1975).

"Jackson Plea Bargain Concert a Big Hit for George Jones." *Lakeland Ledger* (September 18, 1983): 2A.

"Jones Alcohol Addict." *Tuscaloosa News* (October 12, 1978): 30.

"Jones Cancels Performance." *Newburgh Beacon-News* (November 5, 1983): 2.

"Jones Divorce Suit Dropped." Gainesville *Sun* (December 19, 1987): 2A.

"Jones Faces Arrest and Extradition." *Spartanburg Herald-Journal* (June 13, 1982): C2.

"Jones Released." Florence, AL, *Times-Daily* (August 20, 1988): 2A.

"Jones to Make an Appearance." *Southeast Missourian* (April 23, 1982): 15.

"June 3 Grand Ole Opry Show, Added Attractions George Jones and Sonny Burns." *Tucson Daily Citizen* advertisement (May 26, 1954): 17.

"Jones to Perform in Lieu of Jail Term." *Bangor Daily News* (February 11, 1983): 2.

Levine, Jo Ann. "Country Music in the Big City." *Beaver County Times.*

Keel, Beverly. "A Survivor's Tale." *Nashville Scene* (May 27, 1999).

Kienzle, Rich. "Stone Cold Sober at Last." *Pittsburgh Post-Gazette* (November 27, 2001): D1.

King, Caitlyn R. "Country Star Lashes Out at Daughter." Associated Press (April 25, 2012).

"No Business Like Show Business—Except Politics." *St. Petersburg Times* (June 13, 1972): 6B.

"Ohio State Fair Cancels George Jones Concert." Norwalk, CT, *Hour* (June 2, 1981): 10.

Palmer, Robert. "Nashville Sound: Country Music in Decline." *New York Times* (September 17, 1985): 1.

Pareles, Jon. "His Life Was a Country Song." *New York Times* (April 26, 2013).

Patterson, Jim. "George Jones: Alcohol Impaired Driving." *Lakeland Ledger* (May 13, 1999): A4.

———. "George Jones Flourishes with New Album." *Bangor Daily News* (September 17, 2001): D1.

———. "Jones Thrives at 70." *Bangor Daily News* (September 17, 2001): D1.

———. "Singer Critical after Car Crash." Associated Press (March 7, 1999).

"Police: Vodka Found in Singer's Wreckage." *Spartanburg Herald-Journal* (March 13, 1999): A2.

Richter, Bob. "Drunk Singer Cycles Off with Girlfriend, Tequila." *San Antonio News* (August 16, 1982).

Rose, Bob. "Country Music Star's Drinking Spoils Show." *Toledo Blade* (September 27, 1981): F4.

Safford, Peggy. "Jones Makes His Move." Florence, AL, *Times-Daily* (October 1, 1981): 12.

Schwed, Mark. "George Jones: A Journey Back from the Brink." *Ottawa Citizen* (June 23, 1984): 31–32.

"Sheriff Seizes George Jones' Guitar." *Washington Morning Star* (September 23, 1983): 6B.

Shockley, Rebecca. "Orange County Balks at Naming Bridge after Singer." *Beaumont Enterprise* (July 22, 1994).

"Show Business." *Milwaukee Journal* (November 30, 1981): 5.

"Show Promoter Sues George Jones." Fredericksburg, VA, *Free-Lance Star* (December 17, 1981): 28.

"Singer Faces Lawsuit for $10.1 Million." *Montreal Gazette* (June 3, 1981): 32.

"Singer Is Charged." Henderson, NC, *Times-News* (December 18, 1976).

"Singer George Jones Ailing with Severely Infected Sinus." *Tuscaloosa News* (August 19, 1988): 8.

"Singer George Jones in Rehabilitation." *Victoria Advocate* (April 2, 1982): 5D.

"Singer George Jones Said He Doesn't Remember Accident." Associated Press (April 3, 1999).

"Singer Is Indicted on Cocaine Charge." *Toledo Blade* (July 14, 1982): 12.

"Singer Hospitalized after Auto Wreck." *Tuscaloosa News* (March 31, 1982): 8.

"Singer May Give Concert to Carry Out Court Order." *Gadsden Times* (July 16, 1982): 5.

"Singer Out of Hospital after Double Pneumonia." *Tuscaloosa News* (May 11, 1988): 9.

"Singer's Assets Seized to Pay Debt." Fredericksburg, VA, *Free-Lance Star* (October 28, 1982): 3.

"Singer's Charges Dismissed." *Ocala Star-Banner* (July 30, 1983): 2A.

"Singer's Ex-Mate Charged." *Pittsburgh Post-Gazette* (September 23, 1978): 7.

"Songwriter Ivory Joe Hunter Dies." *Milwaukee Journal* (November 9, 1974).

Stuckrath, Dave. "George Jones Showed Up, Just Barely." *Lakeland Ledger* (February 1, 1983): 2C.

"Texas Ruby Dies in Fire; George Jones Hurt in Auto Crash." *Billboard* (April 13, 1963): 22.

"The Cajun Life Changes Jones." *Lexington Dispatch* (October 23, 1982): 2.

"The Return of George Jones." *Lakeland Ledger* (October 14, 1980): 4C.

Toal, Margaret. "Vidor to Add Walk of Fame. Possum Might Attend." *Beaumont Enterprise* (February 4, 2010).

Turner, Milton. "He Plays His Guitar Enthusiastically, Breaking Strings, Gaining Stardom." *Beaumont Enterprise* (June 3, 1956).

"$24 Million Lawsuit by 'Ex' Surprises Tammy Wynette." *St. Petersburg Times* (October 25, 1980): 3A.

Van Dusen, Ray. "Former Sheriff Recalls Run-In with Old Possum Jones." *Monroe County Journal* (May 3, 2013).

Wallich, Dan. "Beaumont City Council Favors Renaming Span." *Beaumont Enterprise* (July 13, 1994).

———. "'Jones Bridge' Wins 2nd OK." *Beaumont Enterprise* (July 19, 1994).

———. "Just Call It 'Possum Bridge': Bureau Wants to Name I-10 Bridge After George Jones." *Beaumont Enterprise* (July 9, 1994).

"Western Bandleader George Jones Hurt." *Daytona Beach Morning Journal* (March 31, 1963): 4A.

"What's in a Name? Jones Deserves Honor." Letters, *Beaumont Enterprise* (July 21, 1994).

MAGAZINE ARTICLES

Carr, Patrick. "George & Tammy: The Never Ending Story," "George Jones Survives the Country Wars," "Tammy Wynette Turns Yet Another Corner." *Country Music* (July/August 1995): 28–42.

Fay, Byron. "FayFare's Opry Blog" (http://fayfare.blogspot.com).

Gabree, John. "Tammy Wynette: Songs of Heartbreak from a Happy Home." *Country Music* (April 1973): 26–34.

"George Jones." *Country Music* (July/August 1987): 42.

Hickey, Dave. "George Jones: Country's Supreme Stylist." *Country Music* (December 1975): 36.

Liddane, Jim. "ISA Gene Pitney Interview." International Songwriters Association, Ireland (http://www.songwriter.co.uk/page71.html).

Nash, Alanna. "Cool Reunion: George Jones & Tammy Wynette." *Entertainment Weekly* (June 30, 1995).

Nusser, Richard, and Patrick Carr. "George Jones: Problems, Problems, Problems." *Country Music* (December 1975): 30–34, 59.

Parker, Melissa. "George Jones Interview: Country Icon on His Country Crossing Involvement and Latest Recording." *Smashing Interviews* (January 21, 2010).

Plowman, Pepi. "A Singin' Fool." *Texas Monthly* (June 1982): 145–149, 232–239.

Tucker, Ken. "Brad Paisley, Mel Tillis and Other Grand Ole Opry Stars Honor George Jones." *Billboard*, April 28, 2013.

Tosches, Nick. "The Devil in George Jones." *Texas Monthly* (July 1994).

Wynette, Tammy. "The George Jones Interview." *Country Music* (June 1980): 32–40.

LINER NOTES

Brown, Andrew. *Benny Barnes: Poor Man's Riches: The Complete 1950s Recordings* (Bear Family Records, 2007).

———. *Eddie Noack: Gentlemen Prefer Blondes: The Complete 1950s Recordings* (Bear Family Records, 2012).

———. *Sonny Burns: A Real Cool Cat: The Starday Recordings* (Bear Family Records, 2011).

Escott, Colin. *George Jones: Cup of Loneliness: The Mercury Years* (Polygram Records, 1994).

Jones Sings Haggard, Haggard Sings Jones: Kickin' Out the Footlights . . . Again! (Bandit Records, 2006).

Kienzle, Rich. *George Jones: A Good Year for the Roses: The Complete Musicor Recordings: 1965–1971,* part 2 (Bear Family Records, 2009).

———. *George Jones: Heartbreak Hotel: Gonna Shake This Shack Tonight* (Bear Family Records, 2011).

———. *George Jones: She Thinks I Still Care: The Complete United Artists Recordings: 1962–1964* (Bear Family Records, 2007).

———. *George Jones: Walk Through This World with Me: The Complete Musicor Recordings: 1965–1971,* part 1 (Bear Family Records, 2009).

GOVERNMENT RECORDS

Beaumont, Texas, City Directories, 1954–1956.

National Park Service, Big Thicket National Preserve (http://www.nps.gov/bith/index.htm).

US Department of Commerce, Bureau of the Census, Population Schedule 1920, Hardin County, Texas.

US Department of Commerce, Bureau of the Census, Population

Schedule 1930, Hardin County, Texas.

US Department of Commerce, Bureau of the Census, Population Schedule 1940, Hardin County, Texas.

US Marine Corps Personnel Records, 1952–1953.

BILLBOARD ARTICLES

"A Great Artist Now Exclusively on United Artists" advertisement. February 24, 1962: 9.

"BMI Certificate of Achievement." November 14, 1959: 19.

"Favorite Male Artists of C&W (Disc) Jockeys." November 9, 1959.

"15th Annual Country Music Disc Jockey Poll." November 10, 1962.

"First Release Is a Socko Starter on Mercury Starday: 'Don't Stop the Music' and 'Uh Uh No.'" February 3, 1957: 33.

"Folk Talent & Tunes." May 4, 1959: 95.

Friedman, Joel. "Folk Talent & Tunes." March 27, 1954: 33.

———. "Folk Talent & Tunes." January 23, 1954.

"Hold Everything: George Jones" review. May 14, 1955.

"Hot on Starday," "Why Baby Why" advertisement. November 12, 1955: 118.

"Jackie Young Murder Victim." December 11, 1965.

"Jones, Owens Featured in Neal Package." May 9, 1964: 18.

"Mercury Staging Singles Hype." July 27, 1959: 2, 46.

"Musicor Contract Pits RCA vs. Epic in Releasing Geo. Jones." January 15, 1972: 3, 8.

"Review Spotlight: 'Don't Stop the Music.'" January 19, 1957.

"Review Spotlight: 'Flame in My Heart with Virginia Spurlock.'" February 1, 1957.

"Reviews of New C&W Records." September 25, 1954: 58.

Sachs, Bill. "Folk Talent & Tunes." December 29, 1962: 18.

"This Week's Best Buys: 'Why Baby Why'" review. October 29, 1955: 48.

"UA Adds Classical, Now Full Circle." August 18, 1962: 5.

Waddell, Ray. "George Jones: The Billboard Interview (2006)." April 26, 2013.

"What Am I Worth" and "Still Hurtin'" review. January 4, 1956.

"What Am I Worth" and "Why Baby Why" advertisement. February 4, 1956.

"'Y'All Come' by Arlie Duff" advertisement. December 19, 1953.

VIDEOS

George Jones and Tammy Wynette. "Milwaukee Here I Come." *The Wilburn Brothers Show,* 1969.

George Jones and Tammy Wynette. Commercial for Badcock Home Furnishing Centers, c. 1971–72.

Telecast, CMA Awards, 1981.

George Jones. "Who's Gonna Fill Their Shoes?" Music video, 1985.

George Jones: Same Ole Me: The Authorized Video Biography DVD (White Star Video), 1989.

George Jones. "I Don't Need Your Rockin' Chair." Music video, 1992.

Country Music Hall of Fame Induction, CMA Awards, 1992.

George Jones. Country Gold Dog Food Commercial, c. 1990s.

The George Jones Show, episode 6. Guests: Loretta Lynn, Sara Evans, Billy Ray Cyrus (Nashville Network, 1998).

The George Jones Show, episode 7. Guests: Merle Haggard, Trace Adkins, Lorrie Morgan (Nashville Network, 1998).

The George Jones Show, episode 8. Guests: Little Jimmy Dickens, Vince Gill, Patty Loveless (Nashville Network, 1998).

George Jones family. Commercial for George Jones Country Sausage, October 2003.

George Jones: 50 Years of Hits (PBS Soundstage Special Event), 2004.

Kennedy Center Honors, featuring Laura Bush, Brad Paisley, Randy Travis, and Alan Jackson, 2008.

Audience videos of George's concert appearances during the final tour, 2012–2013.

Nancy Jones. WZTV Nashville interview, April 29, 2013.

George Jones Funeral Coverage, May 2–3, 2013: Laura Bush eulogy; Charlie Daniels, "Softly and Tenderly"; Vince Gill and Patty Loveless, "Go Rest High on That Mountain"; Alan Jackson, "He Stopped Loving Her Today"; Bob Schieffer, comments, *CBS News This Morning*; Bob Schieffer eulogy.

Bob Schieffer, comments on *CBS News This Morning*, May 3, 2013.

ABOUT THE AUTHOR

Veteran country music critic, journalist, and historian RICH KIENZLE is the author of *Southwest Shuffle: Pioneers of Honky-Tonk, Western Swing, and Country Jazz* and *Great Guitarists: The Most Influential Players in Blues, Country Music, Jazz and Rock*. A contributing editor and columnist at *Country Music* magazine for nearly twenty-five years, he also edited their history publication *The Journal*. He was formerly a contributing editor at *No Depression* and *Guitar World* and is now a regular contributor to *Vintage Guitar Magazine*. His work has appeared in *Fretboard Journal*, *Guitar Player*, *Request*, *The Journal of Country Music* and the *Austin American-Statesman*. The author of liner notes for almost four hundred reissue albums, Kienzle is among the few country journalists profiled in *The Grove Dictionary of American Music*. He received the International Country Music Conference's Charlie Lamb Award for Excellence in Country Music Journalism in 2012.